RACE AND INEQUALITY

Race and Inequality
World Perspectives on Affirmative Action

Edited by

ELAINE KENNEDY-DUBOURDIEU
University of Nantes, France

ASHGATE

Published by
Ashgate Publishing Limited
Gower House
Croft Road
Aldershot
Hampshire GU11 3HR
England

Ashgate Publishing Company
Suite 420
101 Cherry Street
Burlington, VT 05401-4405
USA

Ashgate website: http://www.ashgate.com

British Library Cataloguing in Publication Data
Race and inequality : world perspectives on affirmative
    action
    1.Affirmative action programs - Case studies
    2. Discrimination - Government policy - Case studies
    I.Kennedy-Dubourdieu, Elaine
    305

Library of Congress Cataloging-in-Publication Data
Race and inequality : world perspectives on affirmative action / edited by Elaine Kennedy-Dubourdieu.
    p. cm.
    Includes index.
    ISBN-13: 978-0-7546-4839-0
    ISBN-10: 0-7546-4839-7
    1. Race discrimination. 2. Affirmative action programs. I. Kennedy-Dubourdieu, Elaine.

    HT1521.R235215 2006
    305.8--dc22

                                                                                    2006018450
ISBN-13: 978 0 7546 4839 0
ISBN-10: 0 7546 4839 7

Printed and bound in Great Britain by MPG Books Ltd. Bodmin, Cornwall.

Contents

Notes on Contributors   *vii*
Foreword   *ix*
Acknowledgements   *xiii*

Introduction
Elaine Kennedy-Dubourdieu   1

1   Affirmative Action in the United States   11
     Jo Ann Ooiman Robinson

2   Challenging Systemic Racism in Canada   43
     Colleen Sheppard

3   Affirmative Action in India   63
     Ashwini Deshpande

4   From Periphery to Mainstream: Affirmative Action in Britain   77
     Elaine Kennedy-Dubourdieu

5   Affirmative Action in Northern Ireland   103
     Bronagh Hinds and Ciarán O'Kelly

6   Australian Multicultural Equity and Fair Go   127
     Martine Piquet

7   Affirmative Action in South Africa: The Limits of History   153
     Beverly Thaver

Conclusion   173
Elaine Kennedy-Dubourdieu

Bibliography   *177*
Index   *193*

Notes on Contributors

Ashwini Deshpande is Reader in the Department of Economics, Delhi School of Economics, University of Delhi, India. Her research areas include the economics of discrimination, with a special focus on caste and gender in India, international debt, capital flows and aspects of the Chinese economy. She is also the Chair of the Annual Conference of Development and Change, a platform for young heterodox scholars, funded by the Ford Foundation. She has published several papers in established economics journals and is the co-editor, along with William Darity Jr., of *Boundaries of Clan and Color: Transnational Comparisons of Inter-Group Disparity*.

Bronagh Hinds is Senior Fellow at the Institute of Governance, School of Law, Queen's University Belfast with interests in equality, democracy and governance. She previously held posts in the voluntary sector and as Deputy Chief Commissioner of Northern Ireland's Equality Commission and participated in the 1996–1998 multi-party peace negotiations. Publications include *Checks, Balances and Safeguards* (with Loughlin) and *Women and the Review of Public Administration* (with Gray); 'Problem-solving Negotiation: Northern Ireland's Experience with the Women's Coalition', *Journal of Dispute Resolution*, University of Missouri-Columbia School of Law and Centre for the Study of Dispute Resolution, (with Nolan-Haley); 'Mainstreaming Equality in Northern Ireland', *Women Making Constitutions: New Politics and Comparative Perspectives*.

Elaine Kennedy-Dubourdieu began her teaching career in Zambia before coming to live and work in France where she wrote her doctoral thesis on *The Concept and Practice of 'Positive Discrimination' in Britain during the 'Thatcher Years'*. She now works as Senior Lecturer at the University of Nantes where her research interests are in the field of race relations and social policy. She has lectured on different models and manifestations of multiculturalism – in Britain, France and South Africa essentially – and has published widely in this field.

Ciarán O'Kelly is Research Fellow at the Institute of Governance, School of Law, Queen's University Belfast. Dr. O'Kelly's interests lie in the field of political theory and the state. His research specifically focuses on the effects of human identities, professional and institutional self-conceptions and the like on the governance of states. Dr. O'Kelly's publications include 'Being Irish', *Government and Opposition*, and 'Taking Tough Choices Seriously: Public Administration and Individual Moral Agency', *Journal of Public Administration Research and Theory*, (with Melvin Dubnick).

Jo Ann Ooiman Robinson has taught history at Morgan State University in Baltimore Maryland since 1969. Her research interests fall mainly within U.S. Social History and focus especially on political-social protest movements. She is the author of *Abraham Went Out, A Biography of A.J. Muste*; *Affirmative Action, a Documentary History*; and *Education As My Agenda: Gertrude Williams, Race and the Baltimore Public Schools*.

Martine Piquet is Professor of Anglophone Studies at the University of Paris-Dauphine, France. She has published numerous articles on Australian society, in particular on multiculturalism, the socio-economic situation of Aborigines, reconciliation and the Republic Debate. She is the editor of the Journal *Cultures of the Commonwealth* and the author of *Australie Plurielle: Gestion de la diversité ethnique en Australie de 1788 à nos jours*.

Colleen Sheppard is the Research Director for the McGill Centre for Human Rights and Legal Pluralism and an Associate Professor at the Faculty of Law at the McGill University. Professor Sheppard completed her Honours B.A. and LL.B. degrees at the University of Toronto and her LL.M. at Harvard Law School. Her research and teaching focus on equality rights, feminist theory and comparative constitutional law. Prior to commencing her teaching career, she worked as a law clerk with former Chief Justice Brian Dickson of the Supreme Court of Canada. Beyond her teaching and research work in the domain of human rights, Professor Sheppard has been active in public service activities to promote and advance human rights in Canada and internationally. She served as a Commissioner on the Quebec Human Rights Commission from 1991–1996 and has been a consultant with the Federal Department of Justice, the National Judicial Institute, the Canadian Human Rights Commission, the Ontario Métis Aboriginal Association and the International Labour Organization.

Beverley Thaver holds a BA Degree in History from the University of Cape Town, an MA in African History from the University of York (UK) and a Ph.D in Adult Education from the University of the Western Cape. She is the Acting Director of the Centre for the Study of Higher Education (formerly the Education Policy Unit) in the Faculty of Education at the University of the Western Cape, South Africa.

Along with convening a Masters' programme in Higher Education Studies she has worked on several independent and collaborative research projects. Her current research project is on aspects of deracialisation as it pertains to a changing South African academic profession.

Foreword

Paradox can be dealt with in opposite ways. One is to suppress it or to deny its existence. The second is to embrace it and to derive as much creative and positive energy as possible from the contradiction it embodies. This book illustrates in well-researched and thoughtful ways the successes and failures that different societies have had in acknowledging and managing the two basic tensions inherent in the concept of affirmative action.

The first is that in most societies where it has been tried, the majority need consciously to curtail its advantage so as to favour minority advance, something that is usually electorally unpopular, and hence precarious for the minority by its very nature. The second is that it involves conscious use of racial distinctions in order to create a non-racial society.

As far as the first paradox is concerned, the intrinsic tension has been poorly managed throughout the world. It seems that the majority tend not to adopt programmes of affirmative action simply on the basis of a desire to live in a more moral and just society. They do so not to meet widely proclaimed human rights standards but, sadly, because the social and economic costs of change are outweighed by the social and economic costs of policing the status quo. Put bluntly, affirmative action has frequently come about as a rushed and forced response to what have been called race riots.

The second paradox has at least fostered much lively international debate. The key concepts that have emerged are those of redress and balance. The objective is not to establish a form of anachronistic or disjunctive compensation for past injustices. It is to rectify the way in which these injustices continue to permeate the world we live in. Nor can the aim be to replace one form of social inequity with another, that is, to elevate 'now-its-our-turnism' into a principle of equitable redress. The objective must be to overcome all forms of structured advantage. The moral purpose is thereby intrinsically and inextricably bound up with the social function. Structured and institutionalised imbalances in society call for responses that in turn are structured and balanced.

I remember well the intense debates we had in South Africa in the early 1990s, 'Affirmative action? What does it mean, I don't understand it at all'. None of us were taken in by the query put by Govan Mbeki. Recently released after more than two decades in prison on Robben Island with Nelson Mandela, he was a thoughtful writer, a wise and experienced political thinker (and, incidentally, father of the equally intellectual Thabo Mbeki who is now President of South Africa). *Oom Gov* (Uncle Gov), as we called him, was using a pretend puzzlement to make a point. This was at a workshop on affirmative action organised by the Constitutional Committee of the African National Congress, a time of anxious deliberation on the eve of negotiations for South Africa's first democratic, non-racial Constitution. The point he was making was that affirmative action was a fuzzy concept, meaning nothing at all. It neither called for a radical redistribution of resources in favour of the poor and dispossessed, nor did it present the unconstrained market as the instrument of overcoming the massive, racialised disparities of wealth created in our country by centuries of colonialism, segregation and apartheid. Behind his amiable yet unconvincing claim to ignorance, lay his challenge to affirmative action. In his view it was simply too indistinct to be meaningful.

Yet for those of us involved in negotiating a peaceful democratic revolution in our country, it was precisely its ambiguity and plastic quality that gave affirmative action its strength and value. We had embarked upon a process of establishing a constitutional order that for the first time would enable all South Africans to live together as equals in one country. Emerging from decades of struggle in a deeply divided society, we needed to get maximum consensus on the foundations of our new citizenship. Our objective was to empower a democratically elected Parliament, within a framework of a comprehensive and emancipatory Bill of Rights, to take the steps necessary to bring about the envisaged social justice. The more unfettered the competence of Parliament, the better. Social and economic realities would provide the prescriptive framework, not a detailed programme of transformation laid down in advance. Any proposed and detailed blueprint was calculated to entrench inflexibility in the negotiations just at a time when maximum imaginative reaching-out on all sides was required.

Our first task, accordingly, was firmly to establish the principled character of our new society and to entrench the nature of our constitutional democracy. Then, once a transformative Constitution was agreed upon, we could move forward to establishing equally principled and pragmatic ways of overcoming the structures of injustice in our country. The result was that although the words affirmative action, about which *Oom Gov* was so dubious – he would have preferred more radical terminology – appear nowhere in our Constitution, their spirit animates the whole document.

This book shows how flexible, adaptive and contextual affirmative action has in fact been in different parts of the world. Its ambiguity and adaptability are both its strength and its fragility. It is not a fixed formula for governmental action transportable from one country to another, nor is it a precise constitutional or legal arrangement of universal application. Yet it does have a core feature. Wherever it may function and whatever its terminology, it involves focussed and deliberate governmental intervention that takes account of the reality of race to deal with and overcome the problems associated with race. Racism has been so deeply entrenched over centuries by slavery and colonial domination, that its pervasive heritage cannot be wished away simply by invoking constitutional idealism. We have to take account of the actual manner in which race still affects our societies, and give special weight to the experiences of those injured by it. We must also ensure that amelioration is achieved with the active participation of all.

Above all, we should never lose sight of the fact that the goal is to establish a non-racial society in which social and cultural diversity is celebrated and seen as a source of vitality, and in which race as such ultimately has no political or economic significance. That must always be our goal.

Given true equal opportunities we could expect in any society that the profiles of government and economic life would evolve to reflect the demographics of that society. Then to the extent that the programmes succeed, specific attention to race would become attenuated and disappear. Ideally, there should be no need for an express cut-off point, for as the society truly starts to accept diversity, the affirmative action programmes would become naturally obsolete and irrelevant.

The day might still be far off when we can at last say: demography is destiny. But we can take meaningful steps in that direction. This book provides us with invaluable guides to opportunities seized, and opportunities lost. If *Oom Gov*'s query remains with us, it is not because of lack of clarity as to the meaning of affirmative action, but as a result of lack of will to carry it through.

Albie Sachs
Justice of the Constitutional Court of South Africa

Acknowledgements

I would like to thank Ken Millins, Wilma Boisnard and Bernard Dubourdieu for their help and support throughout. I also wish to thank the University of Nantes for the material support which made this research possible.

Elaine Kennedy-Dubourdieu (ed.)

Introduction

Elaine Kennedy-Dubourdieu

Cohesion has long been an objective in most societies. How to achieve that cohesion is another matter, especially in those countries where the population is made up of different racial and ethnic components.

Various approaches have been adopted over the centuries, either in an *ad hoc* manner, or as a deliberate political choice. The most extreme means of achieving cohesion has been by eliminating difference and the 'other', either by direct aggression or by simple neglect. This can then be justified in terms of Social Darwinism and the 'natural' order, where the most adapted race or culture dominates and the fittest survives.

Attempts at social cohesion through annihilation of those perceived as different may not have totally disappeared, but such practices are now ideologically less acceptable in the global village of increased media scrutiny, or when the 'other' may be capable of striking back.

With increased migration, cohesion has also been posited through the 'melting pot' of assimilation, where 'the other' or the newcomer must conform to the social blueprint of the dominant group if they want to be accepted. However where the 'other' remains visibly different from the majority this may never be achieved, no matter how hard the former tries.

In the second half of the twentieth century, some societies moved beyond the steamroller approach of assimilation towards the concept of unity through the recognition of diversity, which came to be designated as 'multiculturalism' – the interactive co-existence of different cultures in the same society, where minorities have the right to be different from the majority and yet are accepted as part of the whole.

'Culture' can be variously defined: in terms of race, ethnicity or language, or in terms of a shared history, religion, cuisine, dress code etc. But how then does the state create cohesion and a sense of belonging out of this multicultural mix? Allegiance to a flag, a monarch, a national sports team, a national anthem or a national dish? Federation through shared values or just agreed principles?

The debate continues, but one constant does seem to emerge and that is the agreement on the need for equality, and equality of opportunity for all citizens of such societies; these egalitarian principles are believed by many to underpin a stable and just society.

The question then arises of how best to achieve this equality?

One of the great innovations in social policy in recent times has been that of 'affirmative action', set up in various parts of the world, with the United States frequently designated as the model and the prime mover, though in reality the Indian policy of 'Compensatory Discrimination' in favour of the Dalits (Untouchables), those who find themselves from birth in the lowest category of the caste hierarchy, is well anterior to this.

As an overt, clearly enunciated practice, this is a policy that came to public recognition in the second half of the twentieth century, though some have argued that inexplicited practices of a similar type (in favour of men, often white and middle class) have long existed.

Affirmative action is one of those icon social policies that engenders an inflamed debate and opinion polls consistently reveal that practically everyone has an opinion on the subject, even though there is a great deal of confusion over what the policy actually entails, and myths and 'saloon-bar' allegations abound. Yet most people believe they have a good grasp of the parameters of the debate – even when this transcends national borders. The French for example regularly discuss the 'Anglo-Saxon' model of affirmative action, (generally believed to encompass North America and other parts of the English speaking world) and the policy is invariably reduced to the imposition of 'quotas' and the 'dictates of positive discrimination'.[1] For this is all too often a debate that is premised on sweeping generalisations and flattening assumptions.

Thus the intention of this work is to take a detailed look at the policy of affirmative action as it has evolved in different, ethnically diverse parts of the world: Australia, Canada, Great Britain, India, Northern Ireland, South Africa and the United States. Although affirmative action has operated in favour of various segments of the population (such as women, the disabled and war veterans) this work will concentrate essentially on the policy as it has been used in favour of racial/ethnic groups, i.e. essentially those groups somatically identified as different and who have suffered from overt and covert racism and disadvantage. These are mostly minorities, though in the case of post-apartheid South Africa it is the black majority that has been singled out as the beneficiary of this policy.

The Terminology

One of the first difficulties that arises in this debate is the question of the terminology. Even within the same country the semantic content of a term and the connotations that latch on to it may vary widely, which means that although the discussion may seemingly revolve around the same term – the concept and practices contained in that term differ. In short, people may think they are discussing the same thing when in fact they are not.

The policy has been variously described over the years as Affirmative Action, Protective Discrimination, Compensatory Discrimination, Positive Discrimination, Positive Action, Positive Positioning, Preferential Treatment, Reverse Discrimination,

---

[1]   Laurence Girard, *Le Monde*, 21 February 2004, p.30.

Multiculturalism – and more still. All of these terms have different semantic resonances, which are often highly idiosyncratic – indeed the very choice of terminology may at times indicate the ideological standpoint of the speaker.

There are similar complexities to be noted as regards the groups singled out as the beneficiaries of such a policy. The nuances of the terms and categories used in South Africa for example have been minutely addressed by Thaver: notice the intricacies of the term 'black' and 'Black', and the difference even a capital letter can make. This problem of terminology may be further compounded by the fact that some distinctions have simply been lost in translation when rendered in English. Deshpande points out that the two distinctive Indian systems of *Varna* and *Jati* have been translated into English by the single expression 'the caste system'.

Special care therefore has been taken to tease out and elucidate the significance of the terminology used in these different countries and thus, it is hoped, minimise confusion.

Affirmative action is not a consensual policy. Though the term had been used earlier in the United States, nevertheless it was felt to be a new term for a new concept when it was introduced in the 1960s. Since then it has picked up all sorts of connotations worldwide, which may explain why there has been a reshuffling of terminology with new discourses throwing up new terms and in various countries we now find a blurring between what is described as 'affirmative action' and 'equal opportunities' or 'equity' programmes. There does indeed seem to have been a reframing of the debate with a change in presentation, intended to produce a different representation of the policy, as these new terms seem generally well accepted, whereas the former may no longer be so.

Does the vehemence of the debate surrounding this policy thus depend on the way it is presented to the public? Sheppard in the section on Canada clearly thinks it does, and other contributors to the book concur with this view.

There are other facets to this shifting linguistic terrain that appear in filigree in the following chapters, such as the pernicious 'linguistic flip-flops' mentioned by Ooiman Robinson. Here she pinpoints those terms that have long been associated in the United States with the struggle against racial injustice, but which have recently been appropriated by those bent on undermining that same struggle. She explains how this topsy-turvy discourse has been used to confuse voters when called to take a stand on this issue of affirmative action.

Words matter in this debate and they should be called into question regularly.

The Rationale for the Policy

The social and political foundations upon which affirmative action policies have been constructed vary with each country. The historical backdrops to the Indian caste system and the racial divisions of South Africa, America or Australia seemingly have little in common. Yet certain constants remain.

Societies' first response to discrimination often comes in the form of anti-discrimination legislation and the declared necessity of treating everyone in the 'same way' and then believing, like the classical economists in the eighteenth century, in the virtues of *laissez-faire*, allowing the system to regulate itself. This they believed would lead to the best of all possible worlds, untrammelled by government interference. Some democracies, like France, still believe that this prescriptive approach should suffice. Others have adopted a more pragmatic stance, and have examined the way the system actually functions. Such scrutiny has revealed the persistence of discrimination that is ingrained, not only in institutional policies and practices, but also in the very fabric and culture of society. Frequently the nature and extent of this disparity and discrimination have been established through the collection of racial / ethnic statistics, although arriving at such systematic monitoring in some countries has been a saga in itself that would warrant the telling. Elsewhere, such as in India, this has never happened as it is believed this would exacerbate caste feelings. France also persistently rejects the idea of such monitoring as being anti-constitutional and a form of discrimination in itself.

Where governments have chosen to collect such statistics the monitoring has generally become more sophisticated, making it now impossible to believe for example that Catholics' disadvantage in Northern Ireland could be explained in terms of higher birth-rates and geographical location (see Hinds and O'Kelly), as was previously the case.

The realities of these statistics are often compelling, such as the dramatically higher unemployment rates of some racial and ethnic communities. There are also those statistics that confound received ideas: for example in Britain and Canada such data has revealed generally higher education levels for people from 'racialized' communities (a term used by Sheppard) but these are coupled with significant disparities between this educational attainment and subsequent employment rates.

Therefore it has become clear for many that a prescriptive approach to discrimination is not enough. If such group differences do persist, then to do nothing – in the name of neutrality or 'fairness' – just perpetuates the status quo and existing disparities and disadvantage. If society wants equal outcomes, then a lever of change is necessary at times to actively achieve this equality.

This then is the catalyst that has moved some societies on to the pragmatic and pro-active stance of adopting affirmative action programmes. Other countries, like France, that persist in an assimilationist, colour-blind approach largely ignore this debate.

Setting up the Policy

The policy then is based on the premise that intervention is necessary to increase the participation of under-represented groups in certain key areas in society. But in what form? By compulsion, persuasion, stealth or other means?

The countries studied in this work have set about doing this in very different ways and the ethnic or racial groups targeted by such policies also vary: some are indigenous, aboriginal populations – the earliest inhabitants of those countries; others are more recent arrivals – some were transported there against their will as slaves, while many others have come as economic migrants or refugees. As already pointed out, the terms describing the policy may not be the same, but all subscribe to basic principles: 'equality of opportunity', 'social justice', or just what the Australians call having 'a fair-go' (see Piquet).

The legislation and codes of practice that define this policy in each country are systematically examined in each chapter, as are the key areas where the different countries have seen fit to concentrate their intervention. In Canada where there has been a great deal of effort to promote equity in the work place through affirmative action, there have been few corresponding measures in education, where the main reliance appears to be on voluntary efforts. Yet broadly speaking, employment and education are the most frequently targeted domains for intervention. Employment may be tackled in the public sector only (as in India) or in both public and private sectors, where some governments have devised methods of putting direct and indirect pressure on private employers, such as through the practice of 'contract compliance'/ 'procurement' for example. Thus when seeking to redistribute access to employment, education and other services, authorities may choose from a panoply of methods, such as training, encouraging applications, or using numerical goals, quotas, targets and timeframes. Here again terminology is often finely drawn. When does a goal become a quota? This is undoubtedly the aspect of the policy that has focalised most attention over the years and these points are scrutinised in each chapter.

The next question raised is that of the enforcement or not of the relevant measures. Is it enough to stipulate, suggest and educate? Is education really the key, with full compliance to legislation only coming, as some suggest, when organisations themselves see the benefits and rationale for change? Is enforcement unnecessary, even counter-productive, leading perhaps to a hardening of attitudes and increased resentment by those groups who are left out of the policy, or who feel it actively discriminates against them? Or will policies of this nature never be taken seriously if not actively enforced? India has no such enforcement procedure and Deshpande declares that compensatory discrimination remains a dead letter in many cases, as the Constitution is simply not adhered to.

At the time of the setting up of Britain's first enforcement agencies in the 1960s and 1970s, those working in this area looked enviously across the Atlantic to America's watchdog institutions that were seen as having real power. Ooiman Robinson gives a more nuanced view of this, pointing out the importance of who was actually in charge and how different key appointments have led to some startling 'U' turns in policy in the United States.

The enforcement agencies that have been created in the various countries are described, as well as the way the policy fits into the complex whole of central and local power structures and the competing interests of key institutions. The question becomes even more complex in those countries with a federal structure where the play between the federal and state/provincial institutions and legislations may appear convoluted for the outsider. In the US for example Ooiman Robinson carefully explains the push and pull of Congress, the different courts and the interventions of the executive branch.

The Impact

People have tried in various ways to evaluate the impact of these policies. First of all by quantitative measurements: how many people from targeted groups at a given time in a given organisation, and some such studies have indeed shown redistributive effects (see for example Deshpande). However the statistics increasingly consider not the sheer numbers of the targeted group in an institution or business, but the actual positions held and the long-term chances of success of such a policy. Qualitative studies, such as those done on workplace cultures, are now being used increasingly to flesh out this debate.

For Hinds and O'Kelly the police service may be considered as a metaphor for a state's attitude towards equality. In order to serve the public and enforce the law, it is necessary for it to be representative of the society it polices, if it wants legitimacy and sustained support from that society as a whole.

In Britain, where the racist 'canteen culture' of the police has been well documented, it is difficult not only to recruit officers from the racial minorities, but more problematic still, to retain those who have been recruited. The policy statements on non-discrimination and equality of opportunity coming from the upper echelons of the police hierarchy do not seem to have filtered down to the ranks. So it has been argued that other strategies must be used to change this culture from the grass roots upwards through the introduction of a 'critical mass' (usually situated at somewhere between 15 per cent and 30 per cent of the workforce) capable of creating its own dynamic, modifying from within the shared body of practices and values that make up the dominant culture of that organisation. Indeed the importance of constituting such a 'critical mass' is increasingly prominent in the debate, especially in response to the question of how long the policy of affirmative action should be maintained. As long as it takes to establish this 'critical mass'?

Affirmative action is, by its nature, a blunt instrument aimed, not at an individual, but at a group. It is said to favour those who are better placed in that group, not those at the bottom end of the scale. Does this then necessarily invalidate the policy? Those who have benefited not only contribute to the constitution of this 'critical mass' but also provide a model of social mobility that is within the grasp of others. It is useful to remember that it was for this very reason that President P.W. Botha did not want 'The Cosby Show' on South African television, believing that this portrayal of middle class Black Americans was highly subversive and would undermine apartheid and white minority rule in the country.

The View from One Country to Another

Countries may look to one another for positive (and negative) examples of social policy. In the 1960s and 1970s Britain looked to the American civil rights model as an example. After the riots in Britain's northern towns in 2001, the British Commission for Racial Equality once again looked to America, but also to Northern Ireland for examples of good practice and ways of achieving community cohesion.

Countries of the Commonwealth provide abundant illustrations of this crisscrossing of influences: South Africa and Australia have looked to Canada, whereas the British Raj in India set up what were perhaps the first ethnic quotas.

Living and working in France has helped me understand the nature of British social policy in this area and realise how different it is from that of the French Jacobin state. Comparisons of this type can be illuminating, not least when they force a defining of those constituent elements taken for granted perhaps in the home context. Thus the idea emerged of putting together a work on affirmative action as it has been used in various parts of the world.

Specialists for each country were invited to draw out the social and historical basis for this policy, as well as its functioning in each specific context. Thus the book is not just a statement of one person's view, but a collective endeavour – although the opinions expressed are the responsibility of the individual contributors.

At times direct comparisons are made between these countries, but mostly the work simply provides a detailed juxtaposition of various case studies as snapshot audits of the state of affirmative action in a number of countries at a particular time. These different chapters reveal the complexity and multiplicity of form this policy has taken on in different parts of the globe. It is hoped that this will enable the readers, should they so wish, to make comparisons or highlight the disparities between these different countries. The overall intention is to contribute to a deeper understanding of the policy, and to open up discussion.

The collection starts with the United States of America, generally believed to provide the matrix for this policy. Popular wisdom has it that it was set up by President Kennedy – a generous policy that became embroiled in quotas and claims of reverse discrimination. The reality of American affirmative action is in no way as clear-cut as it is believed to be from the outside. The subtleties of the policy, as well as its complex historical background, are detailed by Ooiman Robinson who tells of forgotten earlier attempts at proportional hiring of African Americans by the Tennessee Valley Authority for example. Ooiman Robinson also charts the complex route taken by that emotively charged term of 'quota' and explains in detail those frequently referred to legal cases that are claimed as a victory by both sides of the ideological fence. She also carefully deconstructs the Californian referendum on the future of affirmative action in that state.

For geographical coherence we then move north of the 49th parallel to Canada, part of the same continent, but with a completely different history and view of 'multiculturalism'. This country initially set itself the task of fostering the peaceful co-existence of the two major linguistic communities (French and English) of the rival European colonisers, before responding to the needs of other groups, some of whom were Canada's first inhabitants. Sheppard highlights the complexities of this rapidly changing scene and suggests that Canada has tried to minimise the potential backlash against this policy by presenting it in a context that affirms, not only its legality as inscribed in the new Constitution, but also the beneficial effects for the society as a whole.

From Canada to India, the earliest documented case of affirmative action where the situation also has highly specific complexities with a huge number of caste divisions and categories (estimated at between 2,000–3,000), which also have regional and state variations. Deshpande takes us through the range of terms frequently encountered (Scheduled Castes, Harijans, Dalits, Scheduled Tribes, Other Backward Classes ...) but which are rarely so coherently explained. India is a country where 86 per cent of the population is Hindu and religion and religious affiliation plays an extremely important role. Here the affirmative action programme is quota based to give a proportional share of government jobs, places in educational institutions and electoral constituencies to the targeted groups. The policy was enshrined in the 1952 Constitution so that it could not be subsequently challenged. (Canada and South Africa were later to follow this same course of action.) This was the theory, but the practice, as Deshpande points out, has been very different.

In India, qualifying marks for admission to educational institutions are lowered for beneficiaries of affirmative action, but no special assistance or remedial teaching is available and the dropout rate is considerable.

Britain on the other hand, operates differently with special training courses and remedial teaching which are part of the arsenal of measures targeted at certain racial groups. Until recent times affirmative action in Britain was merely tolerated by the law and was thus only put into practice in an *ad hoc*, sporadic way when individual local authorities or institutions were convinced of its necessity. The country has only recently moved on to a more systematic, pro-active stance with the passing of the Race Relations Amendment Act in 2000.

Along with Great Britain, the other constituent part of the United Kingdom is Northern Ireland, which is somewhat atypical in this collection of countries, as just under one per cent of its population are from the racial minorities. Nevertheless it has been included in this study as it is a society long divided by a sectarian, Catholic/Protestant rift, which has led to extreme forms of violence and instability. As discrimination and exclusion of the Catholic community have been at the heart of the conflict, so the issues of civil rights and equality are now central to the resolution of this same conflict. This has made Northern Ireland a testing ground for a whole range of initiatives, described in detail by Hinds and O'Kelly, some of which have since been extended to the racial minorities living there.

On the other side of the globe the Australian case is different again. Here the term 'affirmative action' has been earmarked exclusively for gender and not race, as it is reserved for the policy of promoting equal opportunities for women. Policies in favour of the racial minorities, including Australia's indigenous population, which are designed to redress unequal access to services and resources, are deemed to be 'multiculturalism'. Piquet shows the close interconnection of the policies of immigration and integration and points out that although Australia has come a long way since the days when it believed that the Aboriginal peoples were heading for extinction (as in Tasmania) and when it unashamedly operated a race-based, British White Australia policy, nevertheless much remains to be done and commitment to this policy of multiculturalism is patchy and ambivalent.

The work closes with the latest addition to the club of countries using affirmative action, which is South Africa, a society long engineered on racial lines under colonialism and apartheid. The white minority governments constantly sought to split up the 'non-white' majority by exacerbating difference and hostility among the various racial and ethnic groups. This policy of 'divide and rule' has left a terrible legacy, not least that which Thaver calls the 'entitlement tension' which endeavours to establish which group suffered most under apartheid, and so is entitled to the most help now.

The first democratically elected South African government provided in the 1996 Constitution for the use of affirmative action, with the detailed legislation enabling it to be set up following on afterwards. The Employment Equity Act makes affirmative action measures including preferential treatment and numerical goals legal, but excludes quotas, so once again, the case is unique and Thaver takes us through its intricacies.

The jury is still out on this particular social policy and whether it will survive well into the twenty-first century. It may be hoped that it will simply outgrow its usefulness, with the achievement of a 'critical mass' being created where possible. Or perhaps it will continue in other less openly declared forms of action, with its terminology metamorphosing accordingly. If dropped altogether, it is to be feared that this would allow established, though undeclared, modes of discriminatory behaviour in favour of dominant groups to operate with little counterbalancing effect.

In India, the Dalits (Untouchables) are still highly over-represented in the under-paid and unpopular jobs. In the United States children of the rich with mediocre grades can still obtain places in the most prestigious institutions of higher learning when their parents pay out considerable sums in legacies to these same institutions. In the twenty-first century it is obvious that birth, not worth, is still a key determinant of life's chances in many places worldwide.

Bringing together the different chapters of this book has been an ambitious task, which has called for considerable perseverance. In the time it has taken to do so the contemporary scene in different parts of the world may have changed somewhat. Nevertheless it is hoped that the work will prove to be a useful reference against which later developments may be evaluated, providing the necessary markers of time and context and elucidate the underlying principles of the policy of affirmative action as it has been practiced around the world.

Chapter 1

Affirmative Action in the United States

Jo Ann Ooiman Robinson

Affirmative action is one instrument by which African Americans, as a 'class', have sought to secure citizenship rights and to erase the stamp of inferiority with which they were branded historically. Finding racial inequality to be embedded in the political, economic and social institutions of the nation, affirmative action advocates insist that it cannot be extirpated by laws and policies that simply promise fair and equal treatment from a given time forward. They argue that some redistribution of political power, social standing, and/or economic resources is necessary to attain what the 36th President of the United States, Lyndon Baines Johnson, identified as the ultimate goal: 'not just equality as a right and a theory but equality as a fact and equality as a result'. The specific means by which these ends are sought include a wide range of race conscious initiatives and reforms, in both the public and the private sectors, and in such areas as school admissions, industrial apprenticeship and training programs, and hiring and promotion practices in the areas of business and manufacturing. It has also been argued that affirmative action should take the form of 'a kind of open-ended reparations'.[1]

Opponents of race conscious initiatives and policies (including some African Americans and members of other disadvantaged groups) decry them as violations of an allegedly 'color blind' Constitution, as 'reverse discrimination' against whites, and as demeaning to the individuals they are intended to elevate.

---

[1] 'Class' is used here as the legal designation that means a 'group as a whole', not just on an individual basis.

Lyndon B. Johnson, 'To Fulfill These Rights', Commencement Address at Howard University, 4 June 1965, *Public Papers of the Presidents, 1 June to 31 December 1965,* 638.

Regarding the link to reparations see Philip F. Rubio, *A History of Affirmative Action, 1619–2000*: 190 (Jackson: University Press of Mississippi, 2001).

The struggle of African Americans for equal economic opportunity and fair access to the centers of power so long monopolized by whites has inspired and provided a model for other groups within the United States who historically have been stigmatized and oppressed. Women, the disabled, American Indians, Latinos and numerous other ethnic minorities, are among those who have sought equality through affirmative action.

1.

In the contradiction between United States' claims of 'freedom and justice for all' and historical records of slavery, exploitation and brutal death for untold numbers lie the roots of the struggle for affirmative action. Following their war of independence against Britain, the new states, in 1787, formed a federal government that sanctioned slavery and assumed that the status of 'citizen' was synonymous with 'white male'.[2] Nearly three quarters of a century later, and at the conclusion of a bloody and bitter Civil War, the United States Congress – briefly controlled by a coalition of white and black reformers – amended the federal constitution, outlawing involuntary servitude (Thirteenth Amendment, 1865); establishing citizenship and guaranteeing 'equal protection of the laws' for 'all persons born or naturalized in the United States' (Fourteenth Amendment, 1866); and extending voting rights to men of color (Fifthteenth Amendment, 1869).[3]

In addition to the constitutional amendments, Congress enacted other laws that could be called prototypes for civil rights and affirmative action legislation a century later, including two civil rights acts (1866 and 1875) and laws that created and maintained a Bureau of Refugees, Freedmen and Abandoned Lands, better known as the Freedmen's Bureau. It was this institution that most prefigured the race conscious remedies enacted in the 1960s and after.

In its earliest history (beginning in 1865) the bureau aided both newly freed slaves and white war refugees. Assistance with housing, employment, food, legal aid and education were among its services.[4] When the bureau came up for renewal in 1866, whites were no longer included within its purview. This prompted opponents

---

[2]   The references to slavery in the US Constitution appear in Article I, Section 2, the 'three fifths compromise' determining that representation in the House of Representatives and direct taxes would be apportioned among the states according to the number of free persons in those states and 'three fifths of all other persons' – a veiled, yet obvious reference to slaves; Section 9 of the same article permitting the importation of slaves up to the year 1808; and Article 4, Section 2 mandating that runaway slaves be returned to their owners. Regarding assumptions of white supremacy in the Articles of Confederation, which governed the new nation before the Constitution, see Rubio, 13.

[3]   Women's suffrage was established in the nineteenth amendment, ratified in 1920.

Rubio, *ibid.*, 35, has noted that usage of the terms 'affirm' and 'affirmative' arose in the political debates of the Reconstruction Era, (1861–1876). The earliest use may have been in the context of defining white supremacy as a tool of affirmative action for whites. However, using it to mean an instrument for protecting blacks was more common. In recent times supporters of affirmative action have ironically labeled white privilege as 'white affirmative action'. See Daniel C. Maguire: 'the United States has been operating under a rigid quota system for white males in the principal centers of power in government, business and the professions…'. *A New American Justice* (New York: Doubleday, 1980).

[4]   *Appendix to the Congressional Globe* 35, Pt. 2 (3 March 1865) 141. The first Freedmen's Bureau also authorized distribution of land that had been abandoned, purchased or confiscated by the federal government. References to land distribution were deleted in 1866 since President Andrew Johnson had returned most of such land to the original owners.

of the law to complain that it was 'class legislation – legislation for a particular class of the blacks to the exclusion of all whites'. Concurring with this view and insisting that 'the idea on which the slaves were assisted to freedom was that on becoming free they would be a self-sustaining population', President Andrew Johnson vetoed the second bill.[5]

That bureau supporters were successful in fighting to override Johnson's veto and to pass the Fourteenth Amendment simultaneously has led some scholars to conclude that the amendment was intended 'to provide a constitutional basis for the Freedmen's Bureau Act'. On these grounds of historical context they argue that a sanction for race conscious legislation is inherent in the Fourteenth Amendment. Foes of affirmative action reject this interpretation. For them the 'equal' in 'equal protection' cannot mean special consideration based on race or any other factor.[6] In any case, for a few brief years national policy with regard to race was geared toward providing civil rights for all.[7]

Ultimately, however, Reconstruction failed. A new generation of political leaders was not concerned with racial justice. With a tremendous surge of industrialization occurring throughout the nation they sought compromises and coalitions that would reap the maximum benefit for themselves and their constituents. Reconstruction's collapse was completed in the contested presidential election of 1876. The price paid by the Republican Party for retaining the White House included ordering federal troops that were stationed in the South to stand down, thereby removing the last vestiges of protection for black civil rights.[8]

Calling themselves 'Redeemers', and with the acquiescence of the federal government, the former slave-holding class of southerners returned to power in the South. They replaced Reconstruction laws and institutions with a system of rigid segregation and inequality.[9] Reinforcing this 'redemption' the United States Supreme Court ruled in 1883 that Congress had exceeded its authority in passing the Civil Rights Act of 1875. Presenting the decision of the court majority, Justice Joseph Bradley asserted that it was time for blacks to cease 'to be the special favorite of the laws'.[10]

In 1896 the Court completed its evisceration of the laws intended to protect African Americans by establishing in the case of *Plessy v. Ferguson* that 'separate but equal' public accommodations were constitutional. Justice John Marshall Harlan

---

[5]   *The Papers of Andrew Johnson*, (February–July 1866), 10: 122–123. For congressional debates in which the charges of 'class legislation' were leveled see *Congressional Globe*, (24 January and 31 January 1866) 35 Pt. 1: 544, 401. The quoted complaint regarding 'class legislation' was stated by Nathaniel G. Taylor, Republican from Tennessee.

[6]   Eric Schnapper, (1985), 'Affirmative Action and the Legislative History of the Fourteenth Amendment', *Virginia Law Review*, 71: 753–790.

[7]   W.E. B. DuBois, *Black Reconstruction in America*, (Cleveland: Meridian, 1935, 1968).

[8]   Rayford Logan, *The Betrayal of the Negro*, (New York: Collier, 1954, 1965).

[9]   *Ibid.*

[10]   Civil Rights Cases of 1883, (1883),109 US 3.

dissented. One phrase in that dissent would be cited repeatedly over the years – his assertion regarding a 'color blind' Constitution. Advocates of affirmative action have attacked it as historically untrue, while for their opponents the phrase is a touchstone for every argument against any remedy for discrimination that includes preferential treatment of one group over another.[11]

The period designated the Nadir by historian Rayford Logan (ca.1876–1914) was a time when whites solidified and openly celebrated legalized segregation in the South and de facto segregation in many other parts of the country.[12] Additionally, many academics and social commentators formulated and broadcast 'Social Darwinism', an ideology predicated on the assumption that equality among human beings is impossible, for there will always be some who are strong and 'fit' and some who are weak and inferior. From such dogma would follow the concepts of 'merit' and 'meritocracy'. (Lauded by opponents of affirmative action in later years, these concepts were invoked to associate race-conscious methods of admissions in education, or hiring and promotion in industry and business, with 'lowering standards' that, presumably, only whites or white males could maintain).[13]

Lynchings and riots served as enforcers of segregation. One of the characteristics of the Nadir that is most salient for the history of affirmative action is the concerted effort by organized labor to exclude black workers and rally around white privilege.[14] The tradition of white supremacy that took root within the ranks of organized labor in the post-Reconstruction era (especially the American Federation of Labor) remained entrenched well into the 1960s.

Throughout the Nadir African Americans continued to resist. By the end of World War I academics and journalists were writing of a 'New Negro' who 'was not content to move along the line of least resistance…'.[15] In the following period, encompassing a world-wide depression, the New Deal response thereto by the administration of

---

[11]   *Plessy v. Ferguson*, (1896), 163 US 537, Marshall also dissented in the 1883 Civil Rights cases.

[12]   For more on the term, 'Nadir', see Rayford Logan, *ibid.*

[13]   Rubio, 61–63. An example of unabashed certainty of the rightness of segregation is quoted by Rubio on page 72: 'Speaking at a graduation ceremony at Tuskegee University', [Alabama Governor William C. Oates] declared: 'I want to give you niggers a few words of plain talk and advice. You might as well understand that this is a white man's country as far as the South is concerned, and we are going to make you keep your place…'.

[14]   Historians report nearly 4,000 lynchings between the last decade of the nineteenth century and the first three decades of the twentieth century. Rubio states that there were at least 50 white-worker-inspired riots between 1882 and 1900 and illustrates with a list of 'post-Reconstruction white supremacist programs… in such cities as Danville, Virginia in 1883; Phoenix, South Carolina, in 1898; New Orleans and New York in 1900; Springfield Ohio in 1904; Atlanta and Greenburg Illinois in 1906 and Springfield, Illinois in 1908'; Rubio, 58, 65, 68.

[15]   *Chicago Defender* quoted in *The Literary Digest*, (9 August 1919) 11, 'Methods of resistance included the black press; law suits and boycotts, alliance with the Populist Party and the founding of the National Association for the Advancement of Colored People'.

Franklin Roosevelt, and the Second World War, blacks laid significant ground work for the later emergence of affirmative action.

2.

The upsurge of black consciousness and racial pride indicated by the New Negro included the rise of a new generation of activist black leaders.[16] A number of these leaders mounted campaigns against employers in their communities who followed white-only hiring practices. Some of these campaigns went beyond promoting the philosophy of 'Don't Buy Where You Can't Work' to demanding that white-owned establishments hire African Americans in proportion to their numbers in the community.

Legal challenges to such demands for affirmative action-like proportional hiring made their way to the United States Supreme Court on two occasions. In 1938 that court granted the New Negro Alliance of Washington, D.C. the right to picket the Sanitary Grocery Store chain on behalf of proportional hiring, but left the concept itself open to debate. In 1950, the court ruled against the black Progressive Citizens of America (PAC). The PAC had demanded proportional hiring by the Lucky Grocery Store chain in Richmond, California. Lawyers for the organization rebutted charges that proportional hiring was discriminatory. They maintained that 'special consideration does not become "discrimination" where its beneficiaries are a uniquely oppressed and exploited social group'. The Supreme Court opined that if the PAC had its way 'Hungarians in Cleveland,...Poles in Buffalo..., Germans in Milwaukee,...Portuguese in New Bedford,...Mexicans in San Antonio...and the numerous minority groups in New York, and so on...' would all soon be 'picketing to secure proportional employment on ancestral grounds...'.[17]

In the midst of the Great Depression, with a third of the US labor force unemployed, securing employment of any type became more difficult than ever for minority workers. In 1932 Franklin D. Roosevelt won the presidential election and proclaimed a 'New Deal' for the nation. Roosevelt's New Deal was Janus-faced, putting out a few forward-looking programs that overrode entrenched white privilege

---

[16] Other indications of the new consciousness included the pageantry of black nationalist, Marcus Garvey, and the cultural outpouring of the Harlem Renaissance. On Garveyism see E. David Cronon, *Black Moses: The Story of Marcus Garvey and the Universal Negro Improvement Association*, (Madison, Wisconsin: University of Wisconsin Press, 1972). A basic study of the Harlem Renaissance is Nathan I. Huggins, *The Harlem Renaissance*, (New York: Oxford University Press, 1990). Regarding grass roots economic boycotts and proportional hiring campaigns of the 1930s see Paul Moreno, *From Direct Action to Affirmative Action*, 30–65 and Rubio, 105–106, (Baton Rouge, Louisiana: University of Louisiana Press, 1997).

[17] Moreno (1938), *New Negro Alliance v. Sanitary Grocery Co.*, 303 US 552. *Hughes v. Superior Court* (1950), 339 US 460. Jo Ann Ooiman Robinson, *Affirmative Action: A Documentary History*, 64–65 (Westport Connecticut: Greenwood Press, 2001).

while establishing many others that faced backwards toward traditional practices of discrimination.[18]

Impetus for the forward-looking initiatives came from African American political leaders such as Robert Weaver, race relations advisor to Harold Ickes in the Public Works Administration (PWA). Weaver was instrumental in persuading Ickes to require for all PWA construction that contractors employ at least the same percentage of African American workers as recorded in the 1930 census for each city. In a similar vein, hiring and training quotas for black workers were mandated for the extensive construction undertaken by the Tennessee Valley Authority, one of the most ambitious New Deal projects.[19]

The term 'affirmative action' appeared for the first time in federal law in the Roosevelt administration's landmark labor reform, the National Labor Relations Act (NLRA) of 1935. The law empowered workers to negotiate and bargain collectively. It also created a National Labor Relations Board (NLRB) authorized to investigate unfair labor practices and 'take such affirmative action...as will effectuate the policies of this Act'. Later laws were modeled on this measure.

Ironically, the measure itself became an instrument of discrimination against black and other minority workers by identifying organized labor as workers' sole collective bargaining agent. Because the dominant unions were affiliates of the AFL, which regularly excluded blacks, the new law enhanced opportunities for white workers and reinforced their racism. Even the more progressive Congress of Industrial Organizations (CIO) that emerged in the 1930s to challenge the AFL had within a decade become 'part of the white labor establishment in privileging whiteness'.[20]

As the likelihood of US involvement in World War II increased, African American leaders put forth the wartime goal of a 'double victory' – the securing of democracy and freedom abroad, and within the United States. Philip Randolph (founder of the Brotherhood of Sleeping Car Porters) spearheaded the all-African American March on Washington Movement (MOWM) in 1941 that exacted

---

[18] Basic coverage of this subject is Harvard Sitkoff, *A New Deal for Blacks: The Emergence of Civil Rights as a National Issue*, (New York: Oxford University Press, 1978).

[19] The PWA undertook major building projects– bridges, public auditoriums, etc., thereby creating jobs. On the proportional hiring policy see Marc W. Kruman, 'Quotas for Blacks: The Public Works Administration and the Black Construction Worker', *Labor History* 16, (Winter, 1975), no. 1: 50–51. The TVA entailed the relocation of communities in a 7 state area covering 41,000 square miles, in order to build dams and generate electricity. Nancy L. Grant, *TVA and Black Americans: Planning for the Status Quo*, (Philadelphia: Temple University Press, 1990).

[20] The National Labor Relations Act may be found in *US Code*, (1935), Vol. 29, secs. 160b, 160c.

Rubio, 92–93, Rubio notes that civil rights organizations lobbied for an anti-discrimination amendment to the NLRA but were rebuffed.

Executive Order 8802 from Franklin Roosevelt, mandating black employment in defense industries.[21]

Although at the end of the war Congress squelched the federal Fair Employment Practice Committee that had followed from E0 8802, numerous states took up the practice of providing a government channel to which victims of employment discrimination could appeal. New York led the way with its 1945 State Law Against Discrimination, establishing a Fair Employment Commission authorized to take 'affirmative action' against 'any unlawful employment practice'.[22]

Meanwhile Congress was devising a policy for returning veterans that stands out as an example of federal preferential policy implementation, the Servicemen's Readjustment Act of 1944. Better known as the G.I. Bill, it guaranteed to all returning servicemen with honorable discharges access to federally funded health care, college or vocational education, assistance in obtaining jobs, and loans for home buying and the opening of businesses. In education, the G.I. Bill authorized special college admissions requirements, along with tutorial support, refresher courses, and college credit for certain aspects of military experience.[23] While women and minorities did not benefit from the G.I. Bill as much as white men, interpretations differ regarding the degree to which it was implemented on a discriminatory basis. Irregardless of that discrimination, the Servicemen's Readjustment Act would stand as a major point of reference for supporters of later economic set-asides and targeted college admissions programs.[24]

For black veterans World War II was a pivotal event. They returned to the United States determined that they and their children would no longer be denied in their own country the freedoms that they had fought to secure for other parts of the world. The almost immediate onset of the Cold War supplied new leverage with which to

---

[21]   Paula Pfeffer (1990), *A. Philip Randolph, Pioneer of Civil Rights*, (Baton Rouge: Louisiana State University Press). Later in the forties the Congress of Racial Equality (CORE) pioneered sit-ins against segregated public facilities and an early freedom ride testing a Supreme Court ruling against segregated interstate transportation, presaging future campaigns of nonviolent direct action. August Meier and Elliot Rudwick, CORE (New York: Oxford University Press, 1973).

[22]   *McKinney's Consolidated Laws of New York*, (1950), Book 18, Cumulative Annual Pocket Part, 73.

[23]   The high quality of college work produced by veterans who took advantage of these programs has been said to have 'proved for the first time that tests of ability are not predictive of academic performance when motivation and expectations are high'. Reginald Wilson (1994), 'G.I. Bill Expands Access for African Americans', *Educational Record* 74: 36.

[24]   *US Statutes At Large* 58, Pt. 1 (1944). Following Hilary Herbold, 'Never a Level Playing Field', (1994/1995), *Journal of Blacks in Higher Education* 5: 104–108. Rubio asserts that 'the G.I. Bill helped increase distance between blacks and whites by granting government benefits to returning white veterans…that were beneficial out of proportion to veterans of color', Rubio, 117. Reginald Wilson, *ibid.* stresses the role of the G.I. Bill in 'developing a tiny group of [African American] professionals into the large stable, and growing "black *bourgeoisie*"' that existed by the end of the century, Wilson, 33–39, quotation 38. On women veterans and the G.I. Bill see June Willenz, 'Invisible Veterans', (1994), *Educational Record* 74: 41–46.

apply that determination. Nothing redounded more to the Soviets' advantage than the public airing of racial conflict in the United States.[25]

3.

The time span from the end of World War II into the 1970s was a period of expansive, mass black resistance, augmented in several instances by support from sympathetic whites. This mass movement was spurred in part by the 1954 Supreme Court ruling, *Brown v. Board of Education*, and by the white 'massive resistance' that it provoked.[26]

In *Brown* the nation's top court nullified 'separate but equal' policies in public education, and thereby removed the legal basis for any form of segregation in the United States. The cases on which the ruling was based originated with ordinary black citizens in five US communities who simply wanted for their children the same educational opportunities and resources enjoyed by the children of their white neighbors.[27] Intransigent racists were abetted by a second Supreme Court ruling (*Brown II*) on how the first was to be enforced – by local courts, 'with all deliberate speed'.[28]

With the process of desegregation left in the hands of those who most opposed it, new vigilantes such as the White Citizens Council soon joined older hate groups, of which the Ku Klux Klan was best known, to rally a violent white supremacist opposition. They enjoyed the full backing of demagogues such as Mississippi

---

[25]   Mary L. Dudziak, *Cold War Civil Rights*, (Princeton: Princeton University Press, 2002).

[26]   Richard Kluger, *Simple Justice*, (New York: Random House, 1977). James T. Patterson, *Brown v. Board of Education: A Civil Rights Milestone and Its Troubled Legacy*, (New York: Oxford University Press, 2001).

[27]   In fact, black parents initially made modest requests, such as the petition for a school bus, presented to white authorities in Clarendon County, South Carolina. It was only after that petition was denied and the parents scraped together the wherewithal to buy their own bus and then requested financial support to keep it running – which was also denied – that they turned to the NAACP and instituted legal action that evolved into one of the five cases ruled on in *Brown*, see Kluger. The same progression from being willing to settle for a small improvement to demanding a total change in policy and practice occurred in the Montgomery Bus Boycott of 1956. In the beginning blacks were willing to settle for a modified system of segregated seating. By stonewalling them city officials helped provoke the massive, yearlong boycott. See Stewart Burns (ed.), *Daybreak of Freedom*, (Chapel Hill: University of North Carolina Press, 1997).

[28]   *Brown v. Board of Education*, (1954), 347 US 483; *Brown v. Board of Education* (1955), 349 US 299. Although the *Brown* rulings dealt solely with education, their implications were plain. The federal district court that heard the case brought in 1956 by citizens of Montgomery, Alabama against segregation on the public buses in their community declared that there was 'now no rational basis upon which the separate but equal doctrine can be validly applied to public carrier transportation…'. *Browder v. Gayle*, 142 F. Supp. 707 (M.D. Ala., 1956).

Senator James Eastland. 'School integration', vowed Eastland, '... is something that the white race will not permit under any conditions; and there is not the power of compulsion on the part of the Federal Government to compel it'.[29]

Presidents whose terms coincided with the modern civil rights movement tended to side with movement objectives in theory, while in practice sidestepping forceful action on their behalf. John F. Kennedy is a case in point.[30]

By a narrow margin, in which black votes figured critically, and having made inspiring campaign promises regarding civil rights, Kennedy won the White House in 1960. With Executive Order 10925 in 1961 he continued a presidential tradition of issuing White House fiats prohibiting racial discrimination in federal employment. The Kennedy order called for 'affirmative action' to guarantee that hiring and employment practices would be implemented 'without regard to race, creed, color, or national origins', and went a step further than previous orders by including in its proscription labor unions whose members worked under government contract.[31]

The press of events also forced the President and his brother, Attorney General Robert Kennedy, to deploy federal troops, intervene with federal marshals, and send federal mediators into the South to quell vicious white supremacist attacks on black, nonviolent protestors. However, from the viewpoint of civil rights leaders, these were reluctant and belated responses, a far cry from the pro-active support for their struggle to which they had hoped the Kennedys were committed.[32]

The civil rights bill sent by John Kennedy to Congress in the summer of 1963 was pending and by no means guaranteed of passage when he was assassinated in November of that year. When Vice President Lyndon Johnson stepped in to the

---

[29]   *Congressional Record*, (27 May 1954), 100 PT 1 7252 and (23 July 1954) 11524–11525.

[30]   Roosevelt's successor, Harry Truman, gave rousing pro-civil rights speeches and appointed a Committee on Civil Rights that laid out a strong agenda for succeeding decades. While he did not wrest from Congress even one of the objectives on that agenda, he did, by means of Executive Order 9981 issued in July of 1948, start the process by which the US armed forces would be desegregated. After him came Dwight Eisenhower, who was privately appalled by the *Brown* decision, and who only with great reluctance sent federal troops to uphold it when racist mobs, egged on by Arkansas Governor Orval Faubus, tried to prevent nine black students from attending Little Rock High School. For an accessible overview of US civil rights in the post-World War II era, including a substantive bibliography, see Steven Lawson (1991), Running *for Freedom: Civil Rights and Politics in America Since 1941*, (New York: McGraw Hill). Truman's EO 9981 (the impetus for which was provided by A. Philip Randolph, in a manner reminiscent of his pressuring FDR during World War II) can be found in *Federal Register*, (28 July 1948) 13: 4313.

[31]   *Federal Register*, (1961) 26: 1977. In addition to verbal election promises on civil rights the Kennedy brothers had intervened on behalf of Martin Luther King, Jr. who had been jailed and whose safety was in question. The phone calls John Kennedy made to King's wife and that Robert Kennedy made to the judge, who had sentenced King, facilitated King's release and garnered black support for the Kennedy ticket, See Lawson.

[32]   Mark Stern, *Calculating Visions: Kennedy, Johnson and Civil Rights*, (New Brunswick: Rutgers University Press, 1992).

presidency, he drew upon a wealth of contacts on Capitol Hill, abilities as a 'wheeler-dealer' for which he had been notorious as a Senator, and the high tide of emotion sweeping the country in reaction to Kennedy's death to cinch passage of the Civil Rights Act of 1964, followed closely by the Voting Rights Act of 1965. These and related initiatives by Johnson carried the seeds of affirmative action – as it would be defined, implemented, ruled upon, defended and decried for the rest of the twentieth century.[33]

4.

The Civil Rights Act of 1964, prohibited discrimination in voting, public accommodations, public education, and employment. Three sections of the new law proved to be especially relevant to the development of affirmative action. First, Title VI made discrimination illegal in any federally sponsored or funded activity. Second, Title VII proscribed 'unlawful employment practices' that applied to all employers and labor unions whose work forces numbered twenty-five or more. During Congressional debates this section of the Act was amended to include sex among the categories upon which discrimination could not be based. Third, a subsection of Title VII established a five-member panel called the Equal Employment Opportunity Commission (EEOC), charged with investigating and resolving claims of discrimination and promoting compliance with the law.[34]

Nowhere in the Civil Rights Act did the term affirmative action appear. Attuned to the negative aura that surrounded the concept of 'quotas',[35] sponsors of the bill

---

[33] Johnson's stance on civil rights changed as his constituency broadened. From his early days in Congress, beginning in 1937 until 1957, he had voted with the southern Dixiecrats against all civil rights legislation.

[34] *Laws of the 88th Congress, 2nd session*, (2 July 1964) 287–319. Robinson pp. 96–102. The amendment of Title VII to include 'sex' as a category of prohibited discrimination came from Virginia Congressman Howard Smith. His action has been frequently interpreted as an effort to derail the entire civil rights bill, expecting that the amendment would trivialize the entire process. However, since Smith was a long time supporter of women's rights, an alternative interpretation suggests that the Congressman was acting in accord with racist forces within the women's movement in making sure that black rights would not take precedence over the rights of white women – as had occurred in the nineteenth century when the Fifthteenth Amendment was passed. Some contributions to the congressional debate over Smith's amendment support that interpretation. For example Congresswoman Edith Griffiths of Michigan declared: 'If you do not add sex to this bill … you are going to have white men in one bracket, you are going to take colored men and colored women and give them equal employment rights, and down at the bottom of the list is going to be a white woman with no rights at all …'. *Congressional Record*, (8 February 1964) 110 Pt. 1: 2579–2581.

[35] In some liberal circles 'quotas' brought to mind the practice on the part of prominent US colleges, universities and professional associations that prevailed for a long period of limiting the number of Jews permitted to enter these institutions. Another negative association with the term arose from the history of the US Immigration Service enforcing quotas against

assured their colleagues that the new law would not require employers to hire a certain quota of minority workers. To guarantee that this would not happen Senators Everett Dirksen and Mike Mansfield composed provision 'j' which was added to Title VII, explicitly stating that the law did not require 'preferential treatment' for 'any individual or...any group', even if in a given locale there was an 'imbalance' in the work force related to race, sex, or the other specified categories.[36] In addition, the rights of employers were bolstered with declarations of what were not 'unlawful employment practices'.[37]

In previous legislation and presidential orders, when 'affirmative action' had appeared, the connotation was always that employers must act fairly and treat all workers alike. That bosses would be expected to identify the present effects of past discrimination and fashion remedies for them was not implied. Lyndon Johnson helped to change the old connotation, denoting in his presidential speeches and orders an obligation to recognize and ameliorate the consequences of past injustice. His most striking utterance on this topic came as he addressed a black audience at the June 1965 Howard University Commencement. Acknowledging that recent legislation would not be sufficient to overcome the nation's history of slavery and discrimination, the president admitted that:

> you do not take a person who, for years, has been hobbled by chains and liberate him, bring him up to the starting line of a race and then say, 'you are free to compete with all the others', and still justly believe that you have been completely fair...[38]

---

certain national and ethnic groups. However, the Southern Democrats who opposed quotas in civil rights policy cared as little for Jews and immigrants as they did for African Americans.

[36] *Laws of the 88th Congress, Second Session*, 306.

[37] For example, the law stated that it was not unlawful to maintain a 'bona fide' seniority system and it was not unlawful to test workers when hiring or promoting them, so long as the test was not discriminatory. Regarding the stipulation that employers would not be *required* to hire a certain percentage of workers, etc., would be subject to differing interpretations. Proponents of strong affirmative action policies took it to mean that employers were *permitted* to voluntarily set hiring goals.

Opponents held that congressional intent was to outlaw such practices.

[38] 'To Fulfill These Rights', *Public Papers of the Presidents, 1 June to 31 December 1965*, 636. Johnson's speechwriters for this address were White House aide Richard Goodwin and assistant secretary of labor, Daniel Patrick Moynihan, who drew upon a major report he had just completed concerning black families in the United States. The Johnson speech included sections on 'the breakdown of the Negro family structure' and other passages deemed condescending by later critics. Nonetheless, the address clearly signaled support for compensatory aid for blacks. Conservative critics deplored that signal, foreseeing programs of racial preference for African Americans at the expense of whites. Critics on the left accused Moynihan of trying to avoid political and economic restructuring in the service of equality by focusing attention on family issues. Stephen Steinberg, 'The Liberal Retreat from Race During the Post-Civil Rights Era', Wahneema Lubiano (ed.), *The House That Race Built*, (New York: Pantheon Books, 1997).

That fall Johnson put forth Executive Order 11246. While assigning civil rights enforcement responsibilities to various government agencies, the president also revised what had become the standard injunction against unfair employment practices. His new order required contractors not only to 'take affirmative action' in their present hiring practices but also to compose written affirmative action plans to remedy past discrimination.[39]

Early court rulings on cases brought under Title VII followed the same lines as Johnson's declarations. A federal district court in Richmond, Virginia concluded in a January 1968 decision that the Philip Morris tobacco giant, and Local 203 of the Tobacco Workers International Union, must scrap a seniority system that disadvantaged black workers and establish a new one 'providing equal advancement opportunity'. Although Title VII protected 'a bona fide seniority or merit system', the court found that the Philip Morris system was not 'bona fide'. Title VII, the Richmond jurists averred, 'did not intend to freeze an entire generation of Negro employees into discriminatory patterns that existed before the act'.[40]

In a similar vein, a federal circuit court decision on January 1969 forced Crown-Zellerbach, a paper manufacturer, to revamp its seniority policy. By that policy when a black worker transferred from an historically all-black department to a largely white department, the black worker was placed at the bottom of the seniority list. After the federal ruling, black workers would carry their seniority with them into their new department and in some cases would move ahead of white workers. Because the old system denied blacks 'promotions which *but* for their race, they would surely have won', the court deemed seniority system revision to be an appropriate measure 'to undo the effects of past discrimination'.[41]

Meanwhile, Johnson's Department of Labor, under the direction of Labor Secretary Willard Wirtz, began to promote forcefully the concept of affirmative action in construction trades with particularly bad histories of excluding minority workers. What would come to be known as the Philadelphia Plan was the brainchild of African American engineer, Edward Sylvester, who served as director of the Labor Department's Office of Federal Contract Compliance (OFCC). The first version of the plan required contractors to complete 'manning tables', documenting the number of minority workers assigned to each division of the total work crew on a given federal project. Sylvester targeted a massive construction project in Philadelphia that was designated to receive several hundred million dollars of federal money. An avalanche of court actions brought by furious contractors, and appeals by them to the federal General Accounting Office, swamped Sylvester's initiative.[42]

However, after Richard Nixon's election as president in 1968, his Labor Secretary (George Schultz) and the African American OFCC director whom Wirtz

---

[39]   *Federal Register*, (1965) 30: 12319.

[40]   *Douglas Quarles and Ephriam Briggs v. Philip Morris Incorporated*, (1968), 279 F. Supp., 505.

[41]   *Local 189 Papermakers and Paperworkers v. US*, (1969), 416 F. 2d 980.

[42]   Robinson, *ibid.*, p. 128.

recruited (Arthur A. Fletcher), revised the plan and successfully maneuvered to get it established in federal law. Fletcher tagged seven categories of workers, among whom 'there traditionally has been only a small number of Negroes employed... because of the exclusionary practices of labor organizations'. He circumvented the political hot button of 'quotas' by requiring employers to create a 'target range' – not of numbers of minority workers to be hired but of the number of hours that might be worked by such laborers.[43]

Codified as Department of Labor Order number 4 and issued in February 1970, the Philadelphia Plan became a model for affirmative action policy nationwide. An association of eighty contractors from five counties in the Philadelphia area immediately challenged it in court. They lost in federal district court and on appeal. When the Supreme Court refused to hear their case the plan's legal standing was assured, for the time being.[44]

While the Philadelphia Plan was taking shape, more court action based on Title VII unfolded, including a Supreme Court ruling in *Griggs et al. v. Duke Power Co.* In this case the court invalidated two tests that the company required workers to pass in order to gain promotions. The tests did not apply to white employees ensconced in good positions within what were once all-white departments. Only African Americans striving for promotion to those departments had to pass them.

Interpreting Title VII (which allowed non-discriminatory tests to be used by employers) and following precedent set in the ruling on Philip Morris in 1968, the justices determined that 'tests neutral on their face, and even neutral in terms of intent, cannot be maintained if they operate to "freeze" the status quo of prior discriminatory employment practices'. According 'great deference' to the Equal Employment Opportunity Commission, and to guidelines that that agency had issued relative to employment tests, they also stressed that such tests had to be demonstrably related to job-performance. In the judges' view, the power company tests were not.[45]

The *Griggs* decision was a major break-through for affirmative action. For lower courts, the Supreme Court decision provided precedent for vigorous exercise of judicial power on behalf of blacks appealing for relief from entrenched racism. Of

---

[43] Department of Labor Memorandum reprinted in the *Congressional Record*, (18 December 1969), 112, pt. 2: 39951. The categories were iron workers, plumbers and pipefitters, steamfitters, sheetmetal workers, electrical workers, roofers and water proofers, elevator construction workers, Robinson pp. 128–135.

[44] *Federal Register 35*, (5 February 1970), no. 5: 2587. Four months after order number 4 was issued, it was revised to include sex discrimination. *Federal Register 35*, (9 June 1970), no. 111: 8888–8889. At first glance the association of conservative Republican Nixon with a far-reaching affirmative action measure seems unusual. Political analysts have noted that the Philadelphia Plan served the political purpose of dividing civil rights liberals from organized labor, which by the 1960s had come to be an ally of the civil rights movement. *Contractors Association of Eastern Pennsylvania v. Secretary of Labor*, (1971), 442 F. 2d: 159. By the 1980s affirmative action plans following the Philadelphia model were scrutinized more harshly and frequently struck down.

[45] *Griggs et al., v. Duke Power Co.*, (1971), 401 US 424.

equal significance, the high court's declaration of respect for the EEOC enhanced the authority of that agency. While these developments heartened believers in affirmative action, they dismayed its opponents, who saw the EEOC as already going beyond its congressional mandate by publishing and promoting guidelines on employment policies.

Opponents viewed the *Griggs* ruling as – in the words of economist Daniel Seligman – the 'judicial ratification of ... disregard of congressional intent'. Many employers, union leaders, and conservative critics bemoaned what they predicted to be the end of hiring and promotion based on ability and merit. Seligman warned that 'companies that have high standards and want to defend them' will– when forced to follow complicated EEOC guidelines – 'conclude that it is simpler to abolish their standards than to try justifying them'.[46]

Such opposition notwithstanding, affirmative action supporters were anxious to strengthen the EEOC. From its inception inadequate funding and weak enforcement authority had compromised the agency. In addition, employers and unions with work forces of fewer than 25 members and all state and local government employees were excluded from its oversight. Beginning in 1965 congressional backers of EEOC struggled to put bills through Congress that would reform and expand its operations. Not until 1972 were they successful. The Equal Employment Opportunity Act of that year granted the EEOC the power to institute court proceedings against violators of civil rights laws and extended its range of coverage to include state and local government employees, and employers and labor unions with 15 or more members.[47]

The social and political backdrop, against which federal courts were ruling, the Philadelphia Plan was evolving, and the EEOC was undergoing reform, was a scene of national turmoil. Nonviolent civil rights protests that had swept over the south since the mid-1950s were superceded in the late sixties by angry cries for Black Power by dissidents who found that recent laws had proven to be 'too little, too late'. Martin Luther King, noting the disproportionate number of blacks drafted to kill and die in Vietnam was only one of the most prominent of activists who joined a swelling movement of passionate opposition to that war. Urban ghettos exploded. In 1967 alone, riots erupted in 150 cities, leaving 83 people dead and more than $660 million in property destruction.[48]

---

[46]   Daniel Seligman, 'How "Equal Opportunity" Turned Into Employment Quotas', *Fortune*, (1973), pp. 165–166.

[47]   Bureau of National Affairs, *The Equal Employment Opportunity Act of 1972, a BNA Operations Manual*, (Washington, D.C.: Bureau of National Affairs, 1973), pp. 1–4.

[48]   Lawson. The phrase, 'too little, too late' was used by the chairman of the Student Nonviolent Coordinating Committee, John Lewis, in reference to John Kennedy's civil rights bill. Lewis was addressing the 1963 March on Washington that drew a quarter of a million civil rights supporters.

The most recent scholarship on the civil rights movement is revising the narrative that replaces southern nonviolence with northern black power. The revisionists document on going nonviolent activism after the sixties, evidence of a long and lasting tradition of self-defense

The National Advisory Commission on Civil Disorders, appointed by President Johnson to identify the conditions that 'breed despair and violence', reported back with an ominous warning of a country 'rapidly moving toward two increasingly separate Americas', one white, the other black.[49] Within weeks of the commission's report, King was assassinated and the nation was again shaken by violent outbursts of grief and rage in 110 of its major cities. Two months later yet another assassination, that of Robert Kennedy, intensified the fear and shock that bore down upon the country.

Advocates of affirmative action saw in these frightening events irrefutable evidence of 'systemic' racism, patterns of discrimination so embedded in national institutions that their effects continued even when the intention to discriminate may have ceased. They pressed harder than ever for systemic reform. Addressing a Senate committee on the urgency of giving the EEOC real political muscle, eminent NAACP lobbyist, Clarence Mitchell, advised against token action as a way of answering 'the man about to throw a Molotov cocktail'.[50]

Even with its new authority, the EEOC still operated with limited effectiveness. Five years after the Equal Employment Opportunity Act was signed a legal expert from Georgetown University reviewed the agency's recent record. Noting that it had 'five chairmen in its first ten years, with its last chairman resigning after only eight months', he found 'severe personnel and organizational weaknesses' contributing to 'long delays in resolving complaints'. Along a similar line author Joan Abramson deplored a backlog of cases filed with EEOC that 'grew from 15,000 in 1969 to close to 130,000 in 1977'.[51]

---

within civil rights activism – north and south – and a history of black power consciousness originating far earlier than the 1960s. For a brief overview of these revisions see Evelyn Brooks Higginbotham's 'Forward' to Jeanne F. Theoharis and Komozi Woodard, *Freedom North*, (New York: Palgrave Macmillan, 2003). Nonetheless, the perception that nonviolence and integration were being eclipsed by racial nationalism influenced the enactment and enforcement of such programs as the Philadelphia Plan.

[49]   *Report of the National Advisory Commission on Civil Disorders*, p. 407 (New York: Bantam Books, 1969).

[50]   Mitchell was addressing the Senate Committee on Labor and Public Welfare, Hearings on Equal Employment Opportunity Enforcement Act, (August 11, 1969) 81. In the Senate during debates on the Philadelphia Plan, Edward Brooke, black Republican from Massachusetts, assured his fellow-senators that 'simple prohibition of discrimination is not enough…The real problem of discrimination in America is …"systemic" or "intrinsic" discrimination…built into the very structure of American society'. He sketched the life of a representative black worker, beginning with his education in poor schools, through the barriers he faced in predominantly white unions that operated according to established, discriminatory custom, *Congressional Record*, (18 December 1969), 115, Pt. 2: 39961, 39964–39965.

[51]   Theodore V. Purcell, 'Management and Affirmative Action in the Late Seventies', in *Equal Rights and Industrial Relations*, ed., Farrell El Bloch et al., pp. 80–81, (Madison Wisconsin: Industrial Relations Research Association, 1977). Joan Abramson, *Old Boys, New Women, the Politics of Sex Discrimination*, 57–59, Robinson, pp. 222–225 (New York: Praeger, 1979).

In one set of initiatives that did have impact, the EEOC in the 1970s took the lead to bring class action suits against major US companies on behalf of employees who charged race and/or sex discrimination. The massive communications corporation, American Telephone and Telegraph (AT&T), was the first target. Some 2000 workers had filed complaints against AT&T when the legal action began in December 1970. EEOC pressed in court for a complete overhaul of the company's 'pernicious system' that purposely relegated African Americans and minorities to 'low-paying, dead-end' jobs. The company accepted a consent decree, pronounced by federal district court judge, Leon Higginbotham, in January 1973, avoiding an admission of guilt while agreeing to comply with an ambitious affirmative action plan. The plan called for promotions, transfers, wage adjustments and back pay totaling $30.9 million, affecting about 40,000 employees.[52]

In the next few years EEOC exacted consent decrees from numerous other major corporations. To the ordinary public observer, the settlements coming from these court actions appeared to be real boons for women and minority workers. From the point of view of management they were onerous and unwelcome government mandates. For the workers themselves the consent decrees were often a disappointment.

In the case of the steel industry, for example, the $30.5 million in back pay stipulated by a decree amounted to a few hundred dollars per worker. As one of those workers observed, 'six hundred dollars for twenty years' worth of discrimination' was insulting. Furthermore, in many cases, in the wake of the consent decrees, minority and women workers had to cope with resentment and hostility directed at them by white laborers. Nonetheless, the EEOC class actions opened the way to better paying jobs for tens of thousands of US workers.[53]

Another device that advanced the progress of minorities and women in industry was the 'set-aside', introduced in Congress by Maryland Representative Parren Mitchell as an amendment to the Public Works Employment Act of 1977 (PWEA). Mitchell's amendment dictated that 'at least 10 percentum of the amount of each [federal construction grant] shall be expended for minority business enterprises'. Non-minority contractors were quick to challenge this provision of the PWEA, but to no avail. Federal courts at every level found it to be constitutional.[54]

---

[52]   Phyllis, Wallace A., (ed.), *Equal Employment Opportunity and the AT&T Case*, (Cambridge, MA: MIT Press, 1976). The Department of Labor and the Federal Communications Commission were also involved in the AT&T case. Robinson, pp. 176–181.

[53]   *Struggles in Steel*, video documentary, produced and directed by Tony Buba and Raymond Henderson (Braddock Films, 1996). The experience of women who entered the steel industry under the consent decree is examined by Mary Margaret Fonow, 'Occupation/ Steelworker: Sex/Female', in *Feminist Frontiers III*, ed., Laurel Richardson and Verta Taylor, pp. 217–222, (Highstown, NJ: McGraw-Hill, 1983) . Other corporations that signed consent decrees included Ford Motor Company, General Electric, General Motors, the International Union of Electrical Radio and Machine Workers, Sears Roebuck, the United Auto Workers, the United Electrical Workers, the Big Ten Steel companies and the United Steel Workers.

[54]   The text of the amendment is quoted in *Fullilove v. Klutznik*, 448 US 448 (1980).

In their decision of July 1980 (*Fullilove v. Klutznik*) the Supreme Court assured white contractors that the government was within its authority to 'disappoint the expectations of nonminority firms' by enforcing a 'properly tailored remedy' to cure the effects of prior discrimination. Such a 'sharing of the burden' by innocent parties is not impermissible', they said.[55] Following this lead many US cities and states passed their own set-aside legislation.

5.

Until the mid-1970s affirmative action in the US was primarily a remedy for discrimination against blacks in the business and industrial workplace. In the final decades of the century other minorities and women included it in their quests for equality. At the same time schools, colleges and universities were adopting it in an effort to increase the minority and female populations in their student-bodies. In this period, affirmative action was upheld by the Supreme Court – most notably in the *Griggs* ruling – but it was also curtailed by the same court.

For example, in 1976 the high court found technical reasons to allow to stand both a test for police trainees in the District of Columbia (that African Americans were failing at four times the rate of whites) and a seniority system operating within the Teamsters Union that put black workers at a major disadvantage. These rulings overturned the 1968 and 1969 lower court decisions against Philip Morris and Crown Zellerbach. Interpreting Title VII, the court majority concluded in the teamsters' case that 'Congress did not make it illegal for employees with vested seniority rights to continue to exercise those rights, even at the expense of pre-Act discrimination'.[56]

With the Supreme Court see-sawing between rulings such as this and decisions such as *Griggs,* the legal foundation for affirmative action was far from solid. The extent to which Title VII could be interpreted as a means for compensating past injustices was not clear, nor was it certain just how much 'deference' EEOC rulings could command. Legal scholar Kenneth Lopatka warned in 1977 that the 'imposing web of Title VII law' that had been woven from *Griggs* could easily be 'unraveled'.[57]

---

[55]   *Fullilove v. Klutznik*, 448 US 448 (1980). Robinson, pp. 251–255. Mitchell, the first African American to represent Maryland in Congress, defined 'minority business enterprise' as 'a business at least 50 per centum of which is owned by minority group members, or, in the case of a publicly owned business, at least 51 per centum of the stock of which is owned by minority group members'. He included in the category of minority group members 'US Negroes, Spanish-speaking, Orientals, Indians, Eskimos, and Aleuts'.

[56]   *Washington v. Davis*, 426 US 229 (1976); *International Brotherhood of Teamsters v. US*, 431 US 324 (1976).

[57]   Kenneth T. Lopatka, 'Developing Concepts in Title VII Law', in *Equal Rights and Industrial Relations* (ed.), Farrell E. Bloch *et al.*, pp. 31–33, 69, (Madison, Wisconsin: Industrial Relations Research Association, 1977) .

While the federal courts were adjudicating employment issues, numerous educational institutions had begun to employ race-conscious criteria in their admissions policies. White applicants denied admission under such policies began to appear on court dockets. The most famous of these cases centered on a race-conscious admissions program at the Medical School at the University of California at Davis. Concerned that a miniscule number of minority candidates was enrolled in their school – mirroring and contributing to a grave imbalance in the ratio of minority physicians to minority patients throughout the country – the Davis faculty instituted the special program. They reserved for minority candidates a certain percentage of the slots available for new students. Although the program permitted minorities to enter with grade point averages and Medical Aptitude Test results somewhat lower than their non-minority counterparts, no one was admitted who was judged unqualified, and once admitted, everyone was held to the same standards.[58]

Allan Bakke, a white man in his mid-thirties who had applied to eleven medical schools, knowing that his age would weigh against him, was rejected twice by the Davis institution, in 1973 and 1974. After the second rejection he filed suit in the Superior Court of California whose jurists were not persuaded that the special admissions program was the sole reason why he had been rejected. He gained admission after going on to the state supreme court, whose judges decided that since the school could not prove that it denied him admission for any *other* reason than because of the special admissions program, it must let him in. Both the superior and state supreme courts found the race-conscious program to be a quota system and therefore in violation of federal law. The university appealed to the US Supreme Court, which announced its ruling on 28 June 1978.[59]

The case came down to three questions: 1) Was Bakke entitled to admission to the Davis medical school? 2) Did the school's special admissions program conform to federal law? 3) Is it legal for an institution to take race into account in its admissions decisions? In a series of five to four votes, each one involving a different configuration of justices, the badly splintered court answered that Bakke was to be admitted; that the special program was in violation of the Fourteenth Amendment and must be ended; and that because, in the words of Justice Lewis Powell, 'the attainment of a diverse student body…clearly is a constitutionally permissible goal for an institution of higher education' admissions procedures could take race into account, but not in the manner of the outlawed program.[60]

---

[58]   *Regents of the University of California v. Bakke*, 438 US 265 (1978). In 1974 the Supreme Court had declined to rule on a similar case at the University of Washington Law School. Because lower courts had ordered the admission of the plaintiff in that case, Marco DeFunis, by the time the case reached the Supreme Court DeFunis was ready to graduate. Six justices voted to declare the case 'moot'. However, the five dissenting justices warned that the 'issues which are avoided today…will not disappear'. Justice William O. Douglas also strongly argued, in his dissent, against preferential admissions policies. *De Funis et al v. Odegaard* et al., 416 US 312 (1974).

[59]   *Ibid.*, Bakke was rejected by all of the other schools to which he applied.

[60]   *Ibid.*, Robinson, pp. 200–213.

Thus was affirmative action in higher education left hanging by the slender thread of 'diversity' while more robust and straight- forward means of addressing persistent inequalities stemming from historical injustices were called into question. Departing from the majority on the issue of the Davis program's viability, justices Brennan, White, Marshall, and Blackmun stressed the fact that historically 'the practice of medicine' in this country was, in fact, if not in law, largely the prerogative of whites.[61] A race-conscious effort to provide opportunity for medical training for minorities was therefore, in their view, justified. Justice Blackmun spoke bluntly:

> I suspect it would be impossible to arrange an affirmative action program in a racially neutral way and have it successful. To ask that this be so is to demand the impossible. In order to get beyond racism, we must first take account of race. There is no other way. And, in order to treat some persons equally, we must treat them differently. We cannot – we dare not – let the Equal Protection Clause [of the Fourteenth Amendment] perpetuate racial supremacy.[62]

'It is more than a little ironic', stated Thurgood Marshall in a separate, anguished dissent, 'that, after several hundred years of class-based discrimination against Negroes, the Court is unwilling to hold that a class-based remedy for that discrimination is permissible…'.[63]

While most observers saw the *Bakke* ruling as a blow to affirmative action, no one could predict its long-term impact. As University of Chicago law Professor, Philip B. Kurland, commented:

> This is a landmark case, but we don't know what it marks. We know it's terribly important, but we won't know for many years what the impact will be.[64]

For the time being the most obvious conclusions were that 'diversity' was an acceptable goal and that, under appropriate circumstances, race could be a factor in making policy decisions in higher education. Over the next two decades the courts would go back and forth in defining exactly what those appropriate circumstances could be.

---

[61]   *University of California Regents v. Bakke.*
[62]   *Ibid.*
[63]   *Ibid.*
[64]   'The Landmark Bakke Ruling', *Newsweek*, 31, (10 July 1978).

6.

A year after the *Bakke* decision a five person Supreme Court majority interpreted Title VII with a latitude that cheered civil rights supporters. At issue in *United Steelworkers of America v. Weber* was a training program for employees of a Kaiser Aluminum plant in Louisiana. Through the program – negotiated in a collective bargaining agreement between the company and the steelworkers' union – trainees could become craft workers. Because African Americans made up 39 per cent of the labor force in the area and only 1.83 per cent of the craft workers at Kaiser, 50 per cent of the training program slots were reserved for African Americans, until a balance between potential and actual black craft workers was achieved.

A white laboratory technician, Brian Weber, applied for the program and was rejected while three of the black workers who were accepted had less seniority than he. His claim that the 50 per cent stipulation was a violation of Title VII was upheld in a federal district court and a federal court of appeals. However, when the union appealed to the Supreme Court, it was vindicated. Delivering the majority opinion, Justice William Brennan asserted that 'Title VII's prohibition ... against racial discrimination does not condemn all private, voluntary race conscious affirmative action plans'. The law, he explained, does not force employers to adopt such plans but it permits them to do so. Consequently, the program devised by the United Steelworkers and Kaiser was legal.[65]

Hopes raised among civil rights advocates by the *Weber* decision sagged in 1984 when the court handed down a particularly devastating ruling in favor of white firefighters in Memphis, Tennessee against a lower court injunction. That court was seeking to preserve a consent decree that committed the city to increase the number of African American firefighters within its ranks. To that end, when a budget shortfall required layoffs, it enjoined the city from dismissing recently hired blacks. This meant that white firemen with seniority were laid off instead. When the whites appealed, the Supreme Court (in *Firefighters Local Union No. 1784 v. Stotts*) deemed the injunction to be unlawful, placing in jeopardy similar consent decrees in cities around the country.[66]

Yet the Supreme Court was not completely locked into a pattern of rejecting programs of affirmative action. In 1986 the court upheld a consent decree in Cleveland. Referring to the earlier case of *Stotts*, the court majority explained that their decision then was against an injunction, not a consent decree. In yet another instance of embracing affirmative action by consent decree, the court resolved a long struggle in Alabama over the exclusion of African Americans from the Alabama

---

[65]   *United Steelworkers of America v. Weber*, 443 US 193 (1979).

[66]   *Firefighters Local Union No. 1784 v. Stotts*, 467 US 561 (1984). The conservative assistant attorney general for civil rights at that time, William Bradford Reynolds, took the lead in having the Department of Justice reopen 51 consent decrees involving urban fire and police departments. Two years later in another case involving seniority and lay-offs the court again invalidated a policy that protected minorities. See *Wygant et al v. Jackson Board of Education et al.*, 476 US 267 (1986).

Department of Public Safety, by ruling on the side of the minority plaintiffs seeking to become state troopers.[67]

The Supreme Court made history with a ruling in March 1987 that women as a class were entitled to affirmative action.[68] In *Johnson v. Transportation Agency, Santa Clara County California*) the court supported an affirmative action plan to correct an 'obvious imbalance' between the sexes in a given job classification and validated the hiring of a woman over a man with essentially the same qualifications.[69]

As the decade of the 1980s neared an end, the Supreme Court did settle into a pattern from which they would rarely deviate for the rest of the century, of voting (usually 5 to 4) against all affirmative action programs that came before them.[70] 1989 was an especially bad year for affirmative action. In that one twelve month period the court overturned a consent decree that had been negotiated in 1981 by the city of Birmingham, Alabama with its black fire fighters; turned back charges of discrimination against minority workers in an Alaskan cannery by requiring them to meet a standard of proof higher than any required heretofore; and invalidated a set-aside program in Richmond Virginia, by subjecting a race-conscious policy designed to end discrimination to the strict scrutiny that was previously reserved for policies and practices that perpetrated discrimination.[71]

In a brief respite from these attacks on affirmative action, the court upheld 'diversity', in 1990, in a case involving policies established by the Federal Communications Commission (FCC) and approved by Congress, to further minority ownership of the nation's airways. In *Metro Broadcasting, Inc., v. Federal Communications Commission et al*, the court majority put forth a two-part test for federal affirmative action programs: they must serve an 'important governmental objective' and they must be 'substantially related to the achievement of that objective'. They found that the FCC policies met both tests.[72]

---

[67]   *Local 28 of the Sheet Metal Workers' International Association et al. v. Equal Employment Opportunity Commission et al.*, 478 US421 (1986). *United States v. Paradise*, 480 US 149 (1987).

[68]   On women's legal standing prior to 1987 see Robinson, liii; Parts II and III.

[69]   *Paul E. Johnson v. Transportation Agency, Santa Clara County California* 480 US 149.

[70]   Sandra Day O' Connor, William Rehnquist, Byron White, Anthony Kennedy (appointed in 1988) and Anthony Scalia (appointed in 1986) consistently voted against affirmative action. They were joined in 1991 by Clarence Thomas. White retired in 1993. Marshall, Brennan and Blackmun supported affirmative action, with John Paul Stevens often joining them. After the retirements of Brennan (1990), Marshall (1991) and Blackmun (1994), the pro-affirmative action vote usually consisted of Stevens, Ruth Bader Ginsburg (appointed 1993), David Souter (appointed 1990) and Steven Breyer (appointed 1994).

[71]   *Martin v. Wilks*, 490 US 755 (1989). *Wards Cove Packing Co., Inc. v. Antonio*, 490 US 642 (1989). *City of Richmond v. J.A. Croson Company*, 488 US 469 (1989).

[72]   *Metro Broadcasting Inc. v. Federal Communications Commission et al.*, 497 US 547 (1990).

However, five years later, when Justice O'Connor delivered another majority opinion against set-asides, *Adarand Constructors, Inc. v. Pena*, she incorporated into the opinion a lengthy review of all Supreme Court rulings relative to affirmative action, from *Bakke* through *Metro*. As she read the record, only *Metro* had failed to stipulate 'strict scrutiny' of 'all racial classifications, imposed by whatever federal, state or local governmental actor'. To the extent that it did not conform to such scrutiny, she declared *Metro* 'overruled'.[73]

At this point, public discourse on affirmative action went topsy-turvy. Those who perpetrated and/or benefited from discrimination against minorities were now being cast as victims, and measures taken to reduce discrimination were to bear more judicial scrutiny than the discrimination itself. Conservatives on the Supreme Court were not alone in engaging in what attorney Patricia Williams dubbed 'the infinite convertibility of terms'.[74]

In the lower levels of the federal court system affirmative action was also taking a beating, particularly with regard to race-conscious admissions policies in universities and professional schools. In 1992 in the Fourth Circuit Court of Appeals, Daniel Podberesky, claiming an Hispanic heritage from his Costa Rican mother, won his case against a University of Maryland scholarship program established exclusively for African Americans. Four years later (in *Cheryl J. Hopwood v. State of Texas*) the Fifth Circuit Court of Appeals invalidated a special admissions program for minorities at the Law School of the University of Texas at Austin. By refusing the Law School's appeal to hear the case, the Supreme Court indicated its satisfaction with the ruling.[75]

7.

In the United States' tri-partite system of government, court decisions were one factor affecting the evolution of affirmative action. The US Congress, exercising its legislative authority, was another. It enacted race-conscious laws; authorized the application of race-conscious policies (as in the congressional approval accorded to the FCC policy that was upheld in the *Metro* case) and became a ground upon which the merits and flaws of affirmative action were vigorously debated.

Such debate was occasioned by efforts on the part of some legislators to abolish affirmative action. In 1995, Senator Robert Dole and Congressman Charles Canaday submitted bills in their respective houses that would have eradicated all federal affirmative action programs.[76] After their bills were defeated in 1995 and again in 1997, another senator, Mitch McConnell went after the Disadvantaged

---

[73]   *Adarand Constructors, Inc. v. Pena*, 515 US 200 (1995).

[74]   Patricia Williams, *The Rooster's Egg*, p. 107, (Cambridge: Harvard University Press, 1995).

[75]   *Podberesky v. Kirwan*, 956 F. 2D52, (4th Cir. 1992); *Cheryl J. Hopwood v. State of Texas*, 78 F. 3d. 932 (Fifth Cir., 1996).

[76]   *Congressional Record*, 141, Pt. 6: 7883–7884, (March 15, 1995) .

Business Enterprise Program (DBE), a set-aide program administered by the federal Department of Transportation.

House and Senate deliberations on the McConnell proposal were intense. As legislative watchdogs, Corrine Yu and William Taylor noted, 'Everyone involved understood how critical that vote would be. If the DBE program was lost, there would be a virtual avalanche of attacks on affirmative action programs'. The DBE was saved.[77] Before the dust settled from the confrontation over the DBE, foes and friends of ending discrimination by taking race into account squared off again.

At issue next was a proposal to prohibit 'preferential treatment' of 'any person or group' seeking admission to a public institution of higher education. When the author of this proposal, Congressman Frank Riggs, invoked in its support the well-known words of Martin Luther King Jr., looking toward the day when all people 'would be judged by the content of their character, not the color of their skin', Congressman John Lewis went on the attack. 'I knew Martin Luther King Jr. well', declared the former chairman of the Student Nonviolent Coordinating Committee.

> If he was standing here tonight…he would say he believes in a color-blind society, but he would tell us that we are not there yet and he would not be supporting the Riggs amendment…. [W]e have fought too long and too hard…. People have gone to jail. People have been beaten. People have lost their lives. Now we must fight one more time against those who wave the banner of fairness but really want to slam the door of opportunity in the face of young people across our Nation.

The Riggs' gambit also failed.[78]

Congressional supporters of affirmative action could also – when they were able to muster the necessary votes – counter court decisions and executive branch actions detrimental to their cause. For example, the Civil Rights Restoration Act of 1998, passed over the veto of Ronald Reagan, affirmed congressional intent with regard to a number of civil rights/affirmative action laws that, in the language of the Restoration Act, '…recent decisions and opinions of the Supreme Court have unduly narrowed or cast doubt upon…'.[79]

Two years later – after a major stand-off with President George E.W. Bush – civil rights forces in Congress enacted the Civil Rights Act of 1991 that overturned nine recent Supreme Court rulings and reasserted the interpretation of Title VII of

---

[77] Corrine M. Yu and William L. Taylor, (eds), *The Test of Our Progress: The Clinton Record on Civil Rights*, (Washington, D.C.: Citizens' Commission on Civil Rights, 1999), 175, 177. Votes in the Senate ran 58 to 37 against McConnell's measure and 225 to 194 in the House, where it had been sponsored by Congresswoman Marge Roukema.

[78] *Congressional Record – House* 144, 2894, 2895, (6 May 1998). The proposal was in the form of an amendment to a law titled the Higher Education Act.

[79] *US Statutes at Large*, (1990), 102 Pt. 1: 28–29. Among the acts reaffirmed by the 1998 Restoration Act were Title IX of the Education Amendments of 1972 – a major source of advancement for women, particularly in college athletics – and the Civil Rights Act of 1964.

the 1964 Civil Rights Act upon which the 1971 Supreme Court *Griggs* ruling was based.[80]

As Congress debated, enacted, revisited and, on occasion, defended civil rights law, and the courts interpreted it, the Executive branch of the government could initiate, veto, and, in myriad ways, influence it. One means of influence was through Supreme Court appointments. Presidents naturally selected judges for federal appointments whose records of judicial opinion harmonized with their own political persuasion. Presidents Richard Nixon and Ronald Reagan were especially influential in determining the make-up of the high court . Retirements from that bench gave them each the opportunity to appoint three justices. When Warren Burger retired in 1986 it fell to Reagan to also name a new Chief Justice. His selection, William Rehnquist, was solidly conservative on matters of race, sex and gender. Although some of the Nixon and Reagan appointees proved to be moderate and/or unpredictable in these regards, overall the court's stance toward such issues as affirmative action became increasingly negative. By the same token, judicial appointments at the district and appeals court levels also gave a rightward or leftward tilt to those courts, depending on who was in the White House when there were vacancies to be filled.

Presidential appointments to key federal agencies and departments, such as the EEOC and the Department of Justice also shaped affirmative action/civil rights policies and decisions. Never was this more evident than after the election of Ronald Reagan in 1980. Reagan appointed outspoken critics of race-based civil rights reforms to positions where they would be in charge of enforcing (or dismantling) those reforms. He named Clarence Pendleton as chairman of the US Civil Rights Commission, Clarence Thomas as director of the EEOC, William French Smith as Attorney General, and William Bradford Reynolds as Assistant Attorney General for Civil Rights. To Pendleton, advocates of affirmative action were 'new racists' wanting 'results to be guaranteed without competition'. Clarence Thomas declared affirmative action to be 'a narcotic of dependency', while Smith and Reynolds promised to uproot race conscious policies and programs with every means at their disposal.[81]

Under such leadership federal agencies and departments that had initiated legal action to enforce race-based policies reversed course and joined the opposition. In one such instance, the EEOC, in the administration of Gerald Ford, backed minority members of a sheet metal workers' union in suing the union for excluding minorities. A federal district court upheld the charges and ordered the labor organization to set a specific goal for increased membership and to create a plan for meeting that goal. The union filed numerous appeals, all of which it lost. By the time the case reached the Supreme Court, Ronald Reagan was president and Clarence Thomas headed the

---

[80]   *Congressional Quarterly Almanac*, 47: 258, 259, (1991).

[81]   Robert J. Weiss, *We Want Jobs: A History of Affirmative Action*, pp. 177–178, (New York: Garland, 1997). Herman Belz, *Equality Transformed: A Quarter Century of Affirmative Action*, p. 184, (New Brunswick, N.J.: Transaction, 1994).

EEOC, which now sided with the union against the minority workers. In a six to five vote the court came down on the side of the minority workers.[82]

It could even happen that the position of an agency would change several times over the course of a given legal action. The Department of Justice supported, then opposed, and then supported again the case of Sharon Taxman, a white teacher laid off by the board of Education of Piscataway, New Jersey in 1989. The board informed Taxman that it had 'decided to rely on its commitment to affirmative action' in dismissing her, rather than a black teacher whose credentials and time of service were basically the same as hers. The Justice Department under Republican George E.W. Bush sued the board on Taxman's behalf and won in federal district court. But when the board appealed, new Justice Department leadership, appointed by Democrat William Jefferson Clinton, sided against Taxman and with the school board. Taxman won again at the appeals court level, prompting the board to petition the Supreme Court.

Now the Clinton Justice Department did an about-face, first recommending that the Supreme Court not hear the case, and when that recommendation was ignored, submitting a brief that supported affirmative action but not when layoffs were involved. As the time neared for arguments before the Supreme Court, opponents of affirmative action predicted not only another win for Taxman but – given other recent rulings against race-conscious policies – a high court decision that could sound the death knell for affirmative action. At this point the Black Leadership Forum – a coalition of twenty-one civil rights and other social action groups – intervened to broker an out-of-court settlement.[83]

The management and funding of federal agencies and departments were yet other factors impinging on civil rights and affirmative action law-making and enforcement. Civil rights leaders' perennial disappointment with the EEOC has been noted above. Other agencies received similar assessments. For example in 1996, scholar Barbara Bergmann found the Office of Federal Contract Compliance to be understaffed and poorly managed.[84]

What is more, federal monitoring and enforcement of all civil rights laws and mandates were decentralized and poorly coordinated. In the case of affirmative action, enforcement responsibility and oversight were divided among multiple agencies – the EEOC, the Department of Justice, the Department of Labor, that

---

[82] *Local 28 of the Steel Metal Workers' International Association et al v. Equal Employment Opportunity Commission et al.*, 478 US 421 (1986).

[83] *Sharon Taxman v. Board of Education of the Township of Piscataway*, 832 F. Supp. 836 (D.N.J., 1993).

Sharon Taxman v. Board of Education of the Township of Piscataway, 91 F 3d 1547 (1996). Mark Walsh, 'Supreme Court Case Plays Out in N.J. School Every Day', *Education Week*, 8 October 1997.

'Key Affirmative Action Case Settled', *Baltimore Sun*, November 22, 1997.

[84] Barbara R. Bergmann, *In Defense of Affirmative Action*, pp. 53,54, (New York: Basic Books, 1996).

department's Office of Contract Compliance, and the US Civil Rights Commission, to name the most prominent.

Complaints about the inefficiency of this arrangement were common from the 1970s onward. 'The entire federal compliance program has become a patchwork apparatus beautiful mainly to some lawyers' eyes' observed Georgetown legal scholar, Theodore Purcell, in 1977. He urged Congress to appoint a commission to simplify and unify enforcement. In the same vein, the Civil Rights Commission recommended that coordination of all civil rights enforcement in the area of employment be made the responsibility of a 'single agency'– a recommendation that was never heeded.[85]

Beyond governmental borders, many organizations and associations operated independently to shore-up, alter or undermine the struggle for justice relative to minorities and women. These included long standing civil rights groups, such as the 21 organizations in the Black Leadership Forum that came forward to help settle the Taxman case, and newer alliances that emerged to rally support for specific affirmative action cases, such as the Coalition to Defend Affirmative Action, formed to back University of Michigan admissions programs when they came under attack at the turn of the century.

Opposing groups also proliferated and became increasingly well organized. Prominent among these was the American Civil Rights Coalition (ACRC) headed by Ward Connerly. Republican, conservative, African American, and insistent that affirmative action stigmatized minorities, Connerly launched his campaign to abolish racial preferences of any kind while serving on the University of California's Board of Regents in 1994. He engineered a Regents' vote to abolish the university's race-conscious admissions program and went on to promote the 'California Civil Rights Initiative', a state referendum on 'Proposition 209' prohibiting state and local governments from implementing affirmative action in 'public employment, public education or public contracting'.[86]

The names of Connerly's organizations and campaigns are another illustration of the 'linguistic flip-flops' to which Patricia Williams had called attention. He appropriated terms historically associated with the struggle against racial injustice for an agenda that essentially sought to undermine that struggle. Apparently it succeeded in confusing voters. In a Harris poll before the referendum on 209, nearly 60 percent of those polled were under the impression that the Proposition was intended to preserve affirmative action. Exit polls on the day of the vote indicated the same trend–'[N]early 30 percent of those voting for 209 thought they had cast a vote *in favor* of affirmative action'.[87]

---

[85]   Purcell in Bloch *et al.*, pp. 80–83. US Commission on Civil Rights, *To Eliminate Employment Discrimination: A Sequel, The Federal Civil Rights Enforcement Effort*, (December 1977).

[86]   Robinson, pp. 339–343, 946 F. Supp. 1480 at 1488 N.D. Cal. (1996).

[87]   Tim Wise, 'Is Sisterhood Conditional?', *MWSA Journal*, [National Women's Studies Association] (Fall 1998) 22, note 11. As Connerly carried his campaign to other cities and

While Connerly undertook a state-by-state overturning of affirmative action programs, some twenty-two groups opposed to set-asides were also mounting attacks. The president of one of those groups, the Southeastern Legal Foundation, bragged in 1999: 'There is not one racial preference program in America that has survived a court challenge since 1989'. Doing all they could to strengthen this trend was another opposing force, the Center for Individual Rights (CIR). Based in Washington D.C., and calling themselves a 'public interest law firm', those associated with the CIR led the Hopwood case against the Law School at the University of Texas in 1996 and actively solicited other cases from whites disgruntled by race-conscious admissions policies.[88]

While organized backlash impeded the development of affirmative action, such opposition did not uproot it. In the arena of higher education some admissions offices responded to court prohibitions by couching race-conscious criteria in new contexts. 'Rice [University] says it remains fiercely committed to having a diverse student body', *The New York Times* reported in December 2002. Since the *Hopwood* ruling in 1996 its admissions officers intensified recruiting efforts at high schools with high minority enrollments and

> developed creative, even sly ways to [maintain diversity] and still obey the court.... [W]ith an undisguised wink, [it] has encouraged applicants to discuss 'cultural traditions' in their essays, asked if they spoke English as a second language and taken note, albeit silently, of those identified as presidents of their black student associations.[89]

Hopwood prompted the Texas legislature, at the behest of its Latino and African American members, to enact the 'Ten Percent Plan', guaranteeing tuition-free college admission to the top 10 percent of each senior class in every high school. Other states (including Florida where Governor Jeb Bush had outlawed affirmative action by executive fiat) adopted the Texas plan. However, critics objected to the obvious assumption that the plan would deliver minority students into the colleges because high schools would remain segregated.[90]

---

states, the effect of language-choice was again evident. In Houston, Texas, for example, in 1997, the City Council demanded straightforward wording for a referendum instigated by ACRC forces. The ballot question that began: 'Shall the charter of the City of Houston be amended to end the use of Affirmative Action...' was roundly rejected by the voters. Yu and Taylor, p. 182.

88 Vernon E. Smith, 'Showdown in Atlanta', *Emerge*, 49, (November 1999). CIR placed ads in college newspapers inviting students to look into their schools' policies and distributed free of charge a handbook on how to initiate action against affirmative action. 'Paid Advertisement', *Pitt News*, 19, (26 January 1999). [The same ad appeared in 13 other college papers.] *Racial Preferences in Higher Education, The Rights of College Students, A Handbook*, (Washington D.C.: Center for Individual Rights, 1998).

89 Jacques Steinberg, 'Using Synonyms for Race, College Strives for Diversity', *New York Times*, 8 December 2002.

90 William E. Forbath and Gerald Torres, 'The Talented Tenth in Texas', *The Nation*, 21, (15 December 1997). Executive Order 99–281, [Governor Jeb Bush]. http://sun6.dms.state.

'Calling such methods [as the Texas plan] "race neutral" when their aim is to keep minority enrollments up is disingenuous and obscures the consensus in favor of racial diversity as an important goal in higher education', asserted Harvard College President, Lawrence H. Summers, and Harvard Law Professor, Laurence H. Tribe.[91]

As educators protested, resisted, and circumvented strictures against affirmative action in school admissions, urban mayors fought to sustain minority business and contractor set-aside programs. In some cities where courts had invalidated such programs, local leaders revived them by removing references to race and gender and inserting criteria regarding the size of a company's assets or its urban location. City mayors also formed coalitions to do battle in court against set-aside opponents.[92]

Those on the front lines of its defense could take courage from signs that affirmative action was gaining acceptance in important areas of national life. 'Affirmative Action Is Deeply Ingrained in Corporate Culture', reported *Business Week* in the summer of 1991. They quoted AT&T chairman Robert Allen: 'Affirmative action is not just the right thing to do. It's a business necessity'.[93]

Attorney Patricia Williams pointed out in 1995 how much the results of affirmative action were already taken for granted. Her example was the courtroom in the celebrated murder trial of athlete O.J. Simpson, where she found that the jurors, the lawyers, the defendant, and all the journalists covering the trial were 'affirmative action babies'.[94]

In the new millennium, court challenges to University of Michigan admissions policies (choreographed by the CIR) provoked an outpouring of support for policies that take race into account. On 23 June 2003 the Supreme court ruled on *Grutter v. Bollinger*, addressing admissions procedures of the university's law school, and *Gratz v. Bollinger*, regarding undergraduate admissions. Submitting briefs as 'friends of the court' on behalf of Michigan were, among others, 30 retired military commanders and 65 Fortune 500 companies. The military brass unequivocally tied national defense to affirmative action, as the corporate moguls identified it as vital to 'continued success in the global marketplace'. Commenting on these briefs in its editorial page, *The New York Times* observed: 'The civil rights movement started on

---

fl.us/eog_new/e0g/orders/1999/november/eo99–281.html, November 1999.

[91]   Lawrence H. Summers and Laurence H. Tribe, 'Race Is Never Neutral', *New York Times*, 29 March 2003.

[92]   Vern E. Smith, 'Showdown in Atlanta', *Emerge*, 49, 51, (November 1999). George R. La Noue, 'Hard Choices About City's MBE Program', *Baltimore Sun*, 5 March 2000.

93   'Race in the Work Place: Is Affirmative Action Working?' *Business Week*, 8 July 1991, pp. 53–56.

[94]   Williams, *ibid.*, pp. 94–95. Opinion surveys – including a *Seattle Times* poll in the summer of 1999 and a Ford Foundation survey that fall, appeared to back up these impressions of substantial support for affirmative action. 'Discrimination Fight Goes On', *Baltimore Sun*, 1 August 1999. Theodora Lurie, 'Ford Foundation Report', (Winter 1999), <http://www.fordfound.org/publications>.

the fringes of society, but today its goals of inclusion and diversity are core American values'.[95]

Even so, the Supreme Court was not ready to accept the University of Michigan's policies for admitting undergraduates that automatically assigned 20 points to minority students in a process that required 100 points for admission. Representing a six-person majority of the court, Chief Justice Rehnquist found this to be unduly mechanistic and equivalent to a quota. At the same time, the university's method for selecting among candidates for its law school passed muster with the court. That method included race as one factor among many in what the court deemed to be 'a flexible assessment of ... each student's talents, experiences and potential'. Harking back to the *Bakke* decision of 1978 Sandra Day O'Connor, delivering a five person majority opinion on the law school case, affirmed Justice Powell's finding of 'a diverse student body' to be 'a constitutionally permissible goal'.[96]

To most observers, the opinion recorded by O'Connor represented a 'win' for affirmative action. 'This is the first time that the court has unambiguously said affirmative action is constitutional', observed Larry Gibson, a Professor of Law at the University of Maryland. An Associated Press analysis of *Grutter* predicted that the ruling was 'expected to have a wide ripple through private colleges and universities, other government decision-making and the business world'. Other voices celebrated the affirmation of diversity, but added a cautionary note. Democratic Senator John Kerry of Massachusetts pointed out that affirmative action was upheld 'by only the slimmest of margins', a fact that also concerned the editorial writers of the *New York Times*. 'One resignation on the court could produce the opposite result in a few years', they warned.[97]

Further warnings foresaw 'years of continuing litigation', due to the close vote in *Grutter* and the mandate set forth in *Gratz* calling for 'individualized review' of applicants. These could only inspire the opposition to continue its challenges, a course of action that clearly would be welcomed by the Court's most conservative members, as they made clear in their dissents on *Grutter:*

---

[95] Ellen Goodman, 'Military Provides a Strong Defense of Affirmative Action', *Baltimore Sun*, 31 March 2003. 'Friends of Affirmative Action', *New York Times*, 1 April 2003. The military signers included former chairman of the Joint Chiefs of Staff, Admiral William Crowe, Jr. and General Norman Schwarzkopf of Persian Gulf War fame.

[96] *Gratz v. Bollinger*, [Court Docket Number 02–516], 23 June 2003, [ruling on undergraduate policy].

Grutter v. Bollinger, [Court Docket Number 02–241], 23 June 2003, [ruling on Law School policy].

[97] 'Ruling Creates Thin Legal Line for Colleges', *Baltimore Sun*, 24 June 2003. Untitled Associated Press news report, 23 June 2003, America On Line: AP–NY–06–23–03 1047 EDT. Kerry quoted in Tom Curry, 'Split Decision on Racial Preferences', 23 June 2003, < msbn.com/news/9929326.asp#BODY>. 'A Win for Affirmative Action', *New York Times*, 24 June 2003.

Justice Anthony M. Kennedy called the Michigan law school's holistic approach a 'delusion...indistinguishable from quotas', while Rehnquist characterized it as 'a naked effort to achieve racial balancing'. To Justice Clarence Thomas it was 'a façade' while to Justice Antonin Scalia it was a 'scheme' and a 'sham'. Indeed, Justice Scalia and Justice Thomas could hardly bring themselves to use the term 'affirmative action', preferring 'racial discrimination' instead.[98]

Taking a position outside the circle of reformers who celebrated the court's affirmation of diversity, those who defined affirmative action as a means of exacting reparations for hundreds of years of injustice derided *Grutter* as partly irrelevant and partly detrimental. Civil rights historian, Howard N. Meyer, summarized this position. Diversity, he said, is merely a way for the university to improve its educational functions. It is 'indifferent to past wrongs'. In the court's decision to permit universities to seek a diverse student body, African Americans have 'won nothing', he asserted, while others are 'misled into a belief that less attention [to the struggle for justice] is needed'.[99]

8.

Certainly that struggle was far from over. While civil rights and affirmative action reforms had increased black voting power, dismantled legal segregation, diminished racial exclusion from campuses and workplaces, and enabled minorities and women to gain footholds in professions and centers of influence that once were entirely closed to them, there remained in US society a yawning gap in earnings, assets, and power between races and – within each race – between genders.

The Federal Glass Ceiling Commission, established by the Civil Rights Act of 1991, released its first findings four years later. In spite of advances made by women and minorities in the world of work, white males, while constituting slightly less than 44 percent of the US workforce in 1990 held 95 per cent of all senior-level

---

[98]   Steven Lubet, 'Affirmative Action Battle Has Just Begun', *Baltimore Sun*, 25 June 2003.

[99]   Howard N. Meyer, 'The Diversity Scam: It Isn't Affirmative Action', Historians' News Network, 14 July 2003, <http://hnn.us/articles/1566.html>. For further discussion of diversity and reparations see Rubio who sees diversity as having led to 'a defense of affirmative action as something that would enrich the experience of whites at workplaces and campuses, rather than being promoted principally as a black compensatory measure', pp. 172–173; 187–190. Other advocates of reparations do not link that concept with affirmative action, seeing reparations as a separate and more radical strategy. Richard America, *Paying the Social Debt: What White America Owes Black America*, (Westport, Connecticut: Greenwood, 1993). Randall Robinson, *The Debt: What America Owes to Blacks*, (New York: Dutton, 2000). Yet another point of view looks upon 'diversity' as a step beyond affirmative action, facilitating the emergence of a 'heterogeneous culture' in which all talents are given full expression and respect. See R. Roosevelt Thomas Jr., 'From Affirmative Action to Affirming Diversity', *Harvard Business Review*, (March–April 1990), pp. 107–117.

management positions. White men with no college education drew down salaries that surpassed blacks and white women with college diplomas.[100]

Analysis of race and gender patterns in higher education also revealed lacunae between whites and blacks. Two former college presidents, William G. Bowen of Harvard and Derek Bok of Princeton, examined changes within 28 highly selective colleges and universities by following some 80,000 undergraduates who matriculated in the years 1951, 1976 and 1989. They published the results of their research in 1998. Despite enormous growth in the percentage of black graduates and substantial increases in the scores of black students on the Scholastic Aptitude Test (SAT), they found that 'progress has been painfully slow and the remaining gaps are very large', reflecting deeply rooted 'differences between blacks and whites in resources, environments, and inherited intellectual capital (the educational attainment of parents and grandparents)'.[101]

Wide disparities in financial capital also contributed to racial divisions in the United States. These were exacerbated by discriminatory practices in the banking, real estate and insurance industries. According to scholars Melvin L. Oliver and Thomas M. Shapiro 'blacks control only 1.3 per cent of the nation's financial assets, while whites control 95 per cent'.[102]

The authors of most affirmative action policies put them into practice with the hope that they would become obsolete. Courts ranked that expectation high on the list of criteria for determining if such policies were permissible. In the ruling on affirmative action at the University of Michigan, Justice O'Connor avowed that 'the Court expects that 25 years from now the use of racial preferences will no longer be necessary'.[103]

---

[100] *Federal Glass Ceiling Commission*, 1995.

[101] William G. Bowen and Derek Bok, *The Shape of the River: Long-Term Consequences of Considering Race in College and University Admissions*, (New York: Cambridge University Press, 1987), pp. 9, 22, 23.

[102] Oliver and Shapiro quoted in Rubio, 189. See also Clarence Page, 'Examining the Roots of America's Racial Disparity', *Baltimore Sun*, 2 May 2003. On other major factors contributing to the US racial divide see Gary Orfield and Susan Eaton, *Dismantling Desegregation: The Quiet Reversal of Brown v. Board of Education*, (New York: New Press, 1997). Robert D. Bullard, J. Eugene Grigsby III and Charles Lee, *Residential Apartheid: The American Legacy*, (UCLA Center for African American Studies Publications, 1996). Another school of thought on affirmative action looked toward gearing it to economic class rather than race on the grounds that 'the problems of [the most severely disadvantaged] are not always clearly related to previous disadvantages'. They are more limited by their immediate environment, regardless of their race. See William Julius Wilson, *When Work Disappears, the World of the New Urban Poor*, (New York: Alfred A. Knopf, 1996), pp. 197, 198. Richard Kahlenberg, *The Remedy: Class, Race and Affirmative Action*, (New York: Basic Books, 1996). For a critique of this position see Deborah C. Malamud, 'Class Based Affirmative Action: Lessons and Caveats', *Texas Law Review* 74: 1847–1900 (1996) .

[103] *Grutter v. Bollinger*.

Twenty-five years earlier in his separate opinion on the Bakke case, Justice Blackmun hoped that 'within a decade at the most' affirmative action would be unnecessary. However, his sense of history suggested that such a hope was 'slim'.

'Many who agree with Justice Blackmun's aphorism, "To get beyond racism, we must first take account of race" would be comforted if it were possible to predict... when that will no longer be necessary', wrote William Bowen and Derek Bok in 1998. 'But we do not know how to make such a prediction', they concluded, 'and we would caution against adopting arbitrary timetables that fail to take into account how deep-rooted are the problems associated with race in America'.[104]

More than 40 years have passed since Lyndon Johnson espoused the goal of fully realized equality in his Howard University commencement address. Since that time in the United States there has been no scarcity of laws, regulations, guidelines, decisions, dissents, promises and visions regarding 'equality as a right and a theory'. But for 'equality as a fact and equality as a result' multitudes are still waiting.

---

[104] *University of California Regents v. Bakke*, Bowen and Bok, 289.

Chapter 2

Challenging Systemic Racism in Canada

Colleen Sheppard

Introduction

One of the most challenging dimensions of the struggle for equality for racialized communities[1] and Aboriginal peoples[2] is the systemic character of discrimination. Current inequalities are deeply tied to histories of exclusion and prejudice. So too are they embedded in modern day policies, practices, and appraisals of worth and value, shaped according to the needs and perspectives of dominant groups in society. Such is the continued reality of systemic racism.[3] Ironically, the pervasive nature of racism risks rendering it invisible and seemingly overcome by the fiat of equal treatment mandated in formal human rights laws. Failure and exclusion are seen as individual problems, not political markers of systemic discrimination. Those with power and prestige within institutions often lack the capacity to re-imagine systemic transformation, for to do so would bring into question the legitimacy of current distributions of privilege.

It is upon this social foundation that affirmative action must be constructed. Accordingly, affirmative action has tended to be based on two very different blueprints. One approach leaves the dominant structures and institutional policies and norms in place, while according preferential access to disproportionately excluded groups. Since individuals from racialized communities, women, Aboriginal peoples and persons with disabilities, for example, are widely under-represented in workplaces and educational establishments, they are accorded special treatment to expedite their

---

[1]   The term 'racialized communities' has been used in Canada as an alternative to 'racial minorities' or 'visible minorities'. The term does not presume minority status. It also puts the focus on the social construction of racial differences and the vulnerability of certain communities to racism 'because of the way institutions define and treat them'. Canadian Bar Association, *Racial Equality in the Canadian Legal Profession*, 'A Note on Vocabulary' at vi. (on-line: Canadian Bar Association Reports, <http://www.cba.org/CBA/cba_reports/RacialEquality.pdf>).

[2]   The term 'Aboriginal peoples' is used to describe Canada's indigenous populations, including First Nations (historically labelled Indians), Inuit, and Métis peoples (mixed First Nation and European heritage).

[3]   Joanne St. Lewis, 'Virtual Justice: Systemic Racism and the Canadian Legal Profession', Canadian Bar Association, *supra* note 1, defines 'systemic racism' at 101 as 'exclusionary practices of social and political institutions which may have arisen in a racist context or retain racist values but are no longer explicitly identifiable while continuing to have a disparate impact on racialized communities'.

entry. Historically excluded groups enter, with the help of special treatment, into the dominant and prestigious institutions of society. Once inside, they are expected to conform to established institutional norms and are judged according to those norms. It is not surprising that affirmative action often fails when this approach is taken. The risks of backlash, isolation, alienation and the pressures to assimilate are significant and costly. An alternative blueprint engages excluded groups in transforming institutional norms, policies and practices. The blueprint itself is then subject to change as under-represented groups redefine the objectives of equality and the pathways to eliminating racism. As institutional policies and practices change, inclusion can occur without special exceptional treatment because exclusionary dominant norms themselves are revisited, revised and eliminated.

The Canadian approach to affirmative action is somewhat of a hybrid of the approaches set out above. Significantly, the legal discourse of equality, including very influential judicial decisions and government policy documents, endorses a transformative vision of affirmative action. The implementation of equity initiatives, however, belies the promise of transformation and continues to be premised on the more limited strategy of grafting affirmative action onto an unchallenged institutional status quo. Embedded within this status quo, though often invisible to those who do not experience them, and left unexamined in any sustained and democratic way, one finds the invidious effects of systemic racism.

The Development of Employment and Education Equity in Canada

Recognition of the importance of group-based claims to equality is part of the legal and political culture of Canada. Historically, the focus of concern was securing the co-existence of English and French communities within one national polity; since the 1970s, a discourse endorsing multiculturalism is embedded in national government policies.[4] Additionally, the situation of Aboriginal peoples has long been subject to particularized legal and political arrangements.[5] Though there was some recognition during the early colonial era of the nation status of Aboriginal peoples, from the mid-nineteenth century until relatively recently, government policy was explicitly aimed

---

[4]   See *Constitution Act, 1867* (U.K.), 30 & 31 Vict., c. 3, ss. 93, 133 reprinted in R.S.C. 1985, App. II, No. 5. *Canadian Charter of Rights and Freedoms*, Part I of the *Constitution Act, 1982*, ss. 16–23, being Schedule B to the *Canada Act 1982* (U.K.), 1982, c. 11 [Charter]. For a discussion of the importance of protecting French and English-speaking communities as foundational to Canadian constitutionalism, see *Reference Re Secession of Quebec* [1998] 2 S.C.R. 217. See also Wilfrid Denis, 'Language Policy in Canada' in Peter Li (ed.), *Race and Ethnic Relations in Canada* (2d ed.) (Don Mills, Ontario: Oxford University Press, 1999) 178 at 179–187; Yasmeen Abu-Laban & Christina Gabriel, *Selling Diversity: Immigration, Multiculturalism, Employment Equity, and Globalization* (Peterborough: Broadview Press, 2002). See also Leo Driedger, *Multi-Ethnic Canada: Identities and Inequalities* (Toronto: Oxford University Press, 1996) at 240–242.

[5]   See *Indian Act*, R.S. 1985, c-I-5; George R., Proclamation, 1 October 1763 (3 Geo. III) [*Royal Proclamation 1763*]; Charter, s. 25; Part II of the *Constitution Act, 1982, ibid*, s. 35.

at assimilation.[6] Despite a limited acceptance of group-based pluralism in Canada, therefore, there is also a long history of overtly racist legal and social policies in both public and private law. In addition to the institution of slavery in the British colonies and the historical mistreatment and colonization of Aboriginal communities, post-Confederation provincial and federal laws contained explicitly racist policies vis-à-vis the Chinese and Japanese communities well into the twentieth century.[7] Moreover, common law and civil law doctrines failed to provide adequate protection against racist exclusionary policies in employment, housing and access to public services.[8]

Legal protection against discrimination was largely non-existent until the emergence of anti-discrimination laws in the 1960s and 1970s.[9] The development of these statutory protections against discrimination in the workplace, in housing and in access to public services, therefore, marked an important advance in securing human rights in Canada. During this period, human rights commissions were also established in all jurisdictions across Canada to investigate discrimination complaints, provide publicly funded legal representation to complainants and engage in various educational activities. This public infrastructural support for human rights enforcement was a cornerstone of human rights policy, rooted in concerns with access to justice. Nevertheless, the individual complaints focus of anti-discrimination laws was premised on the assumption that retroactive redress for aberrant human rights violations would suffice to ensure equality in societal institutions.[10]

---

6   The *Royal Commission on Aboriginal Peoples* condemned this historical assimilationist bias in Canadian government policy and articulated an alternative approach premised on respect for the unique heritage of Aboriginal peoples and their 'right to cultural continuity'. It noted, 'Successive governments have tried – sometimes intentionally, sometimes in ignorance – to absorb Aboriginal people into Canadian society, thus eliminating them as distinct peoples. Policies pursued over the decades have undermined – and almost erased – Aboriginal cultures and identities'. See Canada, *Royal Commission Report on Aboriginal Peoples, (RCAP) People to People, Nation to Nation*, (Ottawa: The Commission, 1996) *Highlights* at 2. The Royal Commission Report is available online at: http://www.ainc-inac.gc.ca/ch/rcap/sg/sgmm_e.html.

7   See Christina Sampogna, Sharon Harper & Karen Rudner, 'Historical Overview and Introduction' in E.P. Mendes (ed.), *Racial Discrimination: Law and practice*, (Scarborough, Ont: Carswell, 1995), ch. 1. See also Vic Satzewich, *Deconstructing a Nation: Immigration, Multiculturalism and Racism*, (Halifax: Fernwood Publishing, 1992) at 48–49. See also Peter S. Li, 'Social Inclusion and Visible Minorities and Newcomers: The Articulation of "Race"and "Racial" Differences in Canadian Society'). (Paper prepared for Conference on Social Inclusion, March 27–28, 2003, Ottawa, Canadian Council on Social Development.) See generally, Peter Li, (ed.), *Race and Ethnic Relations in Canada*, 2nd edn, *supra*, note 4.

8   See Constance Backhouse, *Color-Coded: A Legal History of Racism in Canada, 1900–1950* (Toronto: University of Toronto Press, 1999).

9   For an excellent discussion of the emergence of human rights legislation in Canada, see W. S. Tarnopolsky and William Pentney, *Discrimination and the Law*, (Toronto: Carswell, 1995) c. 2.

10   For a more extensive discussion of the limitations of the individual complaints model, see Colleen Sheppard, 'The Promise and Practice of Human Rights Protection: Reflections

Throughout the 1970s and into the 1980s, this assumption came into question. It was recognized that anti-discrimination laws were an insufficient response to deeply embedded and historical patterns of exclusion. Despite fairly comprehensive anti-discrimination statutes, there was continued under-representation of women, Aboriginal peoples, racialized communities and persons with disabilities in the upper echelons of the labour market and continued labour market segregation. In response to the notable lack of progress of these groups in accessing equal employment opportunities, a Royal Commission on Equality in Employment was set up in 1983.[11] Its mandate was to 'inquire into the most efficient, effective and equitable means of promoting employment opportunities, eliminating systemic discrimination and assisting all individuals to compete for employment opportunities on an equal basis'.[12] Cognizant of US developments on affirmative action, the Commission was also asked to assess whether voluntary or mandatory affirmative action initiatives should be adopted by the federal government.[13]

In 1984, Judge Rosalie Silberman Abella released her historic report, *Equality in Employment – A Royal Commission Report*.[14] The Report is a critical starting point for understanding the modern landscape of affirmative action in Canada. Recognition of systemic discrimination was central to the conclusions.

> Systemic discrimination requires systemic remedies. Rather than approaching discrimination from the perspective of the single perpetrator and the single victim, the systemic approach acknowledges that by and large the systems and practices we customarily and often unwittingly adopt may have an unjustifiably negative effect on certain groups in society. The effect of the system on the individual or group, rather than its attitudinal sources, governs whether or not a remedy is justified.[15]

Systemic discrimination is understood as either the product of structures, policies and systems 'designed for a homogeneous constituency'[16] or the result of the negative effects of group-based stereotypes. For Abella, the 'former usually results in systems primarily designed for white able-bodied males, the latter usually results

---

on the Quebec Charter of Human Rights and Freedoms' in *Melanges Paul-André Crépeau* (Cowansville, Quebec: Yvon Blais, 1996). See also A. Blumrosen, 'Strangers in Paradise: *Griggs* v. *Duke Power Co.* and the Concept of Employment Discrimination' (1972) 71 Mich. L. Rev. 59 at 66–75 (outlining three conceptual stages of protection against discrimination).

[11]   Judge Rosalie Silberman Abella, *Report of the Commission on Equality in Employment* (Ottawa: Ministry of Supply and Services, 1984) [Abella Report]. For background on why the federal government designated women, visible minorities, Aboriginal peoples and persons with disabilities as the groups in need of more effective equality protection, see 'Terms of Reference' at i.

[12]   *Ibid.* at ii.

[13]   *Ibid.*

[14]   *Ibid.*

[15]   *Ibid.* at 9.

[16]   *Ibid.*

in practices based on white able-bodied males' perceptions of everyone else'.[17] Affirmative action is understood as a systemic remedial strategy designed to 'put an end to the hegemony of one group over the economic spoils'[18] and to remedy existing inequalities, deeply embedded in the institutional policies and practices of the workplace. Thus, Abella insisted that 'the end of exclusivity, is not reverse discrimination, it is the beginning of equality'.[19] She emphasized that the 'economic advancement of women and minorities is not the granting of a privilege or advantage to them; it is the removal of a bias in favour of white males that has operated at the expense of other groups'.[20]

To reinforce these ideas, Abella began her Report by changing the terms of the debate. Rather than using the US-rooted terminology of 'affirmative action', often inaccurately equated with rigid job quotas and reverse discrimination, Abella preferred the concept of 'employment equity'.[21] For Abella, both terms describe 'employment practices designed to eliminate discriminatory barriers and to provide in a meaningful way equitable opportunities in employment'.[22] The language of 'equity', however, resonates more closely with Abella's understanding that to do nothing in the face of institutionalized inequality and exclusion is to perpetuate systemic discrimination. The Abella Report proceeded to document the inequalities faced by four designated groups: women, visible minorities, native people and persons with disabilities. She then outlined three key strategies for implementing equality at work: training and education, childcare and employment equity. While all three areas were identified as important for policy development to secure equality at work, her recommendations on employment equity received the most sustained attention and legislative implementation.

In the wake of the Abella Report, the federal government introduced the *Employment Equity Act, 1986*.[23] Although the general principles and purposes of the legislation remain the same today, the 1986 Act was significantly amended in 1995 to address widespread criticism about the inadequacy of its enforcement mechanisms.[24]

---

[17]   *Ibid.* at 10.

[18]   *Ibid.*

[19]   *Ibid.* at 10.

[20]   *Ibid.*

[21]   As Abella noted, 'No great principle is sacrificed in exchanging phrases of disputed definitions for newer ones that may be more accurate and less destructive of reasoned debate', *ibid.* at 7.

[22]   *Ibid.*

[23]   *Employment Equity Act*, S.C. 1986, c. 23 (2nd Supp.).

[24]   The National Action Committee on the Status of Women (N.A.C.) criticized the lack of enforcement powers of the *Employment Equity Act, 1986*. See National Action Committee on the Status of Women (N.A.C.), '*Justice Works: Response of N.A.C. to 'Working Towards Equality', Ontario's Discussion Paper on Employment Equity Legislation'*,(February 1992) 1. See also Phebe-Jane Poole and Judy Rebick, 'Not Another Hundred Years: The Failure of the Federal Employment Equity Act' (1993), *I Can.* Labour L.J. 341. See generally Yasmeen Abu-Laban and Christina Gabriel, *supra* note 4 pp. 129–163.

The express purpose of the current *Employment Equity Act* is 'to correct the conditions of disadvantage in employment experienced by women, aboriginal peoples, persons with disabilities and members of visible minorities by giving effect to the principle that employment equity means more than treating persons in the same way but also requires special measures and the accommodation of differences'.[25] It requires federally-regulated employers with over 100 employees to identify and eliminate barriers to equality in their workplaces and to institute proactive positive policies to ensure equitable representation and accommodation of the four designated groups.[26] Employers must develop an employment equity plan that includes the establishment of short term numerical goals for increasing the representation of the designated groups based on an assessment of the 'degree of underrepresentation of persons in each designated group', the 'availability of qualified persons in designated groups within the employer's and the Canadian workforce', and 'the anticipated turnover of employees within the employer's workforce' in the relevant period.[27] Finally, various record-keeping and reporting duties are imposed on employers.[28] The federal Canadian Human Rights Commission is vested with responsibility for monitoring compliance with the legislation.[29]

At the same time that the first employment equity legislation was introduced, the federal government initiated a Federal Contractors' Program, as recommended in the Abella Report.[30] The Federal Contractors' Program applies to employers with over 100 employees that bid for federal goods and service contracts of $200,000 or more.[31] To secure continued eligibility for such contracts, it requires employers to develop employment equity programs aimed at identifying and eliminating discriminatory barriers, increasing representation of designated groups at all levels of the workplace and monitoring equity progress.[32] The initiative effectively extends the reach of proactive employment equity into workplaces that would otherwise be regulated by provincial employment and human rights law.

The expanded reach of proactive equity engagements is particularly important given the relative absence of parallel employment equity legislation at the provincial and territorial level. Most provinces across Canada do not have comparable employment equity legislation applicable to private sector employers; legislative

---

[25]   *Employment Equity Act*, S.C. 1995, c. 44, s. 2.

[26]   *Ibid.*, s. 5.

[27]   *Ibid.*

[28]   *Ibid.,* ss. 17, 18.

[29]   *Ibid.*, Part II.

[30]   Abella Report, *supra* note 11 at 260.

[31]   See online: Federal Contractors' Program <http://info.load-otea.hrdc-drhc.gc.ca/workplace_equity/fcp>.

[32]   See discussion in A.B. Bakan and A. Kobayashi, *Employment Equity Policy in Canada: An Interprovincial Comparison*, (Ottawa: Status of Women Canada, 2000), online: Status of Women Canada < http://www.swc-cfc.gc.ca/pubs/pubspr/0662281608/200003_0662281608_e.pdf> at 15. (Compliance reviews are undertaken by Human Resources Development Canada).

initiatives have been limited to public sector employment.[33] Nonetheless, basic human rights legislation and exemptions do exist to protect the development of voluntary special programs in every jurisdiction. Furthermore, provinces have been at the forefront in the creation of legislated pay equity provisions. Such provisions mandate a proactive review of wages and salaries and the remedying of the systemic undervaluing of remuneration in predominately female job categories.[34] Quebec has also implemented a contract compliance program that is similar to the federal initiative.[35]

Unlike employment, there have been no major legislative initiatives for affirmative action in the educational domain.[36] Instead, policy approaches rely on voluntary initiatives. Education equity programs have been developed with the explicit objective of identifying and redressing systemic problems of exclusion and disadvantage in educational institutions.[37] Such initiatives have been protected from reverse discrimination complaints by exemption provisions in human rights laws for special programs aimed at redressing systemic inequalities.[38]

Though Canada has not been immune to backlash and political discourses against affirmative action,[39] it is important to underscore the extent to which both

---

[33]   *Ibid.* in Appendix II: 'Summaries of Provincial Employment Equity Structures'. Note that since the Report was completed, Quebec has introduced public sector employment equity legislation: see *An Act Respecting Equal Access to Employment in Public Bodies,* 2000, S.Q. c. A–2.01. It is significant that the legislation goes beyond the groups designated in federal employment equity law to include 'persons whose mother tongue is neither French nor English', see s. 1. It is also noteworthy that Ontario had introduced employment equity legislation that was subsequently repealed when a conservative government took office: See the *Job Quotas Repeal Act*, 1995, S.O. c. 4. For an overview of the Ontario legislation, see Yasmeen Abu-Laban & Christina Gabriel, *supra* note 4 at 141–148.

[34]   For an overview of pay equity developments in Canada, see Marie-Thérèse Chicha, *L'équité salariale: mise en oeuvre et enjeux*, 2nd edn (Cowansville: Yvon Blais, 2000).

[35]   See Quebec Human Rights Commission website at <http://www.cdpdj.qc.ca/en/home>. See also M. Bastien et al., *Les programmes d'accès à l'égalité au Québec: bilan et perspectives*, (Québec: Commission des droits de la personne et des droits de la jeunesse du Québec, 1998).

[36]   Some commentators have argued that supply side solutions (particularly training and education initiatives) are more effective in the long run than demand side solutions. See e.g. A.I. Anand, 'Visible Minorities in the Multi-Racial State: Where Are Preferential Policies Justifiable?', (1998), 21, Dal. L.J. 92.

[37]   For a useful explanation of the objectives and components of education equity, see Ontario Confederation of University Faculty Associations, 'Educational Equity', (Spring 1992), 12, Canadian Women's Studies 99.

[38]   See discussion in Colleen Sheppard, *Litigating the Relationship between Equity and Equality*, (Toronto: Ontario Law Reform Commission Report, 1992).

[39]   See Sheila McIntyre, 'Backlash Against Equality: The Tyranny of the Politically Correct', (1993), 38, McGill L.J. 1. See also Frances Henry and Carol Tator, 'State Policy and Practices as Racialized Discourse: Multiculturalism, the *Charter* and Employment Equity' in

educational and employment equity initiatives in Canada have developed in a legal context that affirms their legality and beneficial effects in redressing societal inequalities. Of particular significance in the Canadian context is the inclusion of an explicit affirmative action clause in the constitutional equality guarantees. While s. 15(1) of the *Canadian Charter of Rights and Freedoms* sets out the basic protection against discrimination, s. 15(2) states that 'Subsection (1) does not preclude any law, program or activity that has as its object the amelioration of conditions of disadvantaged individuals or groups including those that are disadvantaged because of race, national or ethnic origin, colour, religion, sex, age or mental or physical disability'.[40] This type of clause parallels many of the special measures provisions found in international human rights documents.[41] The express inclusion of s. 15(2) in the Canadian Charter was designed to ensure the constitutionality of affirmative action programs and to insulate such programs from potential challenges by those claiming they constitute a form of 'reverse discrimination'.[42]

The Supreme Court of Canada has not yet had occasion to apply s. 15(2) to a case involving allegations of so-called reverse discrimination. It has nonetheless provided some guidance as to the meaning and scope of s. 15(2) and its relationship to s. 15(1).[43] The Court has clarified that s. 15(2) 'provides a basis for the firm recognition that the equality right is to be understood in substantive rather than formalistic terms'.[44] It is 'confirmatory of s. 15(1)'.[45] A substantive approach to equality, according to the Court, means that the underlying purpose of s. 15(1) is 'not only to prevent discrimination but also to play a role in promoting the amelioration of the conditions of disadvantaged persons'.[46] Substantive equality does not simply mean the 'elimination of distinctions'[47] – rather, recognizing and accommodating differences may well promote equality – just as identical treatment in the face of difference 'may frequently produce serious inequality'.[48] Understanding when, pursuant to a vision of substantive equality, differential treatment constitutes discrimination has

---

Peter Li, (ed.), *supra* note 4, pp. 88–115 at pp. 103–106 (reviewing the ideological significance of the repeal of employment equity legislation in Ontario).

[40]   Charter, *supra* note 4, s. 15. The *Charter* was enacted in 1982, with the equality rights provisions coming into effect in 1985.

[41]   See, for e.g., *Convention on the Elimination of All Forms of Discrimination against Women*, 18 December 1979, 1249 U.N.T.S. 455; *International Convention on the Elimination of All Forms of Racial Discrimination*, 7 March 1966, 660 U.N.T.S. 195.

[42]   See e.g., Pentney and Tarnopolsky, *supra* note 9; Beatrice Vizkelety, *Proving Discrimination in Canada*, (Toronto: Carswell, 1987); and Colleen Sheppard, *supra* note 38.

[43]   *Lovelace v. Ontario*, [2000] 1 S.C.R. 950 [*Lovelace*].

[44]   *Ibid.* at para. 93.

[45]   *Ibid.* at para. 108. Iacobucci J. is careful to leave open the possibility that the Court's approach might be reconsidered in a future case engaging the role of s. 15(2) more directly.

[46]   *Ibid.* at para. 93.

[47]   *Lovelace, ibid.*, citing to McIntyre J. in *Andrews v. Law Society of British Columbia*, (1989), 1 S.C.R. 143 at 171.

[48]   *Ibid.*

been a central and ongoing challenge of the Court. It has endeavoured to elaborate a purposive and contextual approach, focusing on the effects of government laws or policies on human dignity and respect. Although the Supreme Court of Canada has been widely praised for its commitment to substantive equality, the jurisprudence reveals continued uncertainty about the meaning and application of the complex and contested principle of equality.[49]

Supreme Court jurisprudence interpreting statutory prohibitions on discrimination has also reflected a positive endorsement of special equity initiatives. In an important systemic discrimination case implicating gender-based discrimination in a railway company, the Court endorsed the findings and approach to systemic discrimination set out in the Abella Report, emphasizing that employment equity programs are 'designed to break a continuing cycle of systemic discrimination'.[50] Chief Justice Dickson outlined three ways in which employment equity facilitates equality at work:

> Firstly, by countering the cumulative effects of systemic discrimination, such a programme renders future discrimination pointless ... Secondly, by placing members of the group that had previously been excluded into the heart of the workplace and by allowing them to prove ability on the job, the employment equity scheme addresses the attitudinal problem of stereotyping ... Thirdly, an employment equity programme helps to create what has been termed a 'critical mass' of the previously excluded group in the work place. This 'critical mass' has important effects. The presence of a significant number of individuals from the targeted group eliminates the problems of 'tokenism'... The 'critical mass' also effectively remedies systemic inequities in the process of hiring.[51]

Importantly, according to the Court, the critical mass also makes possible 'continuing self-correction of the system', a process that is consistent with a more transformative vision of equality. The general emphasis in the opinion on redressing systemic inequalities is central to an approach to equity that demands more fundamental institutional change to eliminate historical sources of exclusion. More recently, the Supreme Court of Canada has reaffirmed its understanding of the role of anti-discrimination protections in the workplace. Chief Justice McLachlin cautioned, 'Interpreting human rights legislation primarily in terms of formal equality undermines its promise of substantive equality and prevents consideration of the

---

[49]   See, e.g. Donna Greschner, 'Case Comment: Does *Law* Advance the Cause of Equality?', (2001), 27, Queen's L.J. 299.

[50]   *CN v. Canada, (Canadian Human Rights Commission)*, (1987), 1 S.C.R. 1114 at 1143 [*Action Travail des femmes*].

[51]   *Ibid.*, On the last point, Dickson C.J. cites A. Blumrosen, 'Quotas, Common Sense and Law in Labour Relations: Three Dimensions of Equal Opportunity', in W.S. Tarnopolsky, ed., *Some Civil Liberties Issues of the Seventies*, (Toronto: Osgoode Hall Law School, York University, 1975), 5, emphasizing at 15, the 'informal processes of economic life'. He also cites Carol Agocs, 'Affirmative Action Canadian Style', (1986), 12, Can. Pub. Pol. 148.

effects of systemic discrimination'.[52] It is critical, according to the Court, to ensure that policies, standards and practices that have discriminatory employment effects be carefully scrutinized and revised whenever possible to secure equality.

As this brief overview suggests, the legal framework for advancing equality through proactive initiatives, particularly in the workplace, provides a solid basis upon which one would expect significant progress for racialized communities and Aboriginal peoples in Canada. Available quantitative data reveal some progress for racialized communities and Aboriginal Canadians since 1985 in both public and private sector employment, but progress has been slow, particularly for Aboriginal peoples.[53] While both Aboriginal peoples and racialized communities confront problems of racism at work and in educational contexts, the specificity of each group's situation requires separate analyses. The next sections therefore highlight some of the challenges to the effective implementation of employment and education equity for racialized communities and Aboriginal peoples in Canada respectively.

Racialized Communities: Systemic and Invisible Racism

Racial discrimination has a long history and a continued presence in Canada.[54] Various minority groups continue to be subject to racism, often linked to the colour of their skin – a visible marker of difference from the dominant white norm. The term 'visible minorities' has been defined 'as non-Caucasian in race or non-white in colour'.[55] The *Employment Equity Act* includes the following groups under the

---

[52]   *British Columbia* (Public Service Employment Relations Commission) *v. British Columbia Government and Services Employees' Union* (B.C.G.S.E.U.), (1999), 3, S.C.R. 3 (*Meiorin*) at para. 41. For an extended discussion of the significance of this case, see Colleen Sheppard, 'Of Forest Fires and Systemic Discrimination: A Review of *British Columbia*' (Public Service Employment Relations Commission) *v. British Columbia Government and Services Employees' Union* (B.C.G.S.E.U.) (2001), 46, McGill L.J. 533.

[53]   See Canadian Human Rights Commission, *Annual Report,* 2002, (Ottawa: Ministry of Public Works and Government Services, 2002), pp. 41–44; Canadian Human Rights Commission, *Employment Equity Report*, 2001, (Ottawa: Ministry of Public Works and Government Services, 2003), pp. 27–31. See also Carol Agocs, 'Canada's Employment Equity Legislation and Policy, 1986–2000: Unfulfilled Promises', in Carol Agocs, ed., *Workplace Equality: International Perspectives on Legislation, Policy, and Practice*, (The Hague; New York: Kluwer International, 2002).

[54]   See references cited in notes 7 and 8, and accompanying text. See also Carol A. Aylward, *Canadian Critical Race Theory: Racism and the Law*, (Halifax: Fernwood, 1999); L. Hill, *Black Berry, Sweet Juice: On Being Black and White in Canada*, (Toronto: HarperFlamingo, 2001).

[55]   See Anand, *supra* note 36 at 93, citing T. Sowell, *Preferential Policies: An International Perspective*, (New York: William Morrow, 1990), pp. 13–14. Anand includes Aboriginal peoples in her analysis of visible minorities, while acknowledging that they are usually considered as distinct from the visible minority category, given their unique history and status. See also Statistics Canada, *Making the Tough Choices in Using Census Data to Count Visible*

rubric of visible minorities for the purposes of employment equity: Blacks, Chinese, Japanese, Korean, Filipino, Indo-Pakistani, West Indian, Arab, Southeast Asian, Latin American, Indonesian and Pacific Islander.[56] While the experiences of different communities are unique, the commonality of racism explains the underlying logic of the visible minority terminology. Nevertheless, it is also problematic for a number of reasons. One limitation, noted in the Abella Report, was the risk that combining '... all non-whites together as visible minorities for the purpose of devising systems to improve their equitable participation without making distinctions to assist those groups in particular need, may deflect attention from where the problems are greatest'.[57] A further problem with this terminology is its failure to include individuals from groups subject to systemic discrimination but who do not fit neatly into the visible minority category. The extended coverage in the new Quebec legislation represents a partial response to this problem of underinclusiveness; it expands the designated groups to include individuals whose first language is neither French nor English, thereby including many immigrant communities.[58] The idea of 'racialization', which underscores the social construction of race, rather than its biological determinants, also brings into question the coherence of a legal category based on physical markers of difference.[59] Finally, the complexity and multiplicity of identity render problematic legal categories that often require individuals to fit neatly into discrete identity categories.[60] Despite these limitations, the visible minority terminology continues to be used in the Canadian context and embraces a wide range of racialized communities.

The racial demographics of Canadian society have been changing rapidly over the past 30 years. Statistics from the 2001 Census reveal that visible minorities represent 13.6 per cent of the Canadian population. In some cities, where visible minority populations are concentrated, visible minorities represent up to 37 per cent of the population.[61] The changing demographics of Canadian society may in part be attributed to changing immigration patterns. For decades, Canadian immigration law and policy favoured immigrants from European countries. Federal government documents have reported that 'Thirty years ago, more than 80 per cent of Canada's

---

Minorities in Canada, (Ottawa: Employment Equity Data Program, 1990); *Approaches to the Collection of Data on Visible Minorities in Canada: A Review and Commentary*, (Ottawa: Employment Equity Data Program, 1991).

[56] See discussion of the designated groups in the Abella Report, *supra* note 11, pp. 86–94.

[57] *Ibid.*, at 46, This problem is effectively one of over inclusiveness.

[58] See *supra* note 33.

[59] Religious and ethnic differences may also be sources of racialization. For a discussion of racialization, see Henry and Tator, *supra* note 36, pp. 91–93. See also Sherene Razack, *Looking White People in the Eye: Gender, Race, and Culture in Courtrooms and Classrooms*, (Toronto: University of Toronto Press, 1998).

[60] See Nitya Iyer, 'Categorical denials: equality rights and the shaping of social identity', (1993), 19, Queen's L. J. 179.

[61] See Canadian Human Rights Commission, *Annual Report 2002*, *supra* note 53 at 47.

immigrants came from Europe or countries of European heritage, whereas 70 per cent now come from Asia, Africa, and Latin America, with 43 per cent coming from Asia alone ...'.[62]

Beginning with the Abella Report in the early 1980s, the effects of racism in the employment domain revealed disproportionate exclusion of visible minorities from employment opportunities. The effects of exclusion were felt both by immigrant and Canadian-born visible minorities. The latter tended to name racism as the key problem; whereas recent immigrants attributed discrimination to 'weaknesses in the services and facilities established to integrate them into Canadian life'.[63] Problems ranged from inadequate language training (particularly for immigrant women) to requirements for Canadian-based job experience, non-recognition of professional and education credentials and insensitive government assistance.[64] Multiculturalism policy was seen as fostering recognition of cultural diversity while not addressing problems of racism and non-integration of minority ethnic communities into mainstream Canadian institutions.[65] Thus, Abella concluded: 'The problem is essentially one of racism. Strong measures are therefore needed to remedy the impact of discriminatory attitudes and behaviour flowing from this problem'.[66]

Despite the fact that the Abella Report was published almost 20 years ago, the same problems and patterns of exclusion persist. For example, the Canadian Council on Social Development, in its 2000 report, *Unequal Access – A Canadian Profile of Racial Differences in Education, Employment and Income*, concluded that despite the generally higher education levels of persons from visible minority communities, there is a significant gap between educational levels and job opportunities.[67] An important study on visible minorities in the federal public service documented the significant under-representation of racial minorities. Data revealed that in 1999, only one in 17 employees in the general staff category, and only one in 33 employees in the management and executive categories, were members of a visible minority group.[68]

---

[62]   Cited by Peter S. Li, 'Social Inclusion and Visible Minorities', *supra* note 7 at 8. See also Peter S. Li, *Race and Ethnic Relations in Canada, 2d, supra* note 4, pp. 56–61, (brief review of the Canadian Immigration Policy).

[63]   Abella Report, *supra* note 11 at 47.

[64]   *Ibid.,* pp. 49–51.

[65]   *Ibid.,* at 51.

[66]   *Ibid.*

[67]   J.L. Kunz, A. Milan and S. Schetagne, *Unequal Access: A Canadian Profile of Racial Difference in Education, Employment and Income,* (Report Prepared by the Canadian Race Relations Foundation, 2000). The report reveals, for example, at 22, that the bottom income quintile in 1996 was composed of 23 per cent of individuals from racialized communities born outside of Canada in contrast to 15 per cent of white people born in Canada or abroad. See also C. Agocs and H.J. Michael, *Systematic Racism in Employment in Canada: Diagnosing Systemic Racism in Organizational Culture,* (Canadian Race Relations Foundation, 2001).

[68]   In response to data on under-representation, the federal government set aggressive benchmarks for hiring visible minorities, (one in 5 external recruitment by 2003, one in 5 entries into executive categories by 2005); see Task Force on the Participation of Visible Minorities

Problems of racial exclusion and discrimination were also documented in an important 1997 human rights decision alleging systemic racism in a federal government department. In *National Capital Alliance on Race Relations*, (NCARR) *v. Canada* (Health and Welfare),[69] a human rights tribunal concluded that, 'visible minority groups… are being affected in a disproportionately negative way. There is a significant under-representation of visible minorities in senior management … Visible minorities are bottlenecked or concentrated in the feeder group … and are not progressing into senior management'.[70] The tribunal ordered that special remedial measures be implemented, including permanent measures that would eliminate sources of systemic racial discrimination and temporary measures, such as hiring quotas.[71]

While the challenges of systemic racism make it difficult to identify and remedy, there is important work being done in this domain.[72] Identifying systemic racism requires attentiveness to its multiple dimensions. First, it can result from standards, policies or practices within a particular institution or profession that appear racially neutral on their face but which have a disparate impact on racialized communities (i.e. the non-recognition of foreign degrees, Canadian experience requirements and standardized testing with implicit cultural biases). Second, it can occur when individuals from racialized communities are over-represented in particular categories or groups subject to disadvantaged educational or working opportunities (i.e. domestic workers, foreign agricultural workers and part-time or contingent workers). Third, systemic racism can result from direct prejudice and mistreatment. When problems of direct racial discrimination recur within a professional, workplace or educational setting, it indicates a pervasive and thus systemic problem of racism, rather than an aberrant individual instance of race-based prejudice. One example, which has been the focus of repeated studies in cities across Canada, is racism in policing practices.[73]

---

in the Federal Public Service, *Embracing Change in the Federal Public Service*, (Ottawa: Treasury Board of Canada, 2000).

[69]   *National Capital Alliance on Race Relations v. Canada*, (1997), 28, C.H.R.R. D/179.

[70]   *Ibid.,* at para. 166.

[71]   *Ibid.,* at para. 193. For example, the tribunal ordered the Federal Government Department, within a period of six months, to begin hiring visible minorities into the senior management category at the rate of 18 per cent for five years in order to reach 80 per cent proportional representation.

[72]   See C. Agocs and H.J. Michael, *supra* note 67, which develops a methodology for identifying institutional problems of racism as the first step towards their eradication. See also Employment and Immigration Canada (Commission), *Employment Systems Review Guide*, (Ottawa: Ministry of Supply and Services Canada, 1991), (Manual to assist employers generally in putting equitable practices into place from the recruitment to the termination stage of employment).

[73]   See discussion in *R.D.S v. The Queen*, (1997), 3, S.C.R. 484. See also *R. v. Brown* (2003), O.J. No. 1251; and Ontario Human Rights Commission, *Report of the Commission on Systemic Racism in the Ontario Justice System*, report written by David Cole and Margaret Gittens, (Ontario: Queen's Printer, 1995).

Finally, systemic racism has been referred to as a 'grey area' of discrimination manifesting in 'informal cliques' that foster gendered and racialized exclusion.[74] One US scholar describes the ways in which the phenomenon of 'unconscious racism' permeates the actions and decisions of individuals from dominant groups in ways that disadvantage racial minorities.[75] Emerging critical race theory has also addressed the institutional pressures to conform in ways that risk separating individuals from their communities of origin.[76]

Beyond uncovering the multiple manifestations of systemic racism within particular educational and employment settings, a systemic lens allows us to connect institutional patterns of exclusion to larger structural, historical and societal inequities. For example, the effects of economic restructuring, privatization and globalization have a disparate effect on workers at the bottom of the economic hierarchy or at the margins of the labour force, where individuals from racialized communities are over-represented.[77] Our regulatory approaches to human rights in the workplace have not kept pace with the structural and systemic changes in the Canadian economy, since they tend to target large employers. Regulatory approaches for securing human rights in the workplace, namely employment and pay equity, labour standards, unionization, occupational health and safety, are premised on a traditional employer-employee relationship. As noted by Glenda Simms of the National Committee on Immigrant and Visible Minority Women, there is a concern that 'employment equity actions will improve the status of "visible minority" men and white women, leaving foreign-born women and/or women of colour untouched'.[78] For it is the workers on the margins of the labour market – the immigrant women, the racialized minority youth – who fall outside of the protected sphere of employment law.[79]

---

[74]   Kunz, Milan and Schetagne, *Unequal Access, supra* note 67 at 30.

[75]   Charles Lawrence III, 'The Ego, the Id, and Equal Protection: Reckoning with Unconscious Racism', (1987), 39, Stan. L. Rev. 317.

[76]   Richard Delgado, 'Affirmative Action as a Majoritarian Device: Or, Do You Really Want To Be a Role Model?', (1991), 89, Mich. L. Rev. 1222. See also Adelle Blackett, 'Mentoring the Other: Cultural Pluralist Approaches to Access to Justice', (2001), 8, Int'l J. Legal Prof. 251. See also Leo Driedger and Shiva S. Halli, *Race and Racism: Canada's Challenge*, (Montreal & Kingston: McGill/Queen's University Press, 2000) pp. 186–202.

[77]   James S. Frieders, 'Changing Dimensions of Ethnicity in Canada', in Vic Satzewich, (ed.), *Deconstructing a Nation : Immigration, Multiculturalism and Racism in 90s Canada*, (Halifax: Fernwood Publishing, 1992), 47, pp. 61–2.

[78]   G. Simms, ' Employment Equity into the 1990s and Beyond', Talk presented in the Distingued Lecture Series, Centre for Women's studies and Feminist Research, University of Western Ontario, January 30, 1991, cited in Monica Boyd, 'Gender, Visible Minority and Immigrant Earnings Inequality: Reassessing an Employment Equity Premise', in Satzewich, *supra*, note 7, 279–321 at 280.

[79]   See Adelle Blackett and Colleen Sheppard, 'Collective Bargaining and Equality: Making Connections', (2004), 142 International Labour Review 419. On intersectionality in the Canadian context, see Iyer, *supra* note 60. See also Daiva K. Stasiulis, 'Feminist Intersectional Theorizing', in Li, *supra*, note 4, 346.

Aboriginal Peoples: Resisting Assimilation

Aboriginal peoples in Canada are defined in the Constitution to include Indian, Inuit and Métis persons.[80] The most recent census data indicate that Aboriginal persons constitute 3.3 per cent of the Canadian population.[81] Aboriginal children represent 5.6 per cent of children under age 14. The Royal Commission Report on Aboriginal Peoples noted that 56 per cent of the Aboriginal population is under age 24, a statistic that underscores the importance of educational and employment equity. Recent government studies reveal dramatically higher rates of unemployment in Aboriginal communities and conclude that the 'employment prospects for Aboriginal people need urgent attention'.[82]

The situation of Aboriginal peoples is different from that of other racialized communities in some fundamental ways. The Constitution accords 'Indian, Inuit and Métis' Aboriginal peoples a unique status in recognition of their histories as distinct political communities and of the deleterious effects of colonization.[83] The Royal Commission on Aboriginal Peoples rejected assimilationist policies as fundamentally wrong, and insisted that the starting point for remedying the 'legacy of brokenness affecting Aboriginal individuals, families and communities'[84] was recognition of the distinctive cultural and national identities of Aboriginal peoples.

> ...Canadians need to understand that *Aboriginal peoples are nations*. That is, they are political and cultural groups with values and lifeways distinct from those of other Canadians. They lived as nations – highly centralized, loosely federated, or small and clan-based – for thousands of years before the arrival of the Europeans ... To this day, Aboriginal people's sense of confidence and well-being as individuals remains tied to the strength of their nations. Only as members of restored nations can they reach their potential in the twenty-first century.[85]

---

[80]   *Constitution Act, 1982*, s. 35(2).

[81]   It is important to note that this statistic does not include all Métis and non-Status Indians.

[82]   Canada, *Report of the Royal Commission on Aboriginal Peoples: Restructuring the Relationship*, (R.C.A.P. Report), Vol. 2, *supra* note 6, at 930. See also Renée Dupuis, 'Aboriginal Peoples and Employment Equity', in *Sharing the Harvest: The Road to Self-Reliance*, (Report of the National Roundtable on Aboriginal Economic Development and Resources), (Ottawa: Ministry of Supply and Services, 1993), 165–74; *Strengthening Aboriginal Participation in the Economy*, Report of the Working Groups on Aboriginal Participation in the Economy to Federal-Provincial/Territorial Ministers Responsible for Aboriginal Affairs and National Aboriginal Leaders, May 11, 2001.

[83]   L. Chartrand, 'Re-conceptualizing Equality: A Place for Indigenous Political Identity', (2001), 19, Windsor Y.B. Access Just, 243, pp. 248–249.

[84]   Canada, *Royal Commission on Aboriginal Peoples Report*, Highlights, *supra* note 6 at iii; see also Vol. 2, Part Two, s. 5, (Economic Development), pp 930–58.

[85]   *Ibid.*, at iv.

These important insights were reached following the most extensive commission of inquiry ever to be completed on the situation of Aboriginal peoples of Canada. The collectivist orientation of the Royal Commission's conclusions raises important conceptual issues with respect to the content and character of employment and educational equity initiatives aimed at redressing inequalities facing Aboriginal peoples.

While the unquestioned objective of most equity initiatives directed at non-Aboriginal women, visible minorities, and persons with disabilities, is fair and full integration into mainstream societal institutions (including educational institutions and workplaces), for Aboriginal peoples, integration may in some instances be insufficient or even inconsistent with the cultural and national survival of the community. Special programs intended to redress historical inequities facing Aboriginal communities are often designed to facilitate economic flourishing in separate economic endeavours rather than the integration of Aboriginal peoples into predominantly non-Aboriginal employment contexts. More traditional employment or educational equity initiatives aimed at integration into mainstream non-Aboriginal institutions no doubt also have an important role to play in securing substantive equality for Aboriginal peoples in Canada; however, they are not sufficient on their own.

Thus, it is important to enumerate two types of equity initiatives. The first, which may be referred to as 'self government initiatives', is premised upon retaining separate Aboriginal economic, educational, political and social institutions.[86] The second type of equity initiative, contemplated by the standard definitions of employment or educational equity, is aimed at facilitating participation by Aboriginal persons in non-Aboriginal institutions and organizations. This duality was implicit in some of the observations made in the Abella Report:

> Although native people spent hours with this Commission discussing employment practices that tend to exclude native people, they stressed that ultimately economic self-sufficiency would make them better able to provide job opportunities for native people and develop the bargaining power necessary to realize the goals of their communities.[87]

Thus, redressing systemic economic inequities in the case of Aboriginal communities often engages the government in initiatives to promote Aboriginal economic activities that are critical to collective identity and community renewal.

It is noteworthy that some of the key cases implicating s. 15(2) (the affirmative action provision of the Canadian Charter) and Aboriginal peoples have arisen in contexts where special government programs are aimed at facilitating the retention of difference by according special treatment to traditional Aboriginal

---

[86]   See Chartrand, *supra* note 83, discussing the right to self-determination of Indigenous peoples in international law.

[87]   Abella Report, *supra* note 11 at 34.

economic activities.[88] For example, in *Apsit v. Manitoba (Manitoba Human Rights Commission)*,[89] a provincial government had granted special licensing preferences to Aboriginal wild rice farmers, given the historical importance of wild rice harvesting to the Aboriginal communities in the province. The preferential licensing scheme was challenged as discriminatory by non-Aboriginal wild rice farmers. Much of the discussion in the case concerns legal interpretation issues regarding s. 15(2). One of the key reasons that the courts struck down the program, however, was due to insufficient evidence supporting a rational nexus between the cause of Aboriginal economic disadvantage and the licensing preferences. The real problem was not access to licenses, but rather a lack of resources to purchase the necessary equipment and supplies.[90] This case underscores the importance of ensuring that equity initiatives are carefully developed to redress the key underlying systemic problems.[91]

In another case implicating Aboriginal communities and the question of special ameliorative programs, a provincial First Nations' Fund was established to promote socio-economic development within First Nations communities.[92] Métis and non-Status Indian communities were not included in the list of Aboriginal communities designated to receive a share of the First Nations' Fund. These excluded Aboriginal communities challenged the distribution scheme as discriminatory. Though this case engaged the courts in an assessment of s. 15(2) and the role of special programs in constitutional equality law, it was fundamentally different from classic 'reverse discrimination' challenges to affirmative action initiatives; this case involved a claim that the special program was underinclusive and should be extended to the excluded economically disadvantaged Aboriginal communities. It was not a challenge by non-Aboriginal individuals or groups. The Supreme Court ultimately rejected the threshold argument that it was discriminatory to limit distribution of the First Nations Fund to Indian bands recognized in federal legislation, and did not base its decision on s. 15(2). While its conclusions on the discrimination claim have been criticized,[93] the case again illustrates how government policy on Aboriginal economic equality extends beyond individual employment and educational equity opportunities and focuses on reinvigorating separate economic development within Aboriginal communities.

---

[88] See, e.g., *Apsit v. Manitoba*, (1987), 50 Man. R (2d) 92 (Q.B.) (*Apsit*); *Lovelace, supra* note 43.

[89] *Apsit, ibid.*

[90] *Ibid.*, at 249.

[91] It also illustrates the risk that litigation takes place without the direct involvement of the individuals and groups for whom the program is designed. The parties to the litigation included the Manitoba government and the non-Aboriginal wild rice farmers. There was no independent representation of Aboriginal interests and concerns in the litigation.

[92] *Lovelace, supra* note 43.

[93] See, for e.g., Dianne Pothier, 'Connecting Grounds of Discrimination to Real People's Real Experiences', (2001), 13, C.J.W.L. 37.

Nevertheless, education and employment equity initiatives aimed at integration into non-Aboriginal institutions have consistently included Aboriginal peoples as group beneficiaries. The federal *Employment Equity Act* and federal contractors program exemplify this, listing Aboriginal peoples as one of the four designated groups. Special initiatives in education have also been of particular importance across Canada.[94] The justifications for including Aboriginal peoples in special equity initiatives are widely accepted and endorsed, particularly given the historical record of human rights violations against Aboriginal peoples.[95] The Canadian Human Rights Commission policy statement on Preferential Employment Policies for Aboriginal Peoples provides a succinct enumeration of the legal justifications for developing special equity measures for Aboriginal Canadians, including (i) unique constitutional status, (ii) continued socio-economic disadvantage, (iii) international obligations (i.e. International Labour Organization Convention 169 on Indigenous and Tribal Peoples in Independent Countries and the Universal Declaration on the Rights of Indigenous Peoples) and (iv) special provisions in human rights legislation.[96]

Yet, data on employment equity programs reveal that these initiatives have not been effective in increasing Aboriginal representation in non-Aboriginal institutions. The Canadian Human Rights Commission reported in 2002 that 'Aboriginal peoples and persons with disabilities – are furthest from reaching representation levels proportionate to their availability in the labour force'.[97] Identified barriers to progress include: a lack of jobs, mismatched skills to available jobs, lack of information regarding job opportunities, racial discrimination, lack of child care, and high rates of turnover.[98] According to the *Report of the Royal Commission on Aboriginal Peoples*, the failure of employment equity initiatives 'stems from barriers that are of a different character from those faced by other groups: a combination of racism rooted in long-standing and deeply ingrained stereotypes, and work environments with cultures that alienate Aboriginal employees'.[99] In particular, the Report identified differences between 'Aboriginal cultures and corporate cultures – interpersonal

---

[94]   See, for e.g., L. Chartrand *et al.*, 'Law Students, Law Schools and their Graduates' (2001), 20, Windsor Y.B. Access Just, 211. See also R. Hesch, 'Aboriginal Life Experience and the Fracturing of Multiculturalist Ideology', in Satzewich, *supra* note 7, pp. 423–68.

[95]   For a discussion of pre-Charter legal decisions, see Sheppard, *Litigating the Relationship*, *supra* note 38.

[96]   See Canadian Human Rights Commission Policy Statement on Aboriginal Employment Preferences (25 March 2003), online: Canadian Human Rights Commission, http://www.chrc-ccdp.ca/legislation_policies/aboriginal_employment-en.asp. See also Abella Report, *supra* note 11.

[97]   Canadian Human Rights Commission, *Annual Report 2002*, *supra* note 53.

98 Canada, Royal Commission on Aboriginal Peoples Report, vol. 2, *supra* note 6, Volume 2, Part Two, s. 5, 2.7, pp. 933–34.

[99]   *Ibid.*, at 2.7. See also R. Dupuis, 'Aboriginal Peoples and Employment Equity', in Royal Commission on Aboriginal Peoples, *Sharing the Harvest: The Road to Self-Reliance*, (Report of the National Roundtable on Aboriginal Economic Development and Resources), (Ottawa: Ministry of Supply and Services, 1993), pp. 165–74.

relations, decision-making processes, concepts of leadership, organization of work …'.[100] The unstated assimilationist underpinnings of many employment and education equity initiatives are considered particularly problematic for Aboriginal persons. The resistance of Aboriginal peoples to assimilation provides important lessons to all of us. For in their fundamental questioning of the logic and morality of the status quo within non-Aboriginal institutions and their insistence on collective and not merely individual well-being, we may find a pathway to equality, premised on respect for difference, open to structural and systemic transformation, and guided by compassion and democratic participation.[101]

Conclusion

The story of the struggle to make Canadian society more inclusive and equitable can be told from multiple perspectives. At times, one sees progress – in the community, schools, workplaces, universities and institutions of governance – and a willingness to replace old visions and definitions with new, more diverse, equitable understandings that there are multiple ways of doing things. The legislative and judicial endorsement of equity initiatives reflects a growing societal acceptance of equality and inclusion as foundational norms, grounded in a commitment to substantive equality and the need for systemic and institutional change.

At other times, the entrenchment of privilege and accentuation of inequality appear so deeply embedded in the societal status quo that substantive equality seems to be an unreachable goal. Inequalities are becoming more acute while legislators and policy makers cling to tired strategies and old approaches. Our legislative models for employment equity and basic human rights protection have not kept pace with the structural and systemic changes in the global economy. And the continued difficulties in securing effective enforcement compromises the persuasiveness and impact of positive legislative, judicial and policy endorsements of equity initiatives. Thus, while the Canadian experience provides important lessons on how to begin moving towards a more equitable society in a way that allows for a more transformative approach to equality rights, much work remains to be done in turning the articulated commitment into reality.

---

[100] *Ibid.*, at 938.

[101] See Patricia Monture, 'Roles and Responsibilities of Aboriginal Women: Reclaiming Justice', (1992), Sask. L. Rev. 237. See also John Burrows, '"Landed" Citizenship: Narratives of Aboriginal Political Participation', in Alan C. Cairns *et al.*, (ed.), *Citizenship, Diversity & Pluralism – Canadian and Comparative Perspectives*, pp. 72–86 (Montreal: McGill-Queen's University Press, 1999).

Chapter 3

Affirmative Action in India

Ashwini Deshpande

Intergroup Disparity in India

Intergroup disparity in India is multi-faceted, with several parallel layers of discrimination, which makes the formulation of an ideal plan for compensatory discrimination difficult, if not impossible. At the risk of oversimplification, an attempt will be made in this chapter to summarise some of the important dimensions of intergroup disparity. There is substantial regional variation in indicators of development across states of India, creating a feeling amongst the people of the less developed regions that they are discriminated against and the several violent agitations in the last half- century for secession from the Indian Union are testimony to this feeling of resentment. At the time of independence from the British in 1947, the country was partitioned on religious lines with the creation of a new country, Pakistan that would be home to the Muslims. The consequent migration of Hindus living on the Pakistani side to India and Muslims on the Indian side to Pakistan is the bloodiest and one of the most traumatic events in recent history. However, minority religious groups, including Muslims, continue to be a part of the Indian population.[1] The legacy of the religious divide continues: right wing organisations ostensibly protecting the interests of the majority religion, Hinduism, press for the exclusion of minority religious groups. Minority religious groups are not only the targets of hate campaigns and systematic violence but also have worse social and economic outcomes.

In addition, within Hinduism is embedded the caste system. It must be noted, however, that while the caste system is conventionally associated with Hinduism, all religions in India, including Islam and Christianity, display intergroup disparity akin to a caste system leading to the hypothesis that perhaps caste was a system of social stratification in pre-modern India. This is also true for the so-called egalitarian religions such as Buddhism. 'The term "Brahmana" of the Vedas is accepted by the Buddhists as a term for a saint, one who has attained

---

[1]   According to the 1991 census, on the whole, 86 percent of the Indian population is Hindu, with the rest divided among minority religions, viz., Islam, Christianity, Sikhism, Jainism and so forth.

final sanctification'. (Radhakrishnan, 2004).[2] Thus, Buddhism makes a distinction between Brahmins and others. This is ironic, since Buddhism has been embraced by low castes in large numbers with the belief that it will provide them with the equality that Hinduism denies them. Occasionally, castes with a stigmatised ethnic identity, the 'untouchables', have converted to other religions, including Christianity and Islam, as an escape from discrimination and exclusion. However, such conversions do not necessarily guarantee social equality; for instance, the census label 'neo-buddhist' indicates an ex-untouchable who has converted to Buddhism. Since this is common knowledge, it is unlikely that the social position of this person will improve significantly.

However, only the caste divisions among the Hindus will be highlighted for a variety of reasons, including the fact that these are central to the programme of affirmative action in India. Low castes from other religions, such as Dalit Christians, have been demanding affirmative action, but so far it is restricted to certain low castes among Hindus (explained below). Estimated to be over 2500 years old, the caste system has undergone many transformations, from the ancient *varna* system to the contemporary *jati* system.[3] The *varna* system divided the population initially into four and later into five mutually exclusive, endogamous, hereditary and occupation specific groups: the Brahmins, Kshatriyas, Vaisyas, Sudras and Ati-Sudras. The latter two were those doing the menial jobs with the latter being considered 'untouchables', in that even their presence was considered polluting and thus was to be avoided.[4] The three higher *varnas* are often referred to as 'caste Hindus' (upper caste Hindus) or as 'twice born', since (the men of) these castes enter an initiation ceremony (the second birth) and are allowed to wear the sacred thread. Together, the upper castes constitute 17–18 per cent of the population. The Ati-Sudras are roughly 16 per cent of the population. Numerically, the largest *varna* is Sudra, constituting nearly half of the population.

Clearly, this division of castes corresponded to a rudimentary economy. Over the years as economy and society grew more complex, this system metamorphosed into the *jati* system, with features similar to the *varna* system, but with some differences. Firstly, the number of *jatis* today is estimated to be between 2 to 3000. It is a testimony to the complexity of the system that even the exact number of caste divisions cannot be determined with certainty. Secondly, most *jatis* are regional categories, making inter state comparisons of *jatis* less than straightforward. It must be noted that *jatis*

---

[2]   Radhakrishnan (2004), p.177, quotes J.G. Jennings: 'It should never be forgotten that Buddhism is a reformed Brahmanism, as is evidenced by the invariably honorific use which Gautama makes of the title "Brahmin" and it therefore takes for granted certain Vedic or Vedantic postulates'.

[3]   Unfortunately, these are translated into a single English term, the caste system, which does not enable us to distinguish between these manifestations.

[4]   The ati sudras were considered untouchables because almost the entire range of social interaction with them was to be avoided by other castes. However, the manner in which *jatis* interact with each other used to be according to rather complex rules of social interaction, wherein certain interactions were permitted with some castes and others were not.

are not clear subsets of the *varnas*, thus making the ranking of *jatis* an enormously complicated task, if not an impossible one. Thirdly, the *jati*-occupation link is not as straightforward as the *varna*-occupation link. However, the association between *jati* and *varna* at the topmost level (Brahmin *jatis*, most Kshatriya *jatis*) and at the bottom (Ati-Sudra or former untouchables) is clearer than it is in the middle ranks.

Being at the bottom of the caste hierarchy, the former untouchables not only are poorer, they continue to be targets of discrimination, oppression, violence and exclusion. Thus, the affirmative action programme in India is targeted at these *jatis*, designed both to bring these groups into the mainstream and also to compensate them for centuries of discrimination. The names of these *jatis* are listed in a government schedule and thus in official literature these castes are referred to as Scheduled Castes, or simply as SCs. Mahatma Gandhi referred to them as Harijans, literally, as people of (close to) God, but some view this as a patronising term. Most prefer to use the original Sanskrit, but now Marathi term Dalit, meaning the oppressed, which is seen as a term of pride. It should be noted that in independent India, untouchability is abolished by law and caste based discrimination is a crime, in theory. Also, in keeping with the ideal of a casteless society, an individual is not obliged to disclose his/her caste anywhere. Data is, therefore, not available by caste: the last *jati* based census was in 1931. Since caste is not ascriptive in the same way as race, it is not always possible to ascertain the caste status of an individual if he/she chooses not to reveal it, especially in urban areas.[5] However, overt and covert instances of untouchability continue and caste is used as a basis of both social and economic discrimination.

In addition, more than 50 million Indians belong to tribal communities that are distinct from the Hindu religious fold. These are the *Adivasis*, (literally, original inhabitants) who have origins that precede the Aryans and even the Dravidians of the South. Many have lifestyles and religious practices that are distinct from any of the known religions in India and languages distinct from the official languages of India and their dialects. Most live on the margins of existence, excluded from the mainstream development process. These are also targets of affirmative action, similarly notified in a government schedule and hence referred to as Scheduled Tribes or STs.

Very close to the social and economic position of the Dalits are the erstwhile Sudra *jatis* that, however, have *not* been targets of untouchability. The blanket term 'Other Backward Classes' (OBCs) is supposed to capture these *jatis* that have been described in the constitution as 'socially and educationally backward classes'. The implication of these categories on data availability is the reduction from an extremely high indeterminate number to either three or four categories, making comparisons easier. Up to the early 1990s, government data was available for three categories: SC, ST, 'Others' (everyone who is neither SC nor ST: the residual category). Subsequently, 'Others' got divided into OBCs and 'Others' (non SC/ST/OBC residual). While the narrowing of the number of categories definitely eases analysis, the non-availability

---

[5]   For the differences between race and caste as categories, see 'Introduction to Darity and Deshpande', (eds), *Boundaries of Clan and Color*, (London, Routledge, 2003).

of data by *jati* does not enable us to isolate the status of the upper castes. However, it should be apparent that any estimate of intergroup disparity, based on this three or four way division, will underestimate the gap between the top and the bottom end of the caste hierarchy. This is because 'Others' is a residual term that includes 'everyone else' (as explained above) and, thus, it includes *jatis* that are very close to SCs in economic and social position.

The Indian Affirmative Action Programme

The affirmative action programme in India is quota based and is two-pronged: it is targeted separately towards SC/ST and OBC groups. It is best to examine them separately. 22.5 per cent of all government jobs, seats in educational institutions that have complete or partial government funding and electoral constituencies at all levels of government are reserved for SC and ST persons. This quota is roughly proportional to their share in the population. While this was enshrined in the Indian constitution via Article 15 (4) (reserve places for the under privileged in state run educational institutions) and Article 16 (4) (reservation of government jobs), this programme has a history that precedes independence. In some areas, such as parts of present day Kerala and Karnataka, quotas were introduced almost a hundred years ago by the British. The constitution of independent India was drafted by B.R. Ambedkar, an outstanding theoretician and one of the most important leaders of the Dalit movement. Making affirmative action for SCs and STs a part of the constitution, a move largely due to Ambedkar, ensured that it is mandatory and cannot be questioned in theory. However, in practice, due to the upper caste predominance in all these institutions, its implementation is indifferent and often quotas remain incompletely fulfilled, as will be seen later.

The logic for affirmative action for SC and STs is based on the following set of arguments:

1. Intergroup economic disparity: there are various standard of living indicators that establish persistent intergroup disparity between SC/STs on the one hand and the rest of the population on the other. Deshpande (2001) in addition to summarising the evidence constructs a '*Caste Development Index*' (CDI) based on five indicators of standard of living (land holding, occupation, education, ownership of consumer durables, and of livestock). The all India mapping of the CDI reveals that in the early 1990s, there was substantial regional variation in the status of SC/ST populations, but in no state of India was their CDI higher than that of the Others. Whatever the improvement in their status over 50 years after independence, it has not been sufficient to reverse the economic gap. Deshpande (2004) maps the same index for 1998–1999 and finds that the pattern persists.

2. The Dalits continue to suffer from a 'stigmatised ethnic identity' due to their untouchable past and there is corresponding social backwardness. Human Rights Watch (1999) amply demonstrates the various aspects of violence,

exclusion and rejection that Dalits continue to face in contemporary India.

3. If equality of opportunity between castes is the objective, then affirmative action is needed to provide a level playing field to members of SC/ST communities.

4. Finally (arguably) social policy ought to compensate for the historical wrongs of a system that generated systematic disparity between caste groups and actively discriminated against certain groups.

Founders of modern India, who gave the policy of affirmative action decisive shape, had two approaches to social justice. One was the principle of 'equality in law' whereby the State should not deny any person equality before the law. The second was the principle of 'equality in fact' which gives the State an affirmative duty to remedy existing inequalities.[6] It has been argued that the two constitutional doctrines supplement rather than contradict each other. True equality can be achieved only if the state maintains an integrated society but adopts unequally beneficial measures to help those previously disadvantaged.

OBC Reservations

There has been considerable debate, again going back to the British times, over whether affirmative action should be extended to the OBCs that have not suffered exclusion due to untouchability. In a number of states in British India, educational benefits were given to the OBCs and in some major states, such as Madras, Bombay and Mysore, preferential treatment was given to OBCs that included reservations and welfare schemes.

Unlike in the case of Dalits, where identification is easier and non-controversial, the assignment of the OBC status to *jatis* is an exercise fraught with considerable difficulty. It is true that there are several *jatis* that are very low in the caste hierarchy and therefore face serious material deprivation. However, since the *jati-varna* link is fluid, it is not clear that each of the *jati* that tries to get the OBC status is, in fact, a descendant of the Sudra *varna*, or indeed, is *currently* facing serious deprivation, as several land owning, otherwise prosperous *jatis* claim OBC status. However, as Guhan (2001) argues, the position of OBCs reflects 'graded inequality rather than a sharp distinction between SCs and caste Hindus'. He also points out that OBC status has meaning in local contexts. For the state lists of OBCs, the Central Government has relied upon documents drawn up in 1949–50. In 1965, commissions were appointed in a number of states to identify the OBCs. However, since no caste enumeration has been done since 1931, these commissions had to rely on extrapolations and sample surveys to estimate the numbers and the social and educational backwardness of the OBCs. As Guhan points out, the problem is that preferential schemes cannot be

---

[6]   This latter principle gave shape to some directive principles of state policy, such as Article 46: '… the state shall promote with special care the educational and economic interests of the people, and in particular SC and STs and shall protect them from social injustice…'.

accepted unless they are based on reliable data and reliable data cannot be collected for fear of exacerbating caste feelings! Also, other social categories, such as religion and language can be considered (and indeed are) divisive, but the government has not stopped collecting data on these.

Clearly then, the issue of quotas for OBCs has been on the agenda for decades. As a part of the same quest, in 1981, yet another report, called the Mandal Commission Report (MCR, hereafter) was tabled. The announcement of its implementation was made in 1991 by the then Prime Minister, V.P.Singh. Under the recommendation of the MCR, reservations would be extended to include the OBCs with a quota of 27 per cent, taking the total (SC/ST/OBC) to 49 per cent. The announcement caused a huge public protest and widespread violent and virulent student agitations across university campuses in the country. Interestingly, despite the disruptions caused by the agitations, public sympathy was fully with the striking students. Also, while the agitation was caused by the announcement of the MCR and the extension of reservations to OBCs, the protest was against affirmative action in general, with openly derogatory casteist slogans directed against the Dalit castes.[7] V.P. Singh was widely demonised as having created the OBC monster. However, as the above discussion suggests, the problem existed independently of V.P. Singh.

Women's Reservation

While the bulk of the affirmative action programme is caste based, the last decade or more has seen the articulation of a demand for affirmative action for women. A full analysis of the movement for women's reservation would require a separate paper. However, a few remarks are in order. In 1991, the government of India introduced a proposal to reserve 33 per cent of electoral constituencies for women in local self-governments (the municipality and metropolitan council levels). After much debate, the measure was passed in 1993. Three years later, a bill for extending such reservation to the parliamentary and state legislative councils was introduced. In 2004, it is still pending in parliament, mired in huge controversy. While the novelty of the move lies in a version of affirmative action for half of the country's population, the implementation is complicated by the mechanics of working out the overlap with the caste-based reservation. However, to believe that the delay is due to the mechanics only would be erroneous. The debate over the passage of the bill has seen a vitriolic upsurge of anti-affirmative action sentiment, in addition to intense anti-women tirades.

---

[7]   For instance, during the agitation upper caste student protestors blocked busy streets and started polishing shoes (imitating shoeshine boys) with placards that read 'this is what we will be reduced to because of the reservation system'. Notice the implication: the occupation that they (read upper castes) would be reduced to is a Dalit occupation. In other words, it is all right for Dalits to continue to do the menial jobs, but if upper castes have to descend to this low level, it is unacceptable. Needless to add, the belief that reservations would push the upper castes down to the menial jobs was only a presumption – not supported by any evidence.

Just as major political parties have often revealed an ugly side during this whole debate, a consensus has emerged in the women's movement about the need for affirmative action in the political arena for women. There is a belief that a greater representation of women in parliament would ensure a gender shift in social and economic policies or at least modify the male dominated and male biased realm of policy making. However, there are concerns that some women may be put up as puppets while the real control would lie with their husbands or other male family members. The counter argument is that even if this happened initially, over time the presence of women in decision making bodies would help alter both their self-perception and their actual position in society.

The normal process of economic development, on its own, may not increase women's participation in the political sphere. The continued low presence of women in the political spheres of the industrialized developed countries is testimony to that. India's actual record is impressive compared to most developed countries: a woman prime minister for 19 years, several women chief ministers, ministers of state and other important political functionaries at both the central and state government levels. However, as elsewhere in the world, women are under represented in key decision making bodies, which has prompted the move to introduce affirmative action.

Implementation of Affirmative Action

Unlike in Malaysia and the USA, in India there is no national enforcement mechanism for affirmative action. Thus, civil action is not an available remedy for denial of due benefits (Nesiah, p. 165). However, they have an alternative in the form of a writ jurisdiction under Article 32 and 226 of the Indian constitution but given the dominance of upper castes in the judiciary, there is an upper caste/elite bias in the redressal mechanism. A formal writ application and subsequent appearances by lawyers in a court are too expensive for most potential petitioners. The central government does have a National SC/ST Commission, but so far it has not played a pro-active role in ensuring implementation of quotas.

In the evaluation of how many members of the target group have benefited from the quotas the following must be kept in mind. The quota-based scheme in India is similar to a guaranteed minimum scheme, in that quotas are supposed to be filled first and the rest of the seats are allocated on 'merit'. Thus, the total number of SC/ST individuals in a job or educational institution will overestimate the actual amount of preference, if some members of the target groups get in without availing of affirmative action.

The one area where caste based quotas are completely fulfilled is the electoral sphere. Thus, constituencies that are designated 'reserved' can only elect SC/ST candidates as the case may be. Again a detailed analysis of the political changes is a task best suited to a political scientist. However, given the enormity of this change, a few generalized comments are offered here. The reserved constituencies have led to a noticeable change in the caste composition of the elected representatives that even 40 years ago were dominated totally by upper castes. There are major Dalit political parties as well as key political players, ensuring that Dalit issues remain in the foreground in some fashion. However, it would be wrong to assume that this represents a fundamental betterment in the material and/or social conditions of the majority of the Dalits. Several of those elected from reserved seats are members of mainstream political parties and thus, are committed to the overall agenda of their parties, which may or may not include the reduction of caste disparity. Also, even in reserved constituencies, the voters are both SC/ST and upper caste, and in order to appeal to the latter, the candidates often have to tone down their pro-Dalit agenda. Of course, along the political spectrum, there is a strong tendency to be opportunistic and self seeking, thus Dalit or not, often those elected work primarily to consolidate their own power rather than transfer any real benefits to the people that they seek to represent.

Coming to the two other spheres of affirmative action, government jobs and education, the picture is more complex. Xaxa (2002) attempts an assessment of reservations in the University of Delhi, one of the premier institutions in the country. In 1999–2000, of all the undergraduate students, only 8.6 per cent were SC (with a quota of 15 per cent) and 1.8 per cent ST (quota of 7 per cent). Of the post-graduate students, 5.5 per cent were SC and 2 per cent ST (with actual quotas the same as that at the under-graduate level). Thus, quotas are grossly under fulfilled and if this could happen in the capital city, things might be worse in other parts of the country. The situation in the teaching posts is even worse. Teachers in Delhi University have bitterly opposed the introduction of affirmative action, even though it is a constitutional provision. As a result, reservations were introduced as late as 1996. At that time, out of the 700 teachers in postgraduate departments, seven were SCs and two were STs. Out of the 4512 teachers in university affiliated undergraduate colleges, 11 were SCs and none ST.

The picture in the non-teaching posts conforms to the overall pattern in other government jobs: the higher the representation of SC/ST, the lower paying the job. Xaxa's figures for 1998–1999 show that whereas only three per cent of Group A jobs were filled by SC/ST combined, the corresponding proportions for Groups B, C and D were 7.4, 13 and 29 per cent respectively. The menial jobs (cleaners, sweepers and so on) often are performed almost exclusively by Dalits, in particular those *jatis* whose traditional occupation was cleaning/scavenging. In all the opposition to affirmative action, there is never any protest against *over representation* of low castes in low paying jobs. In other words, as long as Dalits don't compete in traditional upper caste bastions or 'stay where they belong', it is acceptable.

Coming to government jobs, between 1953–1975, on the whole about 75 to 80 per cent posts in lower levels were filled. However, in the higher categories of officers (called Class I and II), quotas remain unfulfilled, revealing a picture quite like Delhi University above. This can be attributed to 'indifference/hostility on the part of the appointing authorities, insufficient publicisation of vacancies and the sheer expense of application'. At the higher levels or promotion stages, formal and informal procedures had operated to keep out the SCs, such as ad hoc and temporary positions, elimination through personal evaluation procedures like interviews, personality tests and unfair adverse entries in confidential records (Guhan, 2001, p. 213).

Galanter (1991) has attempted one of the most comprehensive explorations of the Indian affirmative action programme. A monetary cost-benefit evaluation is not possible because of the manner in which the Indian programme is formulated. However, he undertakes a crude assessment of the SC/ST affirmative action programme and some of his major findings are as follows:

- The programme has shown substantial redistributive effects in that access to education and jobs is spread wider in the caste spectrum than earlier, although redistribution is not spread evenly throughout the beneficiary groups. There is evidence of clustering, but Galanter believes that these reflect structural factors, since the better situated enjoy a disproportionate share of the benefits in any government programme, not just in affirmative action programmes.
- The vast majority of Dalits are not directly affected by affirmative action, but reserved jobs bring a many fold increase in the number of families liberated from subservient roles.
- In the short run, beneficiaries might get singled out and experience social rejection in offices, college hostels[8] and other set ups where they are introduced through affirmative action. However, in the long run, education and jobs weaken the stigmatising association of Dalits with ignorance and incompetence. Moreover, 'resentment of preferences may magnify hostility to these groups, but rejection of them exists independently of affirmative action programmes'.
- Affirmative action has kept the beneficiary groups and their problems visible to the educated public, but it has not motivated widespread concern for their inclusion beyond what is mandated by government policy.

Thus, Galanter concludes that affirmative action has been a partial success. It has accelerated the growth of a middle class and SC/ST members have been brought into central roles considered unimaginable a few decades ago.[9]

Some Major Controversies

As with affirmative action all over the world, there is huge debate in India both over whether affirmative action is needed at all, and if needed, if it should be caste based. The arguments against affirmative action in principle are essentially meritocratic and the implicit belief is that labour markets and other social institutions reward merit and efficiency, if allowed to function without hindrance in the form of affirmative

---

[8]   There is no explicit affirmative action in college hostels; affirmative action in colleges leads to entry of SC/ST students in college hostels.

[9]   However, even this crude calculation will not work for assessing OBC reservations because of the much more complicated nature of the problem.

action. There is extensive literature over this general debate and no summary will be attempted here, except to emphasise the following point. A cross-national comparison reveals that firstly, in the presence of intergroup disparity, labour markets do not function efficiently. Indeed, there are strong discriminatory losses in earnings among the subaltern groups. Secondly, while nowhere in the world has affirmative action proven to be sufficient to close the gaps between the privileged and the oppressed groups, there is enough evidence to suggest that the gaps would be larger in the absence of affirmative action.[10] A good counter example is India's northern neighbour, Nepal, the world's only Hindu state. Its social composition mirrors that of India, even though the number of castes is much smaller. Nepal has no system of affirmative action. Unlike India, labour market data are available by caste and the disparity in the occupational distribution is striking. Dalits in the rural areas are basically subsistence farmers, and in the urban areas are concentrated at the lowest end of the ladder. There is virtually no Dalit middle class in existence. This suggests that while affirmative action may not be the ideal remedy, the absence of affirmative action, i.e., letting labour markets function without hindrance, does not correct for exclusion either.

Turning specifically to India, the Constituent Assembly in Article 335 states that 'maintenance of efficiency of administration' is a specific objective. Based upon this, the Supreme Court has maintained that this article operates as a limitation on reservations. Thus, reservations were viewed as *exceptional* and *temporary* (the State may make adjustments to the roster of classes being given preferential treatment and may even cease making special arrangements when it feels that it is no longer necessary).

Three major constitutional issues have arisen in the court cases over affirmative action:

1. How many places ought to be reserved? Ambedkar was of the view that reservations, in order to be effective, ought to be limited to a minority. In two different rulings, the Supreme Court enacted a ceiling of 50 per cent with the belief that if reserved seats exceed 50 per cent then some other qualified candidates would be excluded. Galanter (1991) disagrees and argues that 50 per cent is a mechanical rule. It will 'not resolve the tension between the right of all to open merit competition and the right of some to merit selection'. Currently, the combined SC/ST/OBC reservations are less than 50 per cent.

2. Designation of beneficiaries: Quotas for SC and ST are constitutionally sanctioned and may not be challenged in court. However, it is not so for OBCs, which explains the huge debate and attack over OBC reservations. Constitutionally, caste is not, in itself, a permissible criterion for discrimination. The Indian constitution is egalitarian, casteless and classless where untouchability has been abolished and caste hierarchy is viewed as a

---

[10]   See Darity and Deshpande, (eds), *Boundaries of Clan and Color*, *ibid*.

retrograde institution that should not be perpetuated. However, the reality is otherwise, necessitating caste-based affirmative action for SC/ST. For OBCs on the other hand, since the issue is not so straightforward, the Supreme Court has developed a set of neutral (i.e. not related to caste) criteria: poverty, place of habitation, occupation, income level *and* caste.

This revived the old debate over whether caste should be an indicator of backwardness, or whether other criteria should be used. There is a belief that reservations should be class based for two reasons. Firstly, if the state accepts caste as the basis for backwardness, it legitimises the caste system that contradicts secular principles. Secondly, the traditional caste system has broken down and contractual relationships have emerged between individuals.[11] Thus, the argument goes, the life chances of an individual in contemporary India are determined by his/her economic condition and not by the membership of any social group. Thus, a poor Brahmin and a poor Mahar (a Dalit caste in Maharashtra) would have similar social and economic outcomes that would be in contrast to a rich Brahmin and a rich Mahar. Based on data from Gujarat, Shah (1985) demolishes the latter argument and demonstrates how the objective conditions of different castes are indeed disparate. For instances, controlling for land holding, there is wide diversity in educational attainment by caste. As for the former argument, there is some concern that eventually our goal should be the effective abolition of the caste system and so any system of affirmative action should work towards a weakening of traditional caste ties and affinities.

A variant of this argument is that given the widespread poverty in India, affirmative action only bestows privileges on the beneficiaries that are denied to the rest of the population. Thus affirmative action is seen not as compensating discrimination, but as the pampering of certain groups for narrow political ends. Needless to state, this implicitly denies systematic intergroup disparity and discrimination.

Recently the Rajasthan state government has introduced a proposal to extend quotas for poor upper castes, openly flouting and questioning the caste-based principle. Interestingly, this has provoked no adverse media/public reaction, in sharp contrast to the hysterically violent reaction to the announcement of the MCR, when an extension of quotas was seen as a deliberate lowering of merit. The implicit assumption is that poor upper castes are intrinsically meritorious, just backward due to adverse circumstances. Notice also that none of the usual rhetoric about pampering/vote-bank politics accompanies this announcement either.

---

[11]   For an exposition of this position, see Desai, I.P., *Economic and Political Weekly*, 14 July 1984.

There is the additional argument that caste matters only in rural areas. In urban areas, due to the possible anonymity and to the prevalence of capitalist contractual relations, labour market outcomes will not be determined by caste affiliation. Indeed for caste to matter in urban labour markets would be irrational. However, both prima facie evidence and the empirical estimates on discrimination in the labour markets in urban India suggest otherwise.[12] Looking at the occupational distribution separately for the rural and the urban areas, it turns out that while some *jatis* may have moved away from the traditional occupations, Dalits tend to be overwhelmingly concentrated in the lower end of the occupational spectrum. Additionally, studies confirm the presence of both wage (differential wages within the same job) and job discrimination (average earnings differ because of occupational segregation) in the private sector, which employs most of the industrial work force and which is free from the purview of affirmative action.

On the whole, caste remains at present an important indicator of backwardness. However, for OBCs, since the *varna-jati* link is more fluid, and because they didn't suffer historical discrimination in the form of untouchability and also because sections of the OBC community are fairly prosperous (the 'creamy layer' as they are known in the Indian discourse), the caste criterion must be combined with an income ceiling.

3. Is affirmative action by the state permissible outside section 15(4) and 16(4)?

This leads to the larger question of what kind of affirmative action is optimal? For instance, should affirmative action be quota based or non-quota based? If it is quota based in educational institutions, should qualifying marks be lowered to accommodate beneficiaries?[13] The current position is that for admission to most courses, qualifying marks for SC/ST students are lower. While this is done in order to increase the presence of SC/ST students, the long run merit of this move could be questioned in view of the fact that these students tend not to be able to cope and hence drop out before the course is over. This could be potentially avoided by special assistance during the course, such as remedial teaching programmes, but none exist.

Should it cover only government institutions or should it extend to the private sector as well? This is an increasingly pressing question in the context of the liberalisation of the Indian economy and the deliberate reduction in the role of

---

[12]   See Deshpande, Ashwini, 'Recasting Economic Inequality', *Review of Social Economy*, Vol. 58, No. 3, October 2000, pp. 381–399, for a review of this literature.

[13]   See, for instance, the two points of view in Pinto, Ambrose, 'Saffronisation of Affirmative Action', *Economic and Political Weekly*, December 25, 1999 and the rejoinder by H. Srikanth, 'No Shortcuts to Dalit Liberation', *Economic and Political Weekly*, March 25, 2000.

the state. The growth of public sector employment has been negligible in the last decade and state funding for educational institutions has been steadily declining. As institutions get privatised, they come outside the purview of affirmative action. Thus, if affirmative action remains confined to Articles 15(4) and 16 (4), then steady privatisation can erode affirmative action significantly.

Concluding Comments

As with affirmative action programmes the world over, the Indian programme is bitterly opposed by the non-beneficiaries both on meritocratic arguments as well as on grounds of non/inadequate performance, elitism, promoting casteism and so forth. Each of these issues have been discussed above and it has been suggested that firstly, labour markets in the real world do not function on the basis of first-best, perfectly competitive principles, but are in fact, discriminatory to the detriment of the marginalized groups. There is sufficient empirical evidence to establish this fact. Secondly, the Indian programme is only partially successful and perhaps flawed in several ways, but in the absence of an alternative, superior proposal, should be continued. As for the charge that affirmative action programmes promote casteism (or racism in other contexts) that they are designed to counter, it is a highly insidious and fallacious argument, also not unique to the Indian context. The completely erroneous assumption this argument makes is that there is no casteism in the absence of affirmative action programmes. If this were true, the material reality of the low-castes would be the complete opposite of what it is at present and affirmative action would be redundant. Eventually, a sincere and serious affirmative action programme would be able to achieve this outcome.

Glossary

Ati-Sudra:	the lowest in terms of ritual purity in the ancient *varna* system (see below). Confined to the most menial tasks, such as scavenging, sweeping etc. Considered 'outcastes', i.e. outside the fold of the *varna* system: so low in status that they were not even fit to be given a *varna*. Were 'untouchables', meaning thereby, that any contact with them (even with their shadow) was considered polluting and was to be avoided.
Brahmin/ Brahman:	priestly caste; on top of the caste hierarchy in terms of ritual purity.
Dalit:	first used in the Marathi language, meaning 'oppressed', is a word from Sanskrit. This is used as a term of pride by the ex-untouchable *jatis*.
Harijan:	literally 'people of (close to) God'; term used by Mahatma Gandhi for the ex-untouchable *jatis*, often seen as a patronising term.

Jati:	generic term for the contemporary caste unit. *Jatis* are regional and share the same characteristics as *varnas* (see below), but *jatis* are not exact subsets of *varnas*. The exact number of *jatis* is not known with certainty; estimated to be between 2–3000.
Kshatriya:	warrior and princely caste in the ancient *varna* system.
Mahar:	one of the major ex-untouchable *jatis* in Maharashtra. Their role in the Indian armed forces is well known. There has been a 'Mahar Regiment' in the Indian Army for a number of decades. The most well known leader from this *jati* is B.R. Ambedkar.
Mandal Commission Report (MCR):	Report presented by the Central Government recommending reservations to the OBCs (see below).
OBC:	Other Backward Castes: non-untouchable *jatis*, fairly low in social and economic status, probable descendants of the erstwhile Sudras (see below).
Reservations:	quotas – the central plank of the Indian affirmative action programme. Refers to reserving seats in government run and aided educational institutions; in public sector jobs and in electoral constituencies at all levels of government.
SC:	Scheduled Castes: ex-untouchable castes that appear in a government schedule, designated as beneficiaries of the affirmative action programme.
ST:	Scheduled Tribes: certain tribes listed in a government schedule, designated as beneficiaries of the affirmative action programme.
Sudras:	*varna* doing all the menial tasks. Later subdivided into Ati-Sudras: the lowliest of the low (see above).
Untouchables:	see Ati-Sudras above.
Vaisya:	*Varna* specialising in trade, retail sales, money lending: all commercial activity.
Varna:	ancient caste divisions, believed to be more than 3000 years old. Initially four categories: Brahmins, Kshatriya, Vaisya and Sudras. Over time, latter further subdivided into Ati Sudras. *Varnas* were hereditary, mutually exclusive, endogamous, occupation based categories.
Vedas:	most ancient scriptures of Hinduism, composed by various sages over centuries.

Chapter 4

From Periphery to Mainstream:
Affirmative Action in Britain

Elaine Kennedy-Dubourdieu

Introduction

Throughout much of their history, the British have declared their belief in the values
of democracy, fair play and social responsibility. These they said were an integral
part of their identity: 'British' values, which they took with them to the four corners
of their Empire, using them to various ends, not least to underpin and legitimise
Britain's imperialism.

In recent times the public debate has turned to the identification of that post-war
decade when things started to fall apart, when this notion of social responsibility
began to fade and the rot set in. Blame has been pinned on the bohemian 60s, the
chaotic 70s (with its oil crisis and 'winter of discontent') or the 'me-generation'
of the 80s, when Margaret Thatcher declared that only the individual counted and
there was 'no such thing as society'.[1] Other commentators have traced the decline of
social responsibility back to earlier times, while some have refused to believe in its
very existence, seeing there only a chimera, a figment of the collective imagination.

Yet at the same time, it is interesting to note the setting up in Britain of the policy
called variously 'affirmative action', 'positive action' or 'positive discrimination'
which will be discussed subsequently and which testifies to this self-same sense of
social responsibility.

Historical Background

The slave trade and the Empire greatly benefited the British and their economy.
The legitimisation of this mercantile imperialism was the belief in the cultural –
and at times biological – superiority of the white coloniser whose mission it was to
'civilise' the savage or backward 'races', who all subsequently became subjects of
the Crown. Though the mother country sent her sons and daughters out to the far-
flung corners of this Empire, the intention was never for members of these colonised
nations to make the return journey and settle in Britain as permanent residents. When

---

[1]   Margaret Thatcher in an interview for *Women's Own*, (31 October 1987).

some African and West Indian servicemen did take up residence after demobilization at the end of the First World War, their presence was met with hostility. 1919 saw 'race riots' around the dock areas in parts of East London, Liverpool, Cardiff and Hull, which consisted in the attack on these 'black' subjects of His Majesty and the damaging of their property. The solution to this 'problem' as it was constructed then, was the repatriation of this irritant presence, back to where it had come from.

In the period that stretches from the post-war years, into the 21st century and up to the present day, commemoration of the Second World War has become of outstanding importance in the definition of the identity of the nation, while the memory of colonial wars or these 'race riots' in Britain has virtually disappeared. Yet during this Second World War, the British Empire was crucial to the war effort, both in the supply of raw materials and man power, but apart from a few exceptions, colonial servicemen and women were kept away from the shores of the mother country. Whereas on British soil, those who were visibly different from the white majority – and generally described at the time, as the 'coloured' community – were small in number[2] and concentrated in restricted areas inside Britain's seaports (such as Limehouse in London, Cardiff's Tiger Bay and Liverpool's Toxteth). The majority of the white population had never seen a 'coloured' person, even though Britain controlled the lives of millions of 'coloured' people living in the Empire.

After the war came the dismantling of this Empire, the creation of the Commonwealth and a totally new trend in migration. The arrival in 1948 of the SS Empire Windrush bringing 492 West Indians (many of whom were ex-service personnel) to Tilbury Docks, marked the beginning of what is now seen as 'non-white' mass migration to Britain, bringing inhabitants of the West Indies and the Indian sub-continent and subjects of the crown 'home' to the mother country: 'We are here because you were there' was the slogan, often used as a reminder. These visibly different migrants had, for the most part, been brought up as British, on a diet of British culture, 'white history and white geography'[3] and a real belief in the mother country. On arrival most did not define themselves in terms of colour, but the consciousness of colour was soon imposed on them by the white 'host' society where racial discrimination, the euphemistically termed 'colour bar' was a fact of everyday life. These migrants were coming to fill jobs in Britain and the rate of arrivals during the 1950s almost matched the level of labour vacancies, year by year. Yet right from the start they were seen as being 'a problem' and this construct was to continue.

Despite the official discourse to the contrary, it is now clear from papers held at the Public Records Office, that right from the 1950s successive governments, encouraged by public opinion, tried to limit this 'black' influx – though they initially attempted to do this without offending the newly independent states of the Commonwealth. The policy however became manifestly clear and hardened throughout the 1960s, 70s

---

[2]   Estimated at between 8,000 and 15,000 in all.
[3]   In the words of Connie Mark in *Caribbean Women in World War II: 4 Black Women's History of War Time Service*, (Caribbean Ex-Service Women's Association and the London Borough of Hammersmith and Fulham, 1993).

and 80s when British governments of both persuasions (Conservative and Labour) passed laws on immigration and nationality, aimed at limiting, then cutting off as far as possible the influx of 'New Commonwealth', (non-white) immigrants.

Governments argued that this was only good sense, a question of limiting excessive numbers which, as a cramped island, Britain could not support. This was considered to be a pre-requisite for 'racial' harmony and the integration of those visibly different migrants and their descendants already living in Britain. However the door was left open to white migrants from the 'Old Commonwealth' (Canada, New Zealand, Australia and South Africa) and when Mrs Thatcher signed the Single Market Act in 1983 this gave the right of entry and abode in Britain to citizens of the European Union.[4]

From the late 1980s and early 1990s onwards the result of this combined legislation on immigration and nationality was to stop the inflow of economic migrants from the new Commonwealth, except for clearly defined family reasons. The main type of entry and residence into Britain then became as a refugee and seeker of asylum, and here numbers have increased considerably from the beginning of the 1990s. These refugees, often trying to escape violence and chaos at home, come for the most part from countries outside the Commonwealth[5] (Afghanistan, Iraq, the Horn of Africa and Eastern Europe). Quite a lot of these groups come with little or no English, and many are not strikingly dissimilar physically from the majority of the British population.

However the earlier immigrants from the 'New Commonwealth' and their descendants have not melted into the mass as migrants before had done, for they remain somatically different from the white majority. As Trevor Phillips, a black broadcaster and recently appointed Chairman of the Commission for Racial Equality put it: 'For most of my life, I have known that when I meet someone new, they see the colour before they see the man'.[6]

This period has also thrown up conflicting theorisations of 'race' and 'ethnicity', as well as a plethora of terminology, which may well be confusing.

Terminology and Theorising: Rule Britannia or Cool Britannia?

Roy Jenkins, one of the great reforming Home Secretaries of the 20th century, attempted to rebrand the sixties, not as the 'permissive society' (as the media generally had it) but as the 'civilised society', and in this vision he included the 'non-white' groups that have come to be designated as Britain's 'ethnic minorities'. This is a particularly British euphemism used not to designate all ethnic minorities as one might suppose (it does not include those of Italian or Ukrainian origin for example) but simply those who were seen to be visibly different from the 'white'

---

[4]   Some 320 million at the time. Since May 2004 the number of inhabitants in the EU, now enlarged to include 25 member states, is 455 million.

[5]   Zimbabwe being the major exception.

[6]   *The Observer Review*, (6 April 2003), p. 13.

majority of the population. This expression has come to replace that of 'coloured', now rejected by many for its derogatory, colonial connotations. More often than not the words 'ethnicity and 'ethnic' in Britain have been used to replace 'race' and 'racial', these being terms sullied by the use made of them by the Nazis and for many people today they carry unpleasant overtones and should be avoided if possible. Thus, as will be explained below, when the British introduced a question in the 1991 Census to determine the skin colour of a respondent, the question was termed 'ethnic'.[7] Nevertheless, if it is a polite euphemism for some, it is derogatory for others. 'Whoever came up with the term was a genius', said Michael Eboda:

> You've got to be clever to lump together in two words people whose heritages range from West Africa to the Asian sub-continent to the Caribbean and back to Britain. (...) the term 'ethnic minority' does a lousy job. And that's still the case when it's broken down further into the constituent parts: 'black' and 'Asian'. To consign more than three million people to just two categories without taking into account their cultural background or religious beliefs is ludicrous.[8]

Though he is undoubtedly right, these short cuts in designation are the most convenient that British English has come up with for the moment and will be used in this chapter – with 'Asian' referring to those of Indian, Pakistani and Bangladeshi origin essentially,[9] and 'black' to refer to those of Caribbean or African origin, with the term 'ethnic minorities' used to encompass all these groups ... despite the fact that some important commentators and organisations, such as the Institute of Race Relations, still use 'black' to refer to all non-white groups in Britain.[10]

In this post-war period Roy Jenkins rejected assimilation and a 'melting pot' which would 'turn everybody out in a common mould, as one of a series of carbon copies of someone's misplaced vision of the stereotyped Englishman'.[11] He argued therefore

---

[7]   'Ethnicity' generally signifies the belonging to a group which feels itself to be distinct from others because of various factors. These can include shared language, religion, history and memories of colonisation or migration. Thus 'ethnicity' expresses this feeling of shared identity.

Question 11 of the 1991 Census, entitled the 'Ethnic Question' in fact set out to determine what in the American Census is called the respondents' 'race', the colour of their skin. The nine categories that it proposed where not aimed at identifying all ethnic groups in Britain, as there was one category only for 'white', with all other distinctions being for 'non-white' groups (Black-Caribbean, Pakistani, Bangladeshi, Chinese etc.). There were no equivalent possibilities for whites (White-Irish etc, this was only to come in the 2001 Census).

[8]   Michael Eboda, 'It's a jungle out there ...', *The Observer*, (25 November 2001).

[9]   It can also be used to encompass those of Chinese origin. However this umbrella term 'Asian' has also been rejected in recent times (particularly since 9 November 2001) by those designated, who would prefer a differentiating form of identification, such as British-Sikh, British-Muslim etc.

[10]   See <www.irr.org.uk/statistics/index.html>.

[11]   Speech by Roy Jenkins made at the launch of the Race Relations Board, (London, 23 May 1966).

in favour of integration that he saw 'not as a flattening process of assimilation but as equal opportunity, accompanied by cultural diversity, in an atmosphere of mutual tolerance'.[12] This view, developed in the second part of the twentieth century came to be referred to as 'multiculturalism', the co-existence within the same society of different 'cultures', although the hidden reference was once again that of 'race'. This tradition was carried on by New Labour and the arrival of Tony Blair in 10 Downing Street in 1997, extolling the virtues of an inclusive multicultural Britain of 'Cool' Britannia – instead of Rule Britannia of the Empire and the overbearing imperialism of the 'little Englanders'.

On the other side of the ideological fence were people such as Enoch Powell who, in his now infamous 'Rivers of Blood' speech[13] in 1968, predicted apocalyptic consequences due to this influx of 'coloured' people (he generally retained the term). Not long before his death in 1998 Powell declared: 'Racism is a good thing, it defines who you are as a nation', obviously by defining who you are not. Powell believed these 'aliens'[14] and their descent could never become British or – in his even more limited definition – 'English'. At the time of the speech, Powell was a member of the shadow cabinet and the Conservative Party leader Edward Heath dismissed him immediately and distanced the Party from these remarks. A few years later, the next leader of the party and subsequent Prime Minister, Margaret Thatcher, took a very different view, declaring that she always listened carefully to what Powell had to say, and that he had only been doing his job as MP by voicing the fears and preoccupations of his constituents. Margaret Thatcher won three successive general elections (in 1979, 1983 and 1987) and before each she promised that her party would 'get tough' on immigration and close off all remaining loopholes that allowed New Commonwealth (non-white) migrants entry into Britain.

The tension between these two opposing visions was to be felt throughout the latter part of the twentieth century and continues to the present day.

The Statistics

Britain differs from most of its European neighbours in the collection of 'ethnic'/ 'racial' statistics of its citizens, and these statistics are a constituent part of the British policy of affirmative (positive) action, as will be demonstrated below.

The first 'ethnic' statistics in Britain were derived from the Census using firstly the place of birth of respondents and then that of their parents. This was not totally reliable as a method of establishing 'ethnicity', and could only be a short-term solution anyway as second and third generations were being born on British soil. Estimations were also made in other ways, notably through the Labour Force Survey

---

[12]   *Ibid.*

[13]   For a detailed discussion of this see Elaine Dubourdieu, 'Enoch Powell, the "Rivers of Blood" Speech' in A Kober-Smith and T Whitton (eds), *Civilisation Britannique*, (Paris, Editions du Temps, 2002), pp. 83–92.

[14]   Powell's term.

and General Household Survey, but in comparison to the National Census, these surveys were small indeed. From the 1970s onwards the question was increasingly raised about the advisability and the necessity of collecting statistics on British citizens' 'ethnicity', and of doing this directly through the Census. It was a debate that raged for twenty years, and was only finally decided with the 1991 Census and the introduction for the first time of an 'ethnic' question. The only aspect of this debate that will be mentioned here is the use that was to be made of such statistics, as this impinges directly on the question of affirmative action.

Some members of the groups that were to be studied in this way expressed concern that these figures would be used to identify them as a 'problem' or in some way 'inferior' to the rest of the population. Indeed one had only to think back to the Eugenics Movement in the United States which 'proved' blacks were less intelligent than whites to realise this was a genuine concern. Others have worried that the collection of such statistics institutionalises racism, creating 'racial' differences when there is no scientific and biological basis for such classification.

There were other protests at the time of a very different nature: in 1986 Enoch Powell declared them to be 'a prize specimen of a disease more dangerous than Aids',[15] not because they were, by their very nature racist, but because they would lead 'straight to the precipice of compulsory quotas'[16] and would be 'used by those who organise themselves in the pursuit of power and for the overthrow of our existing institutions'.[17]

Since that time, and despite such dire warnings, Britain has indeed gone in for the wholesale collection of such statistics. In the document that accompanied the 1991 Census, intended to convince respondents of the necessity of this manoeuvre, there was the following explanation of the 'ethnic' question: 'This question is included in the Census for the first time. It will help assess the extent and nature of racial disadvantage and what needs to be done to overcome it'.[18]

The 1991 Census revealed that the 'ethnic' minorities then made up 5.6 per cent (just over 3 million) of the total population (of just over 54 million) of the United Kingdom, as well as presenting a host of other socio-economic data about these groups. Since that time it has become common practice to collect such statistics, not only in the public sector but also in the private sector where this sort of 'ethnic monitoring' is common in large businesses, such as the automobile industry, banking, retailing etc.

Despite this first Census, which was a reliable count of the population, myths about the size of the ethnic minority population still flourish. A poll[19] carried out

---

[15]   'Powell attacks "colour count"', *The Independent*, (22 November 1986).

[16]   *Ibid.*, Powell is referring to the use of affirmative action.

[17]   *Ibid.*

[18]   Office of Population Censuses and Surveys, *Why is this Information Needed?*, (London, HMSO, 1990).

[19]   MORI poll, quoted by Beverley Bernard, acting Chairperson of the CRE, in Richard Ford, 'Ethnic Minorities become majority in two areas', *The Times*, (14 February 2003), p.4.

just before the 2001 census revealed that many believed that this group made up 22.5 per cent of the British population, whereas the final result for the whole of the United Kingdom was 7.6 per cent, approximately 4.6 million people (out of a total population of 58.7 million). For the first time, over half of this population had been born in Britain and so could in no way be considered as 'foreigners' or 'immigrants'.

The ethnic minorities make up two per cent of Scotland's population, 2.7 per cent in Wales, with the majority living in England where they now make up nine per cent of the population, an increase of approximately three per cent on the 1991 figures. It should be remembered that these groups are considerably younger that the rest of the population (a difference that should disappear by the year 2020), thus many more are of an age to have children. Also, it is not possible to make a direct comparison between these two Censuses as the Registrar General has attempted to keep pace with the evolving nature of identity in twenty-first century Britain and thus the same 'ethnic' categories were not used each time.[20]

The largest ethnic minority group in England and Wales is 'Asian or Asian British' at 4.4 per cent, two per cent of whom are Indian, 1.4 per cent Pakistani and 0.5 per cent Bangladeshi. Those describing themselves as 'Black or Black British' (whether they be of Caribbean, African or other background) form 2.2 per cent of the population of England and Wales, with Black Caribbeans being the largest black group at 1.1 per cent. Finally 0.4 per cent are of Chinese origin, with another 0.4 per cent in the 'Any other' category.

This ethnic minority population remains clustered in certain inner city areas. Approximately half of these minorities live in London, which has the highest proportion of each ethnic group, apart from Pakistanis (only 20 per cent of whom live there). Half of the Pakistani community on the other hand live in Yorkshire, Manchester and the West Midlands, while most of the Bangladeshi community live in East London (where they make up one third of the population of the borough of Tower Hamlets).

Thus Britain's diverse population is not to be found evenly spread throughout the country. In much of the North East and South West of England more than 95 per cent of people described themselves as white, with the 'whitest place' in England being the former mining town of Easington in the North East, where the local economy and community life were hard hit when Prime Minister Margaret Thatcher orchestrated the dismantling of Britain's mining industry and towns like Easington became places of exodus, rather than influx.

The 2001 Census included for the first time in England, Wales and Scotland (although the subject had been included in previous Censuses in Northern Ireland) a

---

[20]   Amongst other changes made in the 2001 Census was the introduction of the category 'mixed' which then offered a choice of 4 boxes to tick: 'White and Black Caribbean; White and Black African; White and Asian; Any other Mixed background, please write in'. It is believed that this category may have been chosen by people who had defined themselves as 'white' in the previous Census.

question on religion,[21] though this was voluntary, more than 92 per cent did choose to answer it. Over 70 per cent of the population said their religion was Christian. Three per cent (1.5 million) are Muslims who thus make up the country's largest religious minority, followed by the Hindus, who reach 1 per cent (559,000), with the other groups accounting for less than 1 per cent (Sikhs: 336,000, Jews 267,000; Buddhists 152,000 and people from Other Religions totalling 179,000). Over 23 per cent of the population stated no religion or said they had no religion.[22] Once again there was a debate over these figures and their collection. On the whole the representatives of all these religions welcomed this initiative, taking it as a form of legitimisation. The Secretary-General of the Muslim Council of Britain, Iqbal Sacranie for example said:

> Up to now, Muslims have been statistically invisible and thus easily marginalized. The census output is a strong signal to central and local government, social services and employers in particular that the needs of all sections of Britain's multicultural society must be fairly and equitably addressed.[23]

The Census has thus provided a wealth of information about the 'ethnic' minorities in Britain, not only on religion and geographical distribution, but also their family structures, living conditions, health, employment and education.

It has also revealed the existence of marked differences with the white population, as well as highlighting differences that exist between these groups themselves.

In 2001–2002, for example, people from some ethnic minority groups in the United Kingdom were more likely to have degrees, or equivalent qualifications, than white people. Those most likely to have degrees were Chinese people, Indians, Black Africans and Other Asians. And yet, despite some ethnic groups being more likely than the white population to have a degree, others were also more likely to have no qualifications at all. Pakistanis and Bangladeshis in particular were most likely to be unqualified: 48 per cent of Bangladeshi women and 40 per cent of Bangladeshi men had no qualifications. Among Pakistanis, 40 percent of women and 27 per cent of men had no qualifications.

In 2003 the unemployment rate for white people was 4.7 per cent, compared with 12.7 per cent for the ethnic minorities as a whole, but again with major differences between the constituent groups:

---

[21]   There were slight differences in the formulation however. Question 10 of the 2001 Census for England and Wales, 'What is your religion?', offered a choice of eight responses: 'None; Christian (including Church in Wales, Catholic, Protestant and all other Christian denominations); Buddhist; Hindu; Muslim; Sikh; Any other religion, please write in'.

[22]   This includes the 400,000 *Star Wars* fans – 0.7 per cent of the population – who declared they were 'Jedi Knights', a religion which the statisticians refused to recognise.

[23]   Quoted by Ruth Gledhill and Richard Ford, 'Christianity remains dominant religion', *The Times*, (February 14, 2003), p. 4.

Indian 8.5%
Pakistani 16.2%
Bangladeshi 22.9%
Black Caribbean 13.1%
Black African 15.2% [24]

Data also suggests that unemployment varies significantly according to religion, with Sikhs and Indian Muslims being twice as likely to be unemployed as Hindus.[25]

It is necessary to have this statistical breakdown of figures, as rising levels of overall prosperity may create the impression of an increasingly fluid society, which camouflages less optimistic trends such as these. Obviously race and ethnicity are not the only factors that explain the disadvantaged position of some of Britain's ethnic minorities. Britain remains a class-ridden society and the impact of the social class that a citizen is born into impacts on her/his life chances in employment, education and housing particularly, however this disadvantage is undoubtedly compounded by race and ethnicity. Seventy per cent of Britain's ethnic minorities live in 88 per cent of the most deprived local authority areas and when ethnic minorities do have the right qualifications, they still face prejudice when trying to improve their circumstances – whether in applying for jobs or mortgages. Statistically, a Pakistani male with a degree has the same likelihood of being unemployed as a white male with no qualifications. For many members of Britain's ethnic minorities it is not just a question of breaking through the glass ceiling, but more prosaically still, of getting off the sticky floor.

These statistics are not only useful as a revealer of disparities and disadvantage, but also a benchmark from which to assess the impact of measures taken to improve 'race relations'.

The Early Legislation

In the post-war period many believed that Britain should aim at good 'race relations' – but the question was how?

As already pointed out, the first priority established was that of cutting off non-white immigration from former colonies. This was done to reassure the white population, otherwise it was felt that hostility to new arrivals was inevitable, even understandable. At the same time, Labour Governments started to pass laws on 'Race Relations', designed to end overt discrimination on British soil. Thus right from the start what Anthony Lester[26] described as the 'Janus face' of British legislation – that of official government discrimination at the point of entry,

---

[24] Labour Force Survey, quarterly supplement, (Summer 2003).

[25] Cabinet Office Strategy Unit Report: *Ethnic Minorities in the Labour Market*, (London, 2003).

[26] Anthony Lester was one of the architects of the *1975 Sex Discrimination Act* and the *1976 Race Relations Act* to be discussed later.

followed by government prohibition of racial discrimination once on British soil – was clearly manifest.

The first two Race Relations Acts, passed in 1965 and 1968, set out to rid Britain of her 'colour bar', by prohibiting most acts of direct discrimination against those who were visibly different, in public places, in housing and in employment – despite the fact that there was little public pressure or demand for these relatively timid pieces of legislation. This legislation also set up enforcement agencies, 'toothless watch-dogs' with little real power, but with the possibility of initiating research that did reveal the widespread nature of racial discrimination in England to the doubting middle classes who still had faith in the 'British values' of tolerance and non-discrimination. In 1967 a report[27] thus commissioned countered the popular belief that ethnic minorities were disadvantaged simply because they lacked the necessary qualifications. The research had been carried out by Political and Economic Planning (the precursor of today's Policy Studies Institute) who sent out a West Indian Immigrant, a Hungarian immigrant and a white Briton with the same qualifications, to test responses by the 'host' community in employment and housing particularly. The black immigrant was the victim of almost systematic discrimination, though there were variations on the theme: in housing for example some white Britons did decide to sell or rent accommodation to the West Indian, but nevertheless asked him to pay a higher rent, or charged him a higher rate of interest for the mortgage. This method used in the 1960s was indeed revealing, as without this approach, it would be difficult for people to prove that they had been victims of discrimination, or even to imagine that such had been the case.[28]

In 1976 the Labour Government passed the third Race Relations Act and abolished the two previous ones. The enforcement agency created this time was the Commission for Racial Equality (CRE),[29] with its Head Office in London and

---

[27] This report had been commissioned by the Race Relations Board (set up by the *1965 Race Relations Act*) in conjunction with the National Committee for Commonwealth Immigrants. It later achieved wide circulation when it was published as a Penguin Special: W.W. Daniel, *Racial Discrimination in England: Based on the PEP Report*, (Harmondsworth, Penguin Books,1968).

[28] The same technique was to be used 30 years later in France by *SOS Racisme* to demonstrate discriminatory practices at camping sites or entry to night-clubs etc. Such tests have been accepted by French courts as proof of discrimination.

[29] The CRE is a government funded organisation whose duties are: working towards the elimination of racial discrimination; promoting equality of opportunity and good relations between people of different 'racial groups'; and keeping under review the working of the *1976 Race Relations Act*. The CRE has powers of investigation and reporting, as well as powers to support complainants in cases that it sees as legal landmarks. It attempts to raise public awareness of the persistence of discrimination and in recent years it has engaged in some innovative advertising campaigns which have attracted a lot of attention. Since its creation this enforcement agency has continued to operate in a frequently hostile environment, criticised by the largely Conservative press, that portrays it as a whingeing trouble-maker. It is often seen as part of the derogatively dubbed 'race relations industry' of those who make a living,

six other offices, including Edinburgh and Cardiff. This Act, which is still in force today (though amended in 2,000 and subsequently modified by European Union directives), provides the legal foundation for the British form of 'affirmative action', although this is not the term used.

Indeed in Britain there has been a great deal of confusion over the terms used to describe this policy, and the policy itself, because when the government created it they did not officially name it and this led to all sorts of difficulties which cloud the debate.

Naming the Policy: 'Positive Action' 'Positive Discrimination' or Affirmative Action ...?

In the 1970s the Labour government debated the question of whether to have separate anti-discrimination legislation for gender and race, or whether to have just one single Equality Act. In the end, and for 'entirely political reasons'[30] the decision was made to pass separate laws, with gender coming first, as it was felt this would attract more popular support and thus make it easier to bring in similar measures for the ethnic minorities in its slipstream.

When the *1975 Sex Discrimination Act*[31] made it possible to use measures in favour of women without being prosecuted for discrimination, the term 'positive discrimination' was used to describe this policy. The same policy re-appeared a year later in the *1976 Race Relations Act* in favour of the 'ethnic minorities' but the term 'positive discrimination' had disappeared. Perhaps this was because it is an oxymoron, an apparent contradiction in terms, as discrimination no matter how positive, remains by its very definition, negative and reprehensible. So this policy, as described in the 1976 Act, remained unnamed: it was not called 'positive discrimination', 'positive action', 'affirmative action' or indeed anything else. It was only in a booklet, published by the Home Office and the Central Office of Information the following year to explain this Act to the general public, that the expression 'positive action' made its appearance. Now 'positive action' is an extremely vague term that can be

---

at the expense of the public purse, by creating problems where there are none. Despite this, it is today a major player in the field of race relations.

[30] Comments made by Sir Anthony Lester, one of the architects of the *1975 Sex Discrimination Act* and the *1976 Race Relations Act*. 'Bringing it all back', *Connections*, (Summer 2001), pp. 6–7.

[31] The *Sex Discrimination Act* makes it lawful to provide training for members of one sex for particular work, or encouragement for such persons to take advantage of opportunities for that work, where members of that sex have been under represented in the previous 12 months: Ss 47 and 48. This means that job advertisements can explicitly encourage applications from one sex and that employment agencies can be told that particular groups are especially welcome. However, no applicant can be excluded or denied information or the opportunity to apply. Any discrimination at the point of selection will still be unlawful in these circumstances.

Sex Discrimination Act 1975, s. 65.

used in all sorts of contexts: at the beginning of the 1990s, for example, the high street multiple store, *Boots the Chemist*, launched a whole range of cosmetics called 'Positive Action'. Thus it is not a term which is immediately evocative or attached to one single domain,[32] as it could be argued for the term 'affirmative action' in the United States ... where it is perhaps difficult to imagine an advertising agency rash enough to brand a whole range of cosmetics 'affirmative action'.

So when the government launched this policy in favour of the ethnic minorities, they did not take the precaution of signalling it with a clearly identifiable term[33] but left it – perhaps deliberately – vague. Moreover, references to this policy in the *1976 Race Relations Act* are not presented collectively in one clear block, but are scattered throughout the Act.

This 1976 Act sets out to define what constitutes racial discrimination, whether it be 'direct' discrimination or 'indirect' discrimination[34] and the law examines the main manifestations of this in the fields of employment, education, advertising and so on. In so doing, this law lists the possible exceptions which would be tolerated, and which collectively make up this British policy of 'positive action'. Thus there are various actions that can be carried out without risk of prosecution for racial discrimination as defined by this Act. It is possible for example, to provide special facilities or services for certain 'racial groups'[35] to meet their special needs, as regards

---

[32]   However it is intersting to note that 'Positive Action' is the term that has since been adopted by the Council of the European Union. Article 5 of its 'Race Directive' (2000/43/Ec of 29 June 2000), entitled Positive action declares: 'With a view to ensuring full equality in practice, the principle of equal treatment shall not prevent any Member State from maintaining or adopting specific measures to prevent or compensate for disadvantages linked to racial or ethnic origin'.

[33]   It is interesting to note however, in the *Fair Employment (Northern Ireland) Act 1989*, that here the British Government actually uses the term 'affirmative action' – perhaps to avoid the confusion generated on the mainland by the terms 'positive action' and 'positive discrimination' ... or perhaps simply because this law was likely to be read by Irish Americans, more familiar with this term? See the following chapter on Northern Ireland by Hinds and O'Kelly.

[34]   Again, these two terms do not actually appear in the Act, they were only used later to explain the Act. 'Direct' discrimination occurs when someone treats a person directly less favourably than he would another person, because of his race or ethnic group. 'Indirect' discrimination is treatment, (often coming in the form of rules, regulations or procedures) which although seemingly race-neutral and egalitarian, nevertheless has a negative impact on a precise racial or ethnic group.

[35]   Thus defined by this law: 'racial group' means a group of persons defined by reference to colour, race, nationality or ethnic or national origins. *Race Relations Act 1976*, s. 3 (1). Although Jews (since 1980), Sikhs (since 1983), Gypsies (since 1989) and Irish Travellers (since 2000) have been classified in British courts as constituting 'racial groups', Rastafarians were not so defined (1993), nor have other religious minorities, such as Muslims, benefited from this definition and thus the legal protection it affords. This gap in British legislation will soon be filled, as in November 2004 the British government announced its intention of introducing legislation to combat discrimination on the grounds of religion.

their education, training or welfare.[36] What is described as 'discriminatory training' is also allowed when used by 'certain bodies' (employers, trade unions, educational institutions, training organisations). Thus it is quite legal to set up training courses specifically for, and indeed limited to, certain racial' groups if under-representation has been demonstrated either in proportion to the population as a whole, or in proportion to the population of a given area.[37] It is also possible to provide specific services, and to target adverts so they will be seen by a specific 'racial group' (or indeed to declare the intention of using 'positive action' as authorised by the law[38]), again as long as the necessity of this action has been quantitatively demonstrated – hence the importance of the collection of these ethnic statistics, as it is this ability to demonstrate disadvantage or under-representation of a specific 'racial group' which then opens up the possibility of rectifying this through the use of 'positive action'.

Thus as it was introduced in Britain, 'positive action' was a policy intended to provide strategies for helping clearly defined ethnic minority groups overcome their disadvantage, through training, education and the provision of facilities which could be specifically targeted. This was an important turning point for Britain as although there had been other, earlier policies aimed at eradicating disadvantage these had all been non-race specific. However, the policy was in no way compulsory, it was simply tolerated by the law. Therefore an employer might, if he so chose, make an effort to encourage applications from members of a specific 'racial group' for a job, or he might even set up training programmes for ethnic minorities to provide them with the skills necessary for certain jobs, but that employer could not take race into account as a factor at the point of selection for a job. It remains illegal to select someone because of his colour, unless it can be proved that race is a genuine qualification for that job[39] (and that too has been a cause of confusion).

This fine distinction has since been reflected in the terminology used essentially by academics and those working in the field of 'race relations' who say that 'positive action' – these different forms of encouragement and support – is legal, whereas 'positive discrimination' – taking race into account as a factor for job selection (choosing someone because of his colour) – is not.

---

[36]   Nothing in Parts II to IV shall render unlawful any act done in affording persons of a particular racial group access to facilities or services to meet the special needs of persons of that group in regard to their education, training or welfare, or any ancillary benefits. *Ibid.*, s. 35.

[37]   where it appears to the training body that at any time within the twelve months immediately preceding the doing of the act – (...)

(ii) the proportion of persons of that group among those doing that work in Great Britain was small in comparison with the proportion of persons of that group among the population of Great Britain.

(2) Where in relation to particular work it appears to a training body that although the condition for the operation of subsection (1) is not met for the whole of Great Britain it is met for an area within Great Britain. *Ibid.*, s. 37.

[38]   *Ibid.*, s. 29.

[39]   *Ibid.*, s. 5.

However it would appear that outside this circle of the initiated, this distinction is far from clear, not only to members of the general public but also to those who should know better.[40] Even the Commission for Racial Equality, the enforcement agency whose job it is to dispel this confusion, asked respondents in a recent survey[41] to give their opinions on 'positive discrimination' doubtless because the term is more immediately recognizable to the general public, even though by its own standards, this is an illegal practice.

Such were the parameters of this policy when it was set up. The Act created an unnamed policy by negative definition (defining those actions which would not be prosecuted as discrimination) and thus paved the way for a certain amount of confusion in its interpretation.

Because it was not imposed, or co-ordinated by the central government, manifestations of positive action tended to surface in a sporadic, *ad hoc* way, appearing in certain local authorities, individual institutions or individual companies. Some local authorities were quick off the mark because of their political commitment, and also because they did have a statutory duty under section 71 of the 1976 Act to promote equality of opportunity and good race relations.

Some examples of British 'Positive Action'

Education and Training

One of the earliest examples of British positive action were the 'Special Access Courses' in education, set up at the end of the 1970s, shortly after the Race Relations Act was passed, and which have continued up to the present time. The initiative came from the central (Labour) government who invited seven Local Education Authorities (LEAs) with large ethnic minority communities, to set up these Special Access Courses with the intention of getting more people from the ethnic minority communities into the 'professions', especially teaching and social work, where it was believed that they were under-represented, (though there were still no comprehensive statistics at the time to prove this). The idea was to set up special preparatory courses 'designed to bring such students up to the standard required for entry to higher education'[42]. Such courses were then set up by Colleges of Further Education whose strategy varied: some simply made a special effort to attract ethnic minority students through specific advertising campaigns, while others chose to limit entry to certain ethnic minority groups. Most of the Colleges who created such courses did so in conjunction with an institution of Higher Education (usually a

---

[40]   For example, Lord Scarman (a law Lord) used the two terms interchangeably in his report into the Brixton 'riots': *The Scarman Report: The Brixton Disorders 10–12 April 1981*, (Harmondsworth, Penguin Books, 1981).

[41]   Joint survey CRE and *She Magazine*, 'Survey on Race', (London, CRE, April 2002).

[42]   Letter of 2 August 1978 sent by R E Duff, Department of Education and Science, to seven LEAs.

Polytechnic at the time) with whom an agreement had been reached on the type of preparation necessary for a particular Higher Education course. If the Special Access Course was completed satisfactorily then the student was usually guaranteed a place on the course in the Institution of Higher Education. This constituted a form of indirect preferential treatment over the non-Access candidate, who was in no way guaranteed a place and who had to have obtained formal examination qualifications (usually 'A' levels) for entry. However once in the Institution of Higher Education the ex-Access student would then be treated like any other student and subject to the same assessment.

These Special Access Courses have developed and broadened tremendously in scope,[43] but courses reserved for members of specific ethnic groups are still run (for example in teaching, social work and journalism). All this is perfectly acceptable under the *1976 Race Relations Act*, as it provides certain groups with specific training, but does not in any way reserve jobs for them, although it does, in certain cases, indirectly reserve places for them in Higher Education. Though operating frequently with quite small numbers, these courses have proved to be a marked success over the long term by increasing numbers of ethnic minority graduates and professionals in certain sectors.

Since the Act was passed, there have been a variety of such training programmes as well as grants and scholarships aimed specifically at the ethnic minorities and designed to bring them into certain professions. There have also been examples of this in the private sector where *The Financial Times* for example offered a three-month paid internship for a trainee journalist from an ethnic minority background.[44] This was by no means the first initiative in this area; other publications (such as the *Times*, the *Big Issue*, the *Manchester Evening News*, the *Nottingham Evening Post*, the *Bradford Telegraph and Argus*) have already done so – frequently with mixed motivation that ranges from social responsibility to more prosaic market concerns of appealing to the black and Asian consumer.

The Police

Another sector that has also used positive action strategies is that of the police. The need to have a police force that reflects the ethnic composition of the country as a whole (or the higher density of some local authorities) is an issue that goes back to the early 1980s and the 'race riots' that pitted black and Asian youths against the

---

[43] The principle of Access studies was quickly opened up to a much wider public of all those who had not fulfilled their potential at school. Access Courses are now officially recognised nationally as an alternative route into Higher Education.

[44] The deputy managing director Hugh Carnegie declared: 'We are committed to increasing the diversity of backgrounds among our journalists to match the growing diversity of our readers both in the UK and overseas'. 'FT to offer ethnic minority internship', *The Guardian*, (March 13, 2002).

police in certain urban areas.[45] The statistics that have been collected since then have consistently shown an acute under-representation of these groups, which has led to positive action schemes, as recommended for example by Lord Scarman[46] in 1981. The early 80s saw advertising campaigns aimed specifically at the ethnic minorities, such as the recruiting advertisement 'All London coppers are members of a minority (...). Whatever your colour, creed or class, we need you in London's police',[47] which seemed to pass without comment, and also with little effect. Other initiatives met with a far more vociferous response, such as the attempt by the Chief Constable of Derby to take on a very small number of ethnic minority recruits without the minimum qualifications, which was roundly condemned by the Conservatives in Parliament as being a scandalous attack on the policy of 'equal opportunity'.[48]

Ethnic minority recruitment to the police has always been problematic, due in no small part to the poor image the police services have with many of the minority communities and the existence of a racist 'canteen culture' which means that many forces have difficulty retaining ethnic minority officers once they have recruited them. In August 1999 Home Office figures revealed that there were 2,500 ethnic minorities in the police in England and Wales, only two per cent of the force, and the Home Secretary Jack Straw told chief constables that they needed to employ an extra 8,000 black and Asian officers over the next ten years. Without 'the kick-start of targets' he said that he could see little prospect of the police service attaining a proper ethnic balance at any stage over the next quarter century.

However it should be said that in recent times the Black and Asian Police Officers Association has lost confidence in British 'positive action' which has consistently failed to deliver a police force that reflects the society it serves.[49] Superintendent Ali Desai, legal adviser to the Association, believes that targets are not enough and he has been calling for the setting up of quotas, with 'race' being taken into account as a qualifying factor for the employment of officers. (All of this he has described as 'affirmative action' and says it is perfectly legal under the *1976 Race Relations Act*

---

[45]   Notably the St Paul's district of Bristol 1980, Brixton and Southall (London), Toxteth (Liverpool), Moss Side (Manchester) and various parts of the West Midlands in 1981; Handsworth (Birmingham) and Tottenham (London) in 1985.

[46]   Lord Scarman, *ibid*.

[47]   'All London coppers are members of a minority', *The Sun*, (19 July 1982).

[48]   The Chief Constable of Derby had recruited what were described as '12 coloured youths' without the minimum requirement of four 'O' levels. See Oral Parliamentary question by D J Williams to Mrs Thatcher, Session 1981–1982, 28c 919, (2 July 1982).

[49]   Superintendent Ali Desai, legal adviser to the Black and Asian Police Officers Association, was interviewed by John Humphreys on The Today Programme, BBC Radio 4, (4 September 2004). He said the police had lost their legitimacy and efficiency: 'We must be able to obtain community intelligence in order to fight terrorism, in order to fight street crime, and if we don't touch home base with the communities we serve, then simply that's not going to happen'.

– which it is not. So the confusion in the British debate persists to this day – even amongst the members of the police force).[50]

Contract Compliance

While in power in the 1960s and 1970s, the Labour government tried to put in place the American policy of 'contract compliance',[51] that is to say, using the government's buying power as a lever to influence those firms tendering for government contracts to oblige them to eliminate racial discrimination in their own businesses. In 1969 a standard clause was introduced into all government contracts, requiring the suppliers of goods and services to conform to the provisions of the Race Relations legislation in force and stipulating they should take all reasonable steps to ensure that their employees and subcontractors did the same, thus attempting to give this policy an exponential effect. For the most part however, this went unheeded so the Labour government returned to the question in the *White Paper on Racial Discrimination* which preceded the *1976 Race Relations Act*, declaring that contractors should be able to provide the Department of Employment with such information about their employment policies and practices as might reasonably be required. But again this practice never went into widespread use as in 1979 Margaret Thatcher led the Conservatives back to power – where they remained until 1997. A few local authorities did nevertheless try to enforce this, with the most obvious example being the Labour controlled Greater London Council (GLC) with its leader Ken Livingstone, who started to use its considerable purchasing power[52] (as well as the Council, it was also purchasing agent for other organisations – such as Thames Regional Health Authority, the Inner London Education Authority) as a lever for change.

In 1985 the GLC sent out a questionnaire to ensure that its contractors were abiding by the CRE's code of practice (which called for the collection of ethnic statistics on the composition of the workforce). 429 out of the 503 suppliers returned their questionnaires suitably filled in, with 130 companies agreeing to set up 'timetables' to rectify imbalances where these had been revealed by the statistics. When Rowntree Macintosh (makers of confectionary, including *KitKat*) refused to supply such statistics, saying they were an equal opportunities employer and that such statistics had no place in a commercial contract, the issue hit the headlines. Rowntree Macintosh lost its £70,000 a year contract (supplying GLC tuck shops) and the popular press ridiculed the GLC, declaring that this was just another example of the 'loony left'. '*KitKat* ban by Red Ken really takes the biscuit!'[53] exclaimed the *Daily*

---

[50]   Chief Inspector Jan Berry who chairs the Police Federation of England and Wales, interviewed on the same programme, on the other hand identified Superintendent Desai's suggestions as 'positive discrimination' and illegal under British law, *Ibid.*

[51]   See Chapter 1 on the United States by Ooiman Robinson.

[52]   Estimated in 1983 at £100 million.

[53]   '*KitKat* ban by Red Ken really takes the biscuit!' *The Daily Express*, (4 April 1985).

Express, who reminded their readership that the previous year the GLC had not only banned all South African produce, but it had also taken the unprecedented step of banning Robertson's jams because of their golliwog logo (even though the company had attempted to tone this down by referring to it as the 'golly' and dropping the 'wog'). Despite this lambasting by the popular press, the GLC continued to actively pursue this policy till its own demise in 1988, when it was abolished by Mrs Thatcher and the *Local Government Act*.

Margaret Thatcher was particularly opposed to contract compliance declaring amongst other things, that putting such constraints on employers was unacceptable ... so it is interesting to note an unexpected blip in this period of free-marketeering and non-governmental intervention, which occurred surprisingly, just after this *KitKat* incident. In 1985 the Home Office Minister responsible for Race Relations, David Waddington, announced publicly that the Conservative government was considering restricting government contracts to companies that could prove that they employed a representative proportion of 'black people'.[54] The minister apparently felt that action was necessary due to the serious disturbances that had taken place in Tottenham and Brixton (London) and Handsworth (Birmingham) that year. However the Secretary of State for Employment quickly riposted, declaring that such a plan would be 'degrading to blacks and would impose extra burdens on businesses, which would add to unemployment'.[55] In the ensuing public debate, the policy was generally misunderstood, and the subtleties of under-representation, timetables and targets were generally replaced with the flattening rhetoric of 'positive discrimination' and 'black quotas'. 'Nobody benefits from the enforcement of this type of quota system' said a spokesman for the Institute of Directors, while the Confederation of British Industry (CBI) thought the practice unnecessary.

Mrs Thatcher put an end to this ministerial wrangling, killing the fledgling policy, and returning to the official Conservative practice of 'colour blindness'.[56] Her government even toyed for a while with the idea of stopping local government from using this practice in favour of the ethnic minorities; however in the end, the *Local Government Act 1988* did allow local authorities to continue with this if they so chose.[57]

---

[54]   Margaret Van Hattem, 'Government studies black quota plan', *Financial Times*, (14 October 1985).

[55]   John Carvel, 'Ministers clash on fair deal for blacks', *The Guardian*, (15 October 1985).

[56]   It should however be remembered that at the end of the 1980s the same Thatcher government did finally adopt measures similar to those that it had refused for 'mainland blacks', in favour of Northern Irish Catholics, in an attempt to eradicate sectarian discrimination there. See Chapter Five by Hinds and O'Kelly.

[57]   *Local Government Act 1988*, s. 18.

The Act limited to 6 the number of questions a local authority could ask a business concerning their attitude to 'race relations'. This however maintained the right to ask whether a business applied the CRE's 1983 *Code of Practice*, and thereby maintained the right of the

Although Mrs Thatcher disapproved of the *1976 Race Relations Act* and had promised to review it when elected, she never actually did so, neither did her successor John Major, and the *1976 Race Relations Act* remained unaltered till the Labour party returned to power after 18 years in opposition.

The 2000 Race Relations Amendment Act (RRAA)

The CRE carried out three reviews of the 1976 Act and had long been pushing for its amendment, which the Labour party promised on its return to power. However when change finally came to this Act it was more far-reaching than many had imagined, as the political will at that time had been strengthened by public outrage at racial discrimination, crystallised by the murder of a young man.

Stephen Lawrence was a young black 'A' level student who was killed by five white youths in 1993, when he was waiting at a bus stop in South London. They attacked him simply because he was black and they happened to come across him. The Metropolitan police who then investigated the murder assumed that this young black man must, in some way, have contributed to his own demise, either because he was a member of a gang, or because he had been involved in some sort of illegal activity (such as burglary). Neither supposition was in any way founded, the investigation was bungled and the five white suspects remain free to this day. The Conservative government stonewalled and refused to grant a judicial inquiry. This was only to come in 1997 when the Home Secretary of the newly elected Labour government, Jack Straw announced a public inquiry into 'the matters arising from the death of Stephen Lawrence' and 'the lessons to be learned for the investigation and prosecution of racially motivated crimes'. The report of this public inquiry, led by Sir William Macpherson, and published in 1999 found the Metropolitan police service guilty of 'institutional racism',[58] and called for the extension of the *1976 Race Relations Act* to bring the police service within its scope and thus outlaw discrimination within its ranks.

In fact the Government went further and the *2000 Race Relations Amendment Act* (RRAA) banned racial discrimination in all public functions not covered by the original 1976 Act.[59] The Government also agreed with the findings of the Macpherson

---

local authorities to ask both for ethnic statistics, and what policies the companies had adopted if these statistics revealed unequal representation of the different ethnic groups.

[58] Which it defined as 'The collective failure of an organisation to provide an appropriate and professional service to people because of their colour, culture, or ethnic origin. It can be seen or detected in processes, attitudes and behaviour which amount to discrimination through unwitting prejudice, ignorance, thoughtlessness and racist stereotyping which disadvantage minority ethnic people'.

[59] 19D of the Act did initially allow Ministers the right to authorise discrimination in the fields of immigration, asylum and nationality law (thus continuing what Anthony Lester described as the 'Janus face' of British legislation) however this has subsequently undergone modification.

report that discrimination extends well beyond the individual and is embedded in institutional practices and cultures, which were largely unaffected by the *1976 Race Relations Act* with its system of negative prohibitions. Thus the RRAA breaks new ground in British law by creating a statutory 'general' duty for most public authorities (about 42,000 of them)[60] including education institutions, not only to eliminate unlawful racial discrimination but also to promote equal opportunities and encourage good race relations. The intention being to actively promote racial equality, thus moving the debate from the periphery to the centre, from the struggle not to be discriminated against, to the active promotion of inclusion, making it a central preoccupation for these public bodies.

In addition many public bodies have a 'specific duty' (intended to help them meet this 'general' duty) which obliges them to look at the implications of their daily work, identify their priorities and then adopt a systematic approach towards racial equality and good race relations which will deliver tangible improvements. They must look at the way they design and deliver services (not planning for example, health clinics for Pakistani Muslim women on a Friday) and the way they recruit, train and promote their staff. Thus all of these public bodies had to have detailed 'Race Equality' schemes and policies in place by 31 May 2002, making clear how they intended to meet both their general and specific duties.

This new Act does have considerable potential as a lever for change and it is the job of the CRE to oversee all of this – not only through tackling discrimination in these public bodies (ranging from central government departments, the Scottish Parliament, the Welsh Assembly and local government, right down to town councils and community councils) but also providing them with advice and guidance to enable them to comply with these new requirements. If a public authority does fail to meet this duty, then as a last resort, the CRE can issue a compliance notice. However, for the moment the CRE is intent on encouraging and assisting public bodies and has identified 'seven high-level strategic outcomes that should be focussed on', including 'key service outcomes (e.g. educational attainment)' and improvements in 'workforce representation at all levels',[61] which can be brought about by the use of those strategies of positive action as laid down by the *1976 Race Relations Act* – the difference now being that this is no longer left up to individual good will, as the law actively encourages institutions to adopt such measures to enable them to meet their statutory 'general duty'.

---

[60]   These organisations are listed in schedule 1A of the *Race Relations Amendment Act 2000*.

[61]   Schneider-Ross, *Towards Racial Equality: An evaluation of the public duty to promote race equality and good race relations in England and Wales (2002)*, (London, CRE, 2003), p. 4.

Measures of Change

Legislation is an important expression of the political will, signifying that a government takes an issue seriously enough to want to regulate and modify behaviour, but just because it is enshrined in law, does not always mean that it will necessarily generate compliance, and there is a danger that the 'statutory duty' may just get lost under a mountain of paperwork. In an attempt to counter this and measure the degree of compliance and change, the CRE commissioned research to establish the nature, extent and quality of responses to the statutory duty – with the intention of then using this data to help promote and enforce the duty as efficiently as possible. In England and Wales the survey[62] found that there were three categories of responses: a leading group who were 'responding well to both the spirit and letter of the law',[63] a second group who had put down good foundations but still had some way to go, and a third group where the response was weak, and in some cases did not even comply with the legislation. Research in Scotland[64] had similar findings.

As suggested earlier, this is indeed a field that is increasingly monitored, though the data is not always as precise as one would wish. For example, a poll of public authorities run in September 2002[65] suggested that 64 per cent of local authorities already used some form of 'positive action', whereas only 29 per cent of educational institutions did so. Unfortunately details of the nature of this 'positive action' were not given, nor how the institutions actually defined this. The *Bradford District Race Review*, on the other hand, that came in the aftermath of the violence in some of Britain's northern industrial towns in the summer of 2001, goes into some detail of the strategies that authorities may take as corrective measures to promote racial equality. Under the heading 'employment' it is recommended that public bodies should:

> monitor workforce; provide baseline equality data; determine under-representation; implement positive action programmes in recruitment, advertising, shortlisting, interviewing/selecting, training, mentoring, shadowing, secondment, fast-tracking and promotion.[66]

The question still remains as to how this 'positive action' is actually applied when it comes to recruitment. One insight into this was given in 1995 in the programme *The Moral Maze* when both the late Bernie Grant (former leader of Haringey Council and Labour MP) and Linda Belos (former leader of Lambeth Council) declared quite

---

[62] Schneider-Ross, *Ibid.*

[63] *Ibid.*, p. 5.

[64] CRE, *Towards Racial Equality: Are public authorities meeting the duty to promote race equality?*, (London, CRE, 2003).

[65] UK Secretariat of the European Monitoring Centre on Racism and Xenophobia, September 2002. Results of this poll given in 'Extend the duty, say public bodies', *Connections*, (London, CRE,Spring 2003), p. 4.

[66] Bradford District Race Review, *Community Pride not Prejudice: Making Diversity Work in Bradford*, (Bradford Borough Council, 2001), p. 37.

frankly that where two candidates for a job had similar qualifications they would take race into account as a factor for selection,[67] which is illegal under British law, and would be described by some experts as 'positive discrimination' – even though Grant and Belos both defined this behaviour as 'positive action'.

Thus it would appear that there is still a fundamental confusion in Britain over 'positive action' and 'positive discrimination' – what the law does and does not authorise.[68] Though one wonders just how far it is possible to legislate for interviewing and selection procedures that behind a rational façade, remain a frequently emotional and intuitive exercise (that all too often favour(ed) the white male candidate).

One indication of the change that has occurred in Britain over the last twenty five years can be seen by re-examining some of the positive action measures mentioned earlier and looking at their application and degree of acceptance today.

Two events that would have caused an outcry in the 1980s passed off without much comment in the opening years of the new century. In 2002 a report[69] by the Commission for Black Staff in Further Education revealed that while ethnic minorities made up 6.9 per cent of staff in this field, fewer than 3 per cent were senior managers and less than one per cent were principals in mainstream colleges. The Commission then called on the Department for Education and Skills (DfES) to provide 'fast-track' management training for suitably qualified ethnic minority staff and the ministry agreed to this. In the following year the Education Minister Stephen Twigg launched a new annual schools census to collect yearly national data on school performance by ethnicity. This, the Minister explained, would then enable the government to target resources where they are needed most – and the idea was generally well received.

In the 1980s 'contract compliance' was seen by many as being the reserve of the 'loony left' and an unreasonable constraint on business. The policy nowadays,

---

[67]   Bernie Grant: 'I'm talking about positive action (...) if you have people who are roughly equal applying for a job or whatever, and in order to alleviate a situation where there are no black people, or where historically blacks have been discriminated against, I would give the job to a black person in those circumstances'.

Linda Belos confirmed this, when asked by the journalist Janet Daley: 'So what you're saying is that two equally qualified people – one black and one white – the black candidate should be preferred?'. She replied: 'I often do make such a judgement'. *The Moral Maze*, BBC Radio 4, (23 March 1995).

[68]   The CRE tried yet again to clarify this fine distinction between 'positive action' (legal) and 'positive discrimination' (illegal) after the Arnolfini Gallery in Bristol advertised a post for Senior Curator which it declared was only open to Black, Asian and Caribbean applicants. The advert made it clear that the Gallery believed it was 'taking positive action to tackle the under-representation of these groups among senior curators'. This however was illegal and the CRE advised them to withdraw the advert and reconsider its strategy.

Razia Karim, 'Take care when being positive', *Connections*, (London, CRE, Winter 2004/05), p.17.

[69]   Commission for Black Staff in Further Education, *Challenging Racism: Further Education Leading the Way*, (November 2002).

repackaged as 'equality and diversity contract conditions'[70] or 'procurement strategies' is now a recognised part of the arsenal of measures that can be taken to ensure that the general duty of the RRAA is being met.[71] The CRE has brought out two guides[72] to help all those involved in the procurement process in public authorities to understand what they must do when contracting, as well as what they can do to further promote racial equality without breaching either the *European Union Directives*[73] or the *1976 Race Relations Act*. These guides are also aimed at the contractors (from both private and voluntary sectors) to understand what is expected of them if they are to be considered for the work. In 2003 local authorities in England and Wales were believed to spend over £40 billion on goods, services and works – so obviously this is an important area where pressure for change can indeed be exercised.

All of this the CRE publicises as making good business sense, and the incentive of commercial self-interest does seem a message which is striking home, at least with the large 'flagship' companies. When the 'equality and diversity' consultants Schneider-Ross carried out research into the question, their report[74] revealed that over 71 per cent of those interviewed believed that improving their business was the main reason for the 'diversity and equality' initiatives they had taken and 80 per cent linked business performance to 'diversity practice' as this could bring about improved understanding of the markets, give the companies a competitive edge and a better reputation – with the bottom line being an increase in profits. (It is an oft-repeated figure at the moment that the combined disposable wealth of ethnic minorities in the UK is in the region of £32 billion, and this is a young and expanding market).

How representative this behaviour is of smaller firms across the country is another matter[75] but these 'diversity and equality' measures not only receive support from large companies but also large organisations such as the trade union movement[76]

---

[70] Bradford District Race Review, *ibid.*, p. 3.

[71] Even though the Schneider-Ross report regrets that this is 'a significant lever for change that is currently under-exploited', *ibid.*, p. 6.

[72] Available on <www.cre.gov.uk>.

[73] There have been two important directives in this area (on race and employment) which have been incorporated into British law through regulations (secondary legislation).

[74] *The Business of Diversity*, Schneider-Ross, (London, 2002). 140 representatives from the public and private sector were interviewed for this research which was funded by the Cabinet Office and Barclay's Bank.

[75] Though small businesses have also been the subject of attention from the CRE who recently published a free guide with advice on developing policies and procedures, both to avoid unlawful dscrimination and to ensure equality and fair treatment. CRE, *Racial Equality and the Smaller Business: A Practical Guide*, (London, CRE, 2004).

[76] The Trades Union Congress (TUC) has seven million members, spanning racial, religious and gender divides.

and the Confederation of British Industry (CBI) which were hesitant – if not to say openly hostile – to them in the not too distant past.

Many of these measures now go by unquestioned in the press (though there are occasional flare-ups). If these issues do not raise the sort of emotional response that they did in the 1980s and 90s, this is probably due in no small part to the re-phrasing and re-framing of the debate which avoids, where possible, those inflammatory terms that raise a visceral response. (In 2002 when the CRE and *She Magazine* asked for opinions on 'positive discrimination' the response was overwhelmingly negative).[77]

Thus we find the more obscure terms of 'time-related outcomes' (goals), 'strategic outcomes' (targets), 'fast-tracking' and 'mainstreaming' which tend to go past unnoticed, especially when they are used with the consensual concepts of 'equity', 'cohesion' 'diversity' and 'connecting communities'. Some might say that this burgeoning vocabulary is a reminder of the British liking for euphemism (as expressed in the very term 'ethnic minorities'), others might argue that it is just another facet of New Labour 'spin', but that is another issue.

Conclusion

Britain today is more culturally and ethnically diverse than at any other time in its history. Yet Britain's attitude to race relations remains ambivalent. On the one hand there is now an official recognition of multiculturalism and the need to actively forge a cohesive, tolerant society. On the other hand, there is resistance to this multiculturalism in the country, where in places there is a feeling of defensive embattlement that is punctuated by outbursts of racial violence, both individual and collective. Enoch Powell was no longer alive to witness the 'race riots' that took place in some Northern British towns in 2001 and so could not claim them as a vindication of his vision of a Britain torn apart by the presence of the ethnic minorities (as he had done earlier). Nevertheless his biographer[78] writing in *The Spectator* did this for him, claiming these events should 'be seen as the first blast of the trumpet against the dangers of multiculturalism'.

---

[77]   This was a nationally representative sample of women over 16 years old, with a boost sample of 100 women from the ethnic minorities. The report was based on 1,133 analysed questionnaires which were conducted by telephone (2–7 February 2002). Of these, 72 per cent were opposed to 'positive discrimination' at work, on the grounds of race. (The only slightly higher score in favour of 'positive discrimination' came when the practice was related to its use in the police.) The results were similarly negative (over 70 per cent) for the use of the practice in politics, sport, education, medecine, law and the media. Women from the ethnic minorities were only slightly (a few percentage points) more favourable to the practice. CRE/ She Magazine, *Survey on Race*, (London, CRE, April 2002).

[78]   Simon Heffer, *Like the Roman: the Life of Enoch Powell*, (London, Phoenix Grant, 1999).

Professor Stuart Hall pointed out that 'there has been no slow, steady rise of multicultural spirit in Britain,[79] but he also conceded more optimistically that 'there has been change'. Not least in this practice of 'positive action', which Britain has come a long way towards accepting in the last quarter of a century. The *Race Relations Amendment Act 2000* in particular, with its obligation for the public sector to actively promote good race relations, does seem to be moving the policy from the periphery to the mainstream. But this remains an ongoing debate.

Glossary of abbreviations used:

CBI:	Confederation of British Industry
CRE:	Commission for Racial Equality
DfES:	Department for Education and Skills, previously DES (Department for Education and Science)
GLC:	Greater London Council
LEA:	Local Education Authority
RRAA:	the Race Relations Amendment Act (2000)

---

[79]   Stuart Hall, *History Workshop Journal*, Vol 48, Oxford University Press, 1999.

Chapter 5

Affirmative Action in Northern Ireland[1]

Bronagh Hinds and Ciarán O'Kelly

Introduction

Affirmative action is an essential element in tackling structural inequality. It must be placed on a continuum, as part of a range of egalitarian strategies. The unequal society must be tackled in the round, with affirmative action and equality-mainstreaming focussed on a range of policies and practices simultaneously.[2] The Northern Ireland experience highlights how crucial affirmative action is to achieving fairness in a divided society so that peace and stability can be maintained. We should remember, however, that an unequal society *is* a divided society, even if those divisions do not spill over into the sort of conflict that Northern Ireland has seen. Addressing inequality is fundamental to overcoming division.

In this chapter, we describe the broad range of initiatives that seek to eliminate systemic inequalities between the two main sections of Northern Ireland's community.[3] The initiatives we outline work in concert with each other. Without the drive towards wider social equality, affirmative action legislation would be no more than a constant corrective. It would address one element of disadvantage without alleviating its wider societal causes.

It may seem that Northern Ireland presents an unusual case for this volume. Whereas the other contributions address the issue of affirmative action as it relates to ostensibly 'visible' minorities, this chapter seems to deal with affirmative action in response to political division. The distinction is untenable, however. Divisions

---

[1]   The authors are grateful to Domonic Bearfield, Eileen Lavery and Patrick Speight for helpful comments on previous drafts of this chapter.

[2]   For the purposes of this chapter we take the term affirmative action to include positive action. Equality-mainstreaming refers to the introduction of equality considerations into the centre of policy-making. This is discussed at greater length in section 2.

[3]   It should be noted that, including Irish travellers 0.9 per cent Northern Ireland's population belong to minority groups in the sense understood internationally (e.g., 'visible' or 'ethnic' minorities as defined by UK anti-discrimination legislation), whereas roughly 40 per cent of the population is Catholic, 45 per cent are Protestant and 14 per cent state no religion (Census 2001). Although we primarily address Catholic-Protestant difference, minority groups are included in policies described here. See for example, the reforms to the Police Service of Northern Ireland (PSNI). For terminological distinctions, see Kennedy-Dubourdieu's Chapter on Affirmative Action in Britain.

vis-à-vis visible minorities in the general sense are of course also political. Moreover, Northern Ireland is characterised by processes that are no different from those that characterise societies divided on ethnic – in the more traditional sense – grounds. The 'ethnic' differences upon which disadvantages work in Northern Ireland only seem subtle when viewed from outside the region.

That said, there is growing recognition that, as well as addressing disadvantages suffered by Catholics, equality and affirmative action policies must address Northern Ireland's growing minority groups. A Commission for Racial Equality for Northern Ireland was established under the Race Relations (Northern Ireland) Order, 1997. It was responsible for the elimination of discrimination, the promotion of equality of opportunity and good relations between members of different racial groups and keeping legislation under review (Race Relations Order 1997). The Equality Commission for Northern Ireland took over these responsibilities in 1999 (see section 4 of this chapter). The stipulations of Section 75 of the Northern Ireland Act, as described in section 6, are extended to racial minorities. There are also moves to make special provisions for minorities. We allude to these in the conclusion to the chapter.[4]

The chapter is divided into five sections. In section 2, we expand on the relationship between affirmative action and equality-mainstreaming. In section 3, we outline the historical context in which disadvantage in Northern Ireland is rooted. Then, in section 4, we describe affirmative action in Northern Ireland's labour market. In section 5, we describe the initiatives in police recruitment that have come about as a result of the peace process of the 1990s and the Good Friday Agreement of 1998. Finally, in section 6, we outline some equality-mainstreaming components that lie at the heart of egalitarian strategies in Northern Ireland.

Principles Underlying Affirmative Action

For the purposes of this chapter, we regard affirmative action as referring to those programmes that are explicitly aimed at rectifying inequalities between specific groups. As the North American and other experiences suggest, a number of methods are possible in developing affirmative action programmes. These methods might range from the results-driven imposition of quotas to a less ambitious reactive concern with the abolition of discrimination (See ECNI, 2002, p. 21; Fitzpatrick et al. 1997a; Nalbandian 1989; Tumalla 1999). In Northern Ireland, affirmative action programmes have concentrated on forging agreements and developing programmes aimed at alleviating Catholic disadvantage.

---

[4]   Terminologically speaking, although the Catholic community constitute a minority in Northern Ireland, they are rarely referred to as a 'minority group' but rather as 'the minority' or 'the minority community'. 'Minority group' generally refers to minorities as more generally understood in the UK context. The distinction is purely terminological and should not be taken as suggesting that members of minority groups in Northern Ireland are not members of communities.

We apply the term equality – mainstreaming to equality programmes that aim towards the development of a more equal society in general, through the mainstreaming of equality in the service outcomes of public sector and publicly-funded bodies. Although these actions can be wide in scope and neutral on the surface, they may well be aimed at addressing the systematic disadvantage suffered by one community (in Northern Ireland, the Catholic community) in comparison to the other.

Of course these two sorts of programme – affirmative action and equality-mainstreaming – are neither opposed to each other, nor entirely discrete. Instead, they lie in a continuous relation to each other, differing in emphasis and degree rather than being categorically distinctive.

Affirmative action programmes are aimed at the rectification of past injustices, the construction of a more socially just future or the establishment and maintenance of cultural diversity. In intervening in the labour market, for example, the state might seek to impose new conditions on sources and methods of hiring. Directed programmes may not be sufficient to achieve societal change beyond the scope of those programmes, however, as some aspects of inequality are more fundamental and extensive than can be addressed by directed affirmative action programmes. Individuals may suffer from underdeveloped capacities as a result of fundamental inequalities, such as inherited poverty. These fundamental inequalities may in themselves be a function of patterns and processes of discrimination. Equality-mainstreaming programmes are in part directed at changing the behaviours of policy-makers and managers who, otherwise, would continue with policies and practices that, at best, do not improve and, at worst, undermine the prospects and conditions of excluded and discriminated against groups.

Where it has existed for a long time, affirmative action has had some impact. For example, programmes in recruitment to American colleges and universities have led, over a number of decades to a small shift in the patterns of recruitment. However, if affirmative action programmes were withdrawn, patterns of recruitment would most likely return towards the point they were at before the programmes existed.[5] Derek Bowen and William Bok argue that if the gains achieved by affirmative action are to be sustained, then the programmes would have to stay in place: a return to race-neutrality would lead to 'severe effects' on minority participation in American higher education (Bowen and Bok 1998, 280 ff.).

This observation is also true regarding Northern Ireland. As Bowen and Bok point out, 'Corporations will not be healthy until society is healthy' (Bowen and Bok 1998, 12). And 'social health' requires more than targeted affirmative action programmes. We suggest that Northern Ireland is a good case for examining not only affirmative action programmes, but also wider measures that seek to address inequalities across the society. Northern Ireland is special because it not only has a robust set of affirmative action programmes, but has also taken great strides

---

[5]   On issues surrounding affirmative action in the United States, see the chapter by Jo Ann Ooiman Robinson in this volume.

towards the mainstreaming of equality throughout society. Equality-mainstreaming is essential to forging a society that is characterised by equality of opportunity.

In Northern Ireland, social inequalities in general are concentrated disproportionately in the Catholic community (CCRU 1998, 5). As a result, programmes aimed at addressing inequalities across society have a greater impact on Catholics than they do on Protestants. The fact that equality-mainstreaming programmes are more advanced in Northern Ireland than they are in the rest of the UK suggests a recognition that the conflict in Northern Ireland is, in large part, driven by the systemic inequalities experienced across the society.[6]

The remainder of the chapter is devoted to outlining both the affirmative action and the equality-mainstreaming programmes and policies that shape the social landscape in Northern Ireland. Before moving on to that, however, it is important to understand the political and social context in which structural inequalities became a feature of the region.

Understanding Northern Ireland

Equality and human rights issues have been critical in the conflict in Ireland and are fundamental to maintaining a sustainable peace in the region. At a number of points in Ireland's turbulent history national aspirations were either articulated through or allied with campaigns over social and economic equality. Across the nineteenth century, for example, Irish politics coalesced around such issues as exclusion from land ownership and tenancy, penal laws and voting restrictions (Foster 1989).[7]

Unsurprisingly, disadvantage rooted in a history of economic and social discrimination was reflected in the relative deprivation of Catholics in Ireland. In the area that was to become the Republic of Ireland, however, the late nineteenth Century saw the rise of an urban Catholic middle class and a rise in wealth amongst rural smallholders, who benefited from post-famine population decline and reforms to the system of land ownership. In Northern Ireland, on the other hand, Catholics did not see the same levels of improvement in their living and working conditions.

The North-Eastern region of Ireland had long been distinctive from the rest of the island, both in terms of the economy, religious demographics and, from the 19th century, in terms of political allegiance to the United Kingdom (UK) (Foster 1989,

---

[6]   That is not to say that affirmative action programmes are totally absent in the UK outside Northern Ireland. See Kennedy-Dubourdieu in this volume.

[7]   Questions of land ownership that came to the fore in the nineteenth Century were rooted in the post-reformation Plantations. For example, referring to the seventeenth Century plantation of Ulster, Foster writes that 'No Irish tenants were to be allowed on the lands taken over by major 'undertakers'. Although 'The vast holdings taken over by speculators were dealt with from afar or even resold; administrative problems and the desire for profit meant that native Irish were rapidly accepted as tenants on a rent-paying basis, often simply staying in situ and working the land', (Foster 1989, 61). On Voting restrictions, see Foster 1989, 301.

342; McKittrick and McVea 2000, 3). While the rest of Ireland gained independence in the early 1920s, Northern Ireland became a semi-autonomous part of the United Kingdom.

The Northern Ireland Parliament, established in 1921 under the sovereignty of the British Parliament in Westminster, owes its genesis to the Government of Ireland Act 1920. The Northern Ireland Parliament, and the territory in general, was designed around a dominant Protestant/Unionist majority that was sufficiently large so as to control the political landscape (Bardon 1992, 478; Brewer and Higgins 1998, 115). Dominance was maintained through the formal power of the state, manipulation of election boundaries, discrimination in housing and employment and through state and non-state violence. These actions, combined with a range of informal disadvantages,[8] left the Catholic minority in a significantly disadvantaged position. Elections to the first Northern Ireland Parliament in Stormont 'produced a huge unionist majority and inaugurated what was in effect a one-party state' (Foster 1989, 504).

Northern Ireland's economy was rooted in industrial power, situated predominantly around Belfast (Gaffikin and Morrissey 1999, 36; See also Foster 1989, 342). Of course, economic disadvantage was pervasive across the board. However, the discrimination experienced by Catholics translated, almost inevitably, into more extreme economic and social disadvantage. Many industries, including public services, policing, engineering and shipbuilding, were closed to Catholics. This direct discrimination was undoubtedly exacerbated by the concentration on informal networks in the hiring practices of firms. Protestants not only had access to jobs, but also to the informal networks and other means by which jobs were found. The conflict that arose in Northern Ireland in the late 1960s and that still shapes the social and political landscape has its roots in these systemic inequalities.

Through the 1960s Sheelagh Murnaghan, a Liberal MP in Stormont, made several failed attempts to introduce legislation aimed at outlawing religious discrimination. Her aims ranged from making discrimination a criminal offence to establishing a Human Rights Commission to conciliate and enforce fair standards in employment and property. In proposing a Human Rights Bill in 1967, Murnaghan drew on advice from the United States in relation to the elimination of racial and other prejudices. Speaking against the Bill, the Northern Ireland Attorney-General, 'who quite simply did not believe that there was any discrimination worth talking about in Northern Ireland' said that legislation 'was unnecessary and it was impractical' (*Irish Times*, 1967).

At the very least, this position did not recognise the disadvantages that Catholics faced on the social, economic and political fronts. This lack of recognition added to the alienation of Catholics towards Northern Ireland's system of government. Lord Robin Eames, Church of Ireland Primate of the second largest Protestant denomination in Northern Ireland, writes that:

---

[8] For example, the widespread use of informal social networks in the hiring of staff meant that Catholic simply did not have access to jobs.

... for the nationalist and Roman Catholic community the years leading to 1968 represented a period when their people felt alienated and marginalised from the common course of life in Northern Ireland. Their grievances over the discrimination in the allocation of work and houses, the denial of civil rights and the manipulation of electoral opportunities, resulting in a denial of any chance of a say in the government of their community, had resulted for them in almost universal community frustration (Eames 1992, 6).

The frustrations of Catholics brought them onto the streets in the late 1960s. Inspired by the civil rights movements in the US, they campaigned not for nationalist aspirations, but for equal recognition as citizens within the UK (Purdie 1990, 2). The coalition of a more articulate and assertive, but politically and socially excluded, Catholic middle class (having benefited from the post-war extension of state education) and a disaffected, economically, politically and socially excluded, Catholic working class sought better conditions and attempted to internationalise the issue of injustice in Northern Ireland. A number of civil rights organisations emerged in response to endemic discrimination, the most prominent of which was the Northern Ireland Civil Rights Association (NICRA) formed in 1967. Laws against discrimination by public authorities were among its demands.[9]

Prompted by an egregious example of unfair housing allocation under a Unionist controlled local authority in rural Northern Ireland, civil rights supporters engaged in a series of demonstrations, marches and public meetings. The violent response by the police to peaceful political protest to secure equality led to world attention and a greater level of support in Northern Ireland and beyond.

The brutal response of the political authorities forced the hand of the UK government in Westminster which was compelled to intervene. British troops were deployed in an effort to protect Catholics from Protestant paramilitaries. Direct rule from London was imposed on the region in March 1972, after thirteen people had been shot dead in January by members of the Parachute Regiment at a NICRA Civil Rights march. In effect, the resistance of the Northern Ireland Government to NICRA's equality agenda, and their misunderstanding of NICRA, identifying it with nationalist insurgency, led to the collapse of Northern Ireland as a politically viable entity. Further miscalculations on all sides, fed by mutual suspicion and feelings of threat, and not least by a lack of clear strategic intervention from London, left a political vacuum that saw Northern Ireland descending into a spiral of violence.

The pervasive economic disadvantages faced by Catholics were not properly addressed for almost another 20 years. Until the 1980s many social scientists seemed to assume that 'discrimination was a minor factor and that factors such as the higher birth rate of Catholics and geographical location were far more important'

---

[9]   The Northern Ireland Civil Rights Association demanded one man, one vote in local elections (as opposed to a property-owners' franchise); the ending of gerrymandering of electoral boundaries; laws against discrimination by public authorities and machinery to deal with complaints; fair allocation of public housing; repeal of the Special Powers Act and disbanding of the B Special paramilitary police.

in explaining economic inequalities (Compton 1981, 140).[10] This assumption was comprehensively refuted in later analyses.

Affirmative Action in Northern Ireland's Labour Market[11]

Although inequalities were not top of the political agenda as regards Northern Ireland, some steps were taken early on. With the British Government's introduction of the Northern Ireland Constitution Act (1973), anti-discrimination provisions in relation to religious belief and political opinion came into force. The Act also established a Standing Advisory Commission on Human Rights (SACHR). Control of public housing, the contentious issue that had sparked off the first civil rights protests, had already been removed from local authorities in 1969. This was followed by further local government reform in 1973 that stripped district councils of most of their functions and placed these with new publicly appointed boards.

An initiative aimed at introducing fairer participation in governance in the region led to a short-lived government based on the sharing of political power between Catholics and Protestants. The initiative was brought down by unionist opposition within a year of conception having only been in place for six months. 'Some feared the new arrangements were the start of a slippery slope towards a united Ireland' McKittrick and McVea write, while 'others simply could not abide the thought of having Catholics in government' (McKittrick and McVea, 2000, 99).

State intervention was more successful in the labour market where it set about tackling political and religious discrimination in employment. William van Straubenzee, a British Minister in the Northern Ireland Administration, chaired a committee that reported in 1973, laying the groundwork for the introduction of the 1976 Fair Employment Act. The Act covered both public and private employment (Working Party on Discrimination in the Private Sector of Employment 1973). Although a Fair Employment Agency (FEA) was set up to enforce the legislation, a reliance on voluntary compliance meant that it did not live up to its intent. The FEA had investigative powers but opinion is divided on whether the agency's investigations had impact. While it may be that FEA criticism had some impact on practices in the public sector, for example in the Northern Ireland Civil Service (NICS), it was often the case in the wider economy that, 'investigations by the Fair Employment Agency had little impact beyond the individual organisation investigated' (McCrudden 1999, 1706; On NICS, see Harbison 1991; Osbourne and Shuttleworth 2004).

Certainly, there was little or no effect on reducing the unemployment differentials between the two sections of the community, Catholic male unemployment continuing to stand around 2.5 times that of Protestants. While, unlike the Unionist administration, the British Government had acknowledged the existence of discrimination in Northern Ireland's labour market, its approach was timid. The van Straubenzee report

---

[10] Quoted in Fitzgerald 2004, vii.
[11] A number of the issues in this section are addressed at length in McCrudden 1999 and in Osborne and Shuttleworth 2004.

had rejected the use of quota-based affirmative action. As Osborne and Shuttleworth note, quotas were generally taken to entail unjust discrimination, no matter what the noble intentions behind them. Moreover, such a policy, people believed, would not improve relations between the communities (Osbourne and Shuttleworth 2004, 3).

In the 1980s, the British Government came under increasing pressure, particularly from the United States, to tackle the issue more forcefully. The 1984 MacBride Principles were based on methods used by campaigners to undermine the apartheid regime in South Africa (For an account of the campaign in the US see McNamara 2002). Irish-Americans began to campaign for American firms and their subsidiaries to institute affirmative action programmes in Northern Ireland. This was accompanied, in some cases, by legislation at the US state level (McCrudden 1999, 1706).

The British Government vigorously opposed the campaign which took off when endorsed by the powerful AFL-CIO and by the State Comptroller of New York. The Principles became a rallying point for Irish-Americans. As British Labour MP Kevin McNamara noted 'the idea spread like wildfire. It has recast the nationalist case in terms of American democratic experience, civil rights, affirmative action and anti-apartheid solidarity' (McNamara 2002, 77). Arguments abounded about whether the MacBride Principles were lawful, a matter that was determined in the campaign's favour by a US federal district court (New York City Employees' Retirement System v. American Brands Inc 1986).

The MacBride Principles campaign, in McNamara's view, had an impact on strengthening fair employment legislation (McNamara 2002, 82). In the meanwhile, the FEA was amassing evidence from its investigations, and a SACHR report proposed extensive reform of the legislation after a thorough review of its effectiveness (SACHR 1987). These pressures, plus intensive lobbying during its passage ensured a greatly strengthened Fair Employment Act 1989. The government department responsible for implementing the Act, the Department of Economic Development (DED), stated that 'employers must register, monitor their workforce and regularly review their recruitment, training and promotion practices. They must take affirmative action measures and set goals and timetables where necessary. There are both nominal fines and economic sanctions – involving loss of business and grants – for those guilty of bad practice' (Quoted in Bardon 1997, 799).

The 1989 Act introduced compulsory rather than voluntary compliance (McCrudden 1999, 1708). It outlawed indirect discrimination. It set up a new Fair Employment Commission (FEC) with stronger powers than its forerunner, the FEA. Thus Northern Ireland moved towards a results-focused approach to eradicating inequality in the labour market. Regular compulsory monitoring of all public employers and private companies with more than ten employees meant that progress on achieving a balanced workforce proportionate to the surrounding labour market could be measured – annual monitoring returns had to be returned to the FEC.[12] Large employers and the public sector had also to monitor job applicants.

Although they were not quotas, these goals and targets underscored the need for employers to take deliberate and timely steps to redress imbalances. Employers were required to undertake three-yearly reviews of their workforce composition and employment practices for 'the purposes of determining whether members of each community are enjoying, and are likely to continue to enjoy, fair participation' (*Fair Employment (Northern Ireland) Act 1989* Section 31 (a), replicated in *The Fair Employment and Treatment (Northern Ireland) Order 1998*, Article 55 (1)). If fair participation was found not to exist, employers were required to determine reasonable and appropriate affirmative action and decide what results might be expected over what timeframe (*Fair Employment Act 1989*, Section 31 (b) and (c) and Article 55 (2) and (3)). The FEC was given powers in the Act to recommend and enforce affirmative actions with goals and timetables.

The 1989 legislation defined affirmative action as:

action designed to secure fair participation in employment by members of the Protestant, or members of the Roman Catholic, community in Northern Ireland by means including – (a) the adoption of practices encouraging such participation; and (b) the modification or abandonment of practices that have or may have the effect of restricting or discouraging such participation' (*Fair Employment Act 1989*, Section 58 and Article 4).[13]

Several specific types of affirmative action were specifically permitted: training to redress under-representation, management of redundancy schemes to maintain progress in attaining a representative workforce, encouraging applications from an under-represented community. The FEC instructed employers on incorporating affirmative action measures such as the use of welcoming statements in job advertisements, consultation with trade unions and equal opportunities awareness training.

So, a more comprehensive strategy for tackling discrimination and inequality emerged. Individuals could make complaints to Fair Employment Tribunals and the FEC monitored, investigated and reviewed employers' labour patterns and practices. The Commission published regular reports on monitoring results. The legislative strategy gave a central place to affirmative action, whether as a permitted

---

[12] 'The FEC operationally defined under-representation as meaning any numerical disparity between the availability of a relevant group and the utilisation of that group. *Availability* refers to that community's representation and within the economically active population, while *utilisation* concerns the community's share of the monitored workforce' (Russell 2004, 25). An 'agreement firm' is one that is subject to an FEC agreement, whereas the 'monitored workforce' is made up of those people who are employed by firms that employ more than 10 people.

[13] Additionally, Section 21 (2) and Article 5 (5) says that 'Any reference in this Act (Order) to the promotion of equality of opportunity includes a reference to the promotion of affirmative action and, accordingly, any reference to action for promoting equality of opportunity includes a reference to affirmative action'.

action under the Act or, where the workforce was not balanced, as a lawful special measure envisioned by an employer.[14] The enhanced powers of the FEC enabled the Commission to develop binding agreements with employers and issue enforceable directions to them.

Advances in equality legislation continued under The Fair Employment and Treatment (Northern Ireland) Order 1998 which consolidated and strengthened fair employment legislation on religious and political discrimination.[15] It extended anti-discrimination laws to the provision of goods, facilities, services and premises (although there were some exceptions to provisions regarding premises). Part-time workers were brought within the ambit of monitoring requirements, and information on those ceasing to be employed was to be sought from large private employers (over 250 employees) and the public sector. In addition, special measures were introduced to encourage recruitment from among unemployed people, among whom Catholics are disproportionately represented; and, with the Equality Commission for Northern Ireland's approval (the Equality Commission for Northern Ireland took over the functions of the Fair Employment Commission in 1999, along with the functions of the bodies responsible for gender, race and disability), to permit training for non-employees of a specific religious belief where that section of the community is under-represented in a particular workforce.

In the period between the 1989 Act and the 1998 Order the political situation in Northern Ireland was transformed. Cease-fires were declared in 1994 and Multi-Party Talks started in 1996, culminating in the Belfast/Good Friday Agreement in 1998. For the first time it seemed that achieving a sustainable peace was possible with convergence between agreement on the constitutional future and agreement on equality and human rights – or at least a great measure of acceptance in both areas. Just as discrimination and exclusion had been central to the conflict, equality and human rights was fundamental to its resolution. The House of Common's Northern Ireland Affairs Committee said in 1999 'several witnesses stressed how important to the Peace Process issues of equality of opportunity are, particularly issues of fair employment' (Northern Ireland Affairs Committee 1999).

Affirmative Action and the Police Service of Northern Ireland

As we argue in Section 2, affirmative action policies are not simply intended to equalise recruitment in the labour force. They often aim at more systemic social

---

[14]   Section 20 (3) of the 1989 Act, replicated in Article 5 (3) of the 1998 Order, states that 'a person is not to be treated as not having the same opportunity as another person has or would have by reason only of anything lawfully done in pursuance of affirmative action'.

[15]   The Order repealed the 1976 and 1989 Acts; the Order re-enacted substantial parts of these together with new elements. Under Article 2 (3) of The Fair Employment and Treatment (Northern Ireland) Order 1998 a person's religious belief or political opinion include '(a) his supposed religious belief or political opinion; and (b) the absence or supposed absence of any, or any particular, religious belief or political opinion'.

reform. So, for example, affirmative action in American colleges and universities is aimed at establishing diversity on campus and beyond (as argued, for example, in Dworkin 1977). By the same token, as well as being directed at organisational change, some forms of affirmative action in Northern Ireland are societal in intent. Of these, the introduction of affirmative action procedures in police recruitment is the most notable. This policy is one of the most important political and social changes introduced during the peace process and is integral to its future. The Belfast/Good Friday Agreement recognised the need for 'a new beginning to policing in Northern Ireland with a police service capable of attracting and sustaining support from the community as a whole'. The parties to the Agreement:

> ...also believe that this agreement offers a unique opportunity to bring about a new political dispensation which will recognise the full and equal legitimacy and worth of the identities, senses of allegiance and ethos of all sections of the community in Northern Ireland. They consider that this opportunity should inform and underpin the development of a police service representative in terms of make-up of the community as a whole (*The Agreement* 1998).

In the wake of the Agreement, a Commission on Policing for Northern Ireland (the Patten Commission) was established. It was charged with reporting on ways by which composition, recruitment, culture, ethos and symbols of the Royal Ulster Constabulary (RUC) should be addressed. The central challenge the Commission faced was to increase the proportion of Catholics in the RUC beyond the eight per cent it stood at in December 1998. The tackling of the perception that Catholics were not welcome in the RUC (called the 'chill factor'), which acted as a significant barrier to Catholics applying to join the police, entailed among other things the police demonstrating a commitment to a human rights culture and operating under a name, oath and code of ethics acceptable across the community. In line with the Patten Commission findings, the RUC was renamed as the Police Service of Northern Ireland (PSNI). The Commission proposed that the police service develop outreach programmes, particularly in areas where its relationship with the community needed most development, and place advertisements that made clear its wish to attract more Catholics and women. Most significantly Patten recommended that one Catholic should be appointed for every new Protestant appointee, drawn from the pool of qualified candidates for the service.[16] The Commission stated that 'we believe that the ratio of recruits should be kept to 50:50, at least for ten years of the model' (The Independent Commission on Policing for Northern Ireland 1999, 89).

The Patten Commission approached the question of affirmative action somewhat gingerly, given the sensitivities of the majority Protestant and unionist community. It stressed that 'merit must remain a critical criterion for selection for the police

---

[16]   Although the Patten Report described the arrangement as 50 per cent Catholic and 50 per cent Protestant, the Northern Ireland Policing Bill of 2000 related recruitment as 50 per cent Catholic and 50 per cent *non-Catholic*. This formulation of equality includes minority groups as effectively lying within the Protestant community.

service', and did not propose that 'religious or cultural identity, gender or ethnicity should be treated as a makeweight for merit' (The Independent Commission on Policing for Northern Ireland 1999, 87). For those reasons it recommended that a specified standard of merit should be met with successful achievers entering a pool from which appointments would be made. It further justified its 50:50 selection from the pool as a reflection of the religious breakdown of the population in the normal age range for recruitment (The Independent Commission on Policing for Northern Ireland 1999, pp. 88–89).

Despite this, the passage of the Police (Northern Ireland) Act through the Westminster Parliament in 2000 was highly contentious. There was opposition from unionists who described it as an attack on the police force and its symbols. They also viewed it as instituting a policy of discrimination against Protestants, especially in light of increasing Catholic participation in a service whose numbers were to fall in any case. On the other hand, there were those who considered that the draft Act failed to implement Patten, given that it introduced a ten-year limit (rather than minimum) on 50:50 recruitment plus powers vested in the Secretary of State to review, and renew or revoke the measure, on a triennial basis. These changes could have a significant effect on the affirmative action ambitions of the reforms, given that it would take ten years for 30 per cent of the reformed service to be Catholic, with just 17–19 per cent being reached within four years (see O'Leary 2000).

The compatibility of 50:50 recruitment with domestic and European anti–discrimination legislation was considered by the Human Rights and Equality Commissions. The Patten Commission had rejected the extension of its recruitment proposal to women on the basis that it was incompatible with European legislation. There was no such issue on grounds of religion; with only the Fair Employment and Treatment (NI) Order 1998 requiring amendment to accommodate the Act. However, a potential problem loomed with the European Framework Directive on Equal Treatment, which came into force in October 2004.[17] Opinion was divided on the best way of handling this – by seeking derogation from the Directive in respect of policing in Northern Ireland or by changing the wording of the Police Act to incorporate the kind of flexibility that the European Court of Justice had approved in the use of other affirmative action measures. The Government chose derogation.

Lobbying by the Equality Commission for Northern Ireland and others secured the withdrawal of the ten-year limit and the immediate extension of Section 75 of the Northern Ireland Act 1998 (see below) to the police service. Additionally, special provisions were sought that targeted gender, with women comprising only 12.6 per cent of the police service and there were 16 members of minority groups (who make up 0.9 per cent of the general population of Northern Ireland) in the force, compromising 0.16 per cent of the service.[18] The Government responded by

---

[17]   The Equal Treatment Directive's attachment to non-discrimination could have had an impact on affirmative action interventions in the Northern Ireland labour market, though a specific article was inserted permitting some forms of discrimination in Northern Ireland.

[18]   Correspondence between the Authors and the Equality/Diversity Unit, PSNI.

consolidating within the Act monitoring arrangements and action plans to address the under-representation of women (Harbison 2002; on ECNI lobbying re Patten see ECNI 1999). Minority groups were not included specifically, but questions have since been asked about recruitment from these sections of the community.

The pace of change is seen as slow by some, taking between five and ten years to reach the critical mass of between 15–30 per cent estimated as necessary to change the organisational culture and character of the service. Added to this is the fact that policing remains a contested issue in talks designed to get the political process back on the rails, with policing arrangements not yet supported by the representatives of a large section of the nationalist, mainly Catholic, population.[19] This is a difficult environment in which to reap the full benefits of an affirmative action scheme. Nonetheless, as Hillyard and Tomlinson argue 'never before in the history of three decades of fair employment debates has a British Government backed one-for-one recruitment as a way of remedying an unrepresentative workforce' (Hillyard and Tomlinson 2000, 413).

Reforms to policing signal the Government's intentions to address equality issues in Northern Ireland. Policing reform is a labour market issue as well as being a significant element in driving social and political change. Just as importantly it runs to the core of the state's relationship with its citizens. A police service that does not reflect the socio-economic makeup of citizens struggles to be regarded as legitimate. 'The community as a whole', Patten noted, 'should see themselves as having a stake in the police service as a whole' (The Independent Commission on Policing for Northern Ireland 1999, 81). The police service, a crucial element in the public sphere as well as a major employer, acts as a metaphor for the state's approach to equality.

Equality-Mainstreaming – Towards a More Egalitarian Society[20]

A sustainable and lasting peace necessitates the forging of a consensus around the stability of the region, something that would be close to impossible if structural inequalities remained. This certainly contributed to the government's motives in addressing policing reform. It has also compelled policy-makers to address other structural inequalities that pervade Northern Ireland's society. As a result, the region has become a testing ground for a highly developed egalitarian agenda.

A striking initiative that arose from the 1998 Agreement was the imposition of a statutory obligation on public authorities to 'carry out all their functions with

---

[19] The political process hit deadlock over implementation of the Agreement and the Northern Ireland Assembly was suspended most recently in October 2002. Despite new elections in 2003 the Assembly has not reconvened. Its recall depends upon the successful outcome of current talks. Sinn Fein does not support policing developments; it wishes to see further change first.

[20] Issues related to Section 75 and equality mainstreaming are addressed more fully in Hinds 2003.

due regard to the need to promote equality of opportunity in relation to religion and political opinion; gender; race; disability; age; marital status; dependents; and sexual orientation' (*The Agreement* 1998, 16). This equality duty, outlined below, evolved across the 1990s, arising from dissatisfaction with government inaction on equality proofing in Northern Ireland first introduced into the civil service through administrative circular in 1990. This dissatisfaction continued despite an attempt to strengthen equality proofing in 1994 through Policy Appraisal and Fair Treatment guidelines (PAFT) that proved just as ineffective.[21] The concept behind PAFT was viewed by many of those representing equality interests as an important complement to fair employment and other anti–discrimination legislation, offering the opportunity to introduce equality considerations into the design of public policies. It was a 'substantial shift towards equality and away from the narrow pre-occupation solely with discrimination' (McCrudden 1999, 1712).

Unfortunately, government departments and public bodies took a restricted approach to questions of equality. They concentrated on averting 'discrimination or unequal treatment' rather than positively promoting equality or affirmative action. In any case, PAFT was given insufficient attention across government (Central Community Relations Unit 1994, §2.1; Osborne et al. 1996).

SACHR had argued for the need for new legislation and policies beyond fair employment to eliminate religious and political discrimination and provide for equality of opportunity. Indeed it had pressed in 1990 for the introduction of a 'statutory obligation on Government departments and other public authorities and bodies to monitor their policies and practices' (SACHR 1990, 30 §4.12). In coming to this decision SACHR had noted Section 71 of the Race Relations Act 1976 in Britain, which imposed a statutory duty on local authorities 'to eliminate racial discrimination and promote equality of opportunity and good relations' (SACHR 1990, 24 §4.55).[22] In 1998 SACHR stated 'it is clear that relying on Government Departments and public bodies to implement PAFT on a voluntary basis has failed and SACHR has recommended that it should be placed on a statutory basis' (SACHR 1998, 4 §1.8).

In the light of this criticism from SACHR and the mobilisation of equality activists in the voluntary sector, pressure increased for a more robust approach to mainstreaming equality (SACHR 1997; McCrudden 1996; McCrudden 1997; McCrudden 1998; See also Hutson 1996). During the 1996–98 peace talks, Northern Ireland's political parties, supported proposals to legislate for equality proofing in the subsequent Northern Ireland Act 1998. The Agreement also established new Human Rights and Equality Commissions. The Equality Commission was given responsibility for enforcing a new statutory equality duty placed on public authorities. It was to monitor and to promote 'equality of opportunity in specified

---

[21]   By equality proofing we mean that policy must be examined to ensure that it promotes equality.

[22]   Debates over legislative approaches to equality in Northern Ireland have drawn on legislation and debates in the UK, US and elsewhere.

areas and parity of esteem between the two main communities, and to investigate individual complaints against public bodies' (*The Agreement* 1998).

Section 75 of the 1998 Northern Ireland Act fleshed out the two crucial legal duties given to government departments and public bodies:[23]

1. To have 'due regard to the need to promote equality of opportunity
   a. between persons of different religious belief, political opinion, racial group, age, marital status or sexual orientation;
   b. between men and women generally;
   c. between persons with a disability and persons without; and
   d. between persons with dependents and persons without'.
2. To have 'regard to the desirability of promoting good relations between persons of different religious belief, political opinion or racial group'.

The Act also set out the steps that public authorities, must take to comply with the legislation (*Northern Ireland Act* 1998, § 75 and Schedule 9). Policy makers are required to consider policies from the perspective of the promotion of equality, taking proactive measures rather than merely preventing potential discrimination. Groups affected by relevant inequalities[24] have been encouraged by the obligation on policy-makers to look at the impact of policies on them specifically. Uniquely, through including many different equality interests, the Act recognises and addresses the multi-dimensionality of inequality. It has the potential to tackle the full range of people's experiences of inequality at once.

Using detailed guidelines drawn up by the Equality Commission public authorities are required to produce equality schemes covering all their functions, powers and duties. A scheme must include commitment to leadership, resource allocation, monitoring and review, training and communication. The public authority must review its existing policies and look at new ones in order to determine whether there is evidence 'that different groups have different needs, experiences, issues and priorities' or there is 'an opportunity to better promote equality of opportunity' (ECNI 2000, 36). If so, the policy should undergo an equality impact assessment (EQIA). An EQIA evaluates what effect a policy has, or might have, on particular groups.

Significantly, public authorities are expected to consider each policy comprehensively, paying particular attention to exploring:

a. 'measures which might mitigate any adverse impact of that policy on promotion of equality of opportunity'; and

---

[23]   The legislation covered many public bodies from the outset, with other added through designation by the Secretary of State for Northern Ireland. They include many UK bodies with a remit that includes Northern Ireland.

[24]   Formally known as 'affected groups' or as 'Section 75 groups'.

b. 'alternative policies which might better achieve the promotion of equality of opportunity' (*Northern Ireland Act 1998*, Schedule 9).

Indeed 'if the monitoring and evaluation show that the policy results in greater adverse impact than predicted, or if opportunities arise which would allow for greater equality of opportunity to be promoted, the public authority must ensure that the policy is revised' (ECNI 2000, 46).

Consultation at various points is a central feature of the requirements, underlining the importance attached by the legislation and the Equality Commission to consistent engagement between policy-makers and vulnerable groups. Building blocks laid down for effective consultation by the Equality Commission include: that public bodies begin consultation as early as possible, provide relevant and accessible information, use a variety of engagement methods, train their facilitators, provide an accessible and supportive environment (eg childcare), and allow time for groups to discuss and come to a view. The Commission makes clear that 'formal consultation' should be included as a critical stage in the EQIA, namely immediately prior to decision-making. Less formal consultation should inform the entire EQIA process and 'consultations in general play an integral role in the EQIA and these consultations must be underpinned by a good working relationship with relevant consultees' (ECNI 2001, 23).

The reach of Section 75 is extensive. By March 2003, 177 public bodies had come within the ambit of the legislation and 154 equality schemes had been approved by the Equality Commission (ECNI 2003).[25] Equality schemes, and their EQIAs are intended 'to increase participation and inclusion, to change the culture of public decision making, and to place a more proactive approach to the promotion of equality at the heart of public policy' (ECNI 2001, 5).

Moreover, it is possible that public procurement can be shaped by Section 75. In 1997, for example, SACHR advocated that fair employment legislation should be amended 'to broaden the scope for linking contract compliance to the promotion of affirmative action and fair participation by employers', stating that 'public bodies should be required to satisfy themselves before contracts are awarded that tendering contractors have effective fair employment, equal opportunities and anti-discrimination policies, procedures and practices. If not, then those contractors should be excluded from consideration' (SACHR 1997, 20). 'Contract compliance' was addressed in a review of public procurement published in 2002, proposing the application of Section 75 to public procurement (Central Procurement Directorate Northern Ireland 2002, §2.6).

Despite this, there is controversy over what precisely Section 75 is intended to do. Some people interpret the equality duty as merely prohibiting discrimination, while others believe that it entails absolutely equal treatment. Both approaches effectively deny the use of affirmative action as a Section 75 tool. It is clear, however, that

---

[25] Unofficial figures from March 2004 suggest that 220 public bodies are designated and 168 equality schemes have been approved.

the Government envisioned the legislation going beyond anti-discrimination to the proactive pursuit of equality of opportunity. In fact, when the Northern Ireland Act was being discussed in Parliament, the Northern Ireland Secretary, Paul Murphy stated that Section 75 'in no way calls into question the ability of public authorities to take affirmative action in appropriate cases to correct disadvantage. Affirmative action in appropriate circumstances is an important method of combating inequality, and it is our firm intention that that should remain so'. Indeed, he continued, Section 75 'means that public authorities are bound to have regard to the need for affirmative action when considering their duty under the clause' (House of Commons Official Report 18 November 1998, Mr Murphy). In reference to the compatibility of Section 75 with special measures on targeting social need and promoting social inclusion, Government further said 'the obligation relates to equality of opportunity, not equal treatment' (Official Report, 26 October 1998, Lord Dubs). The Government's intention was reinforced in the guidelines with which public bodies were required to comply. The Equality Commission for Northern Ireland specified that 'the promotion of equality of opportunity entails more than the elimination of discrimination. It requires proactive measures to be taken to secure equality of opportunity as between the groups identified in Section 75' (ECNI 2000, 25).

It is no surprise that equality-mainstreaming is highly controversial in a divided society like Northern Ireland. For some parties to the conflict, questions of equality are wrapped up in fears that every time one group benefits from equality legislation, the other group must lose. They see it as a zero-sum game. As a result of this, and of other, more traditional conservative critiques of the legislation, the Act has met with some resistance both in its essence and in its applications.

In the light of the political debate, it is important to appreciate the direct relationship between the sorts of processes demanded in Section 75 and the just outcomes that are possible from it. That is, implementation of the Section leads to the inclusion of previously excluded and marginalized groups in dialogue and a policy debate that must take account of their needs and views. The detailed steps that public bodies must take are intended to change the culture of policy-making, making it simultaneously more rigorous and effective. Moreover, as McCrudden points out, procedural implementation is crucial where there is a lack of trust (McCrudden 2004, 29). McCrudden argues that equality of opportunity must be interpreted within the context firstly of Northern Ireland, where affirmative action has been used in the pursuit of fair employment and secondly within the context of the European Union, where the lawful co-existence of non-discrimination and positive action are accepted. The legislation will, he suggests, bring about changes to policy outcomes and reduce systemic resource inequalities over time (McCrudden 2004, 13).

Of course, Section 75 does not stand alone as an equality-mainstreaming initiative. For example, Targeting Social Need (TSN), introduced as a public expenditure priority in 1991, can be seen as action to overcome disadvantage, much of which resulted from discrimination and under-representation in economic opportunity. Apparently a traditional welfarist initiative aimed at poverty-reduction rather than specifically targeting particular groups, its intention and effect is more equality-mainstreaming-oriented than is apparent at first glance (see Dignan and McLaughlin 2002, 11).

As evidenced over years in employment, housing and other statistics, poverty and social exclusion is more extensive in the Catholic section of the community than in the Protestant. In this environment, as we said above, conflict and disadvantage go hand in hand. So reducing disadvantage per se will erode a major differential between the two main sections of the Northern Ireland community and result in a reduction of grievance and conflict.

TSN entailed the examining of the impact of existing policies and programmes in order to target them better towards areas and people in greatest need. When it was deemed to be ineffective, it was re-issued as the post-Agreement New TSN and became one of the components for building a cohesive, inclusive and just society in the new Northern Ireland Executive's Programme for Government (Northern Ireland Economic Council, 1998):[26] 'Our vision is set out in the New Targeting Social Need (TSN) Policy by which we are committed to tackling community differentials in unemployment and the significant levels of deprivation, long term unemployment [an area in which the Catholic community is over-represented] and benefit dependency which have blighted our society' (Northern Ireland Executive 2001, 7) In this light, 'While not discriminating in favour of one community and against the other, therefore, New TSN should contribute, over time, to the erosion of differentials between the communities' (Central Community Relations Unit 1998).

Ineffective though it has been in this regard, TSN was developed as a 'facially neutral but purposefully inclusionary' policy to equalise the positions of the Catholic and Protestant communities.[27] So, although it does not have the benefit of its own budget, it does fall within the general ambit of affirmative action. Moreover, while the policy intention was not as radical as that of Section 75, its emphasis on differential resource allocation suggests that it may also be seen as equality-mainstreaming.

Section 75 has led to a more integrated approach to equality issues. This approach will be taken further in the forthcoming Single Equality Act (SEA). The Office of the First and Deputy First Minister (OFMDFM) commenced consultation on the act in 2001, but legislation became a casualty of continuing political deadlock (OFMDFM 2001). Nevertheless, it is likely that it will be introduced by the Northern Ireland Assembly, once it is unsuspended. In the meanwhile, there is an ongoing debate over what precisely it will contain (see ECNI 2002; ECNI 2004; OFMDFM 2004). The act will bring all questions of equality, including affirmative action and equality-mainstreaming programmes, under one legislative roof. In the consultation process many interest groups are seeking to raise all equality practices up to the standards of the most substantial and robust approaches.

---

[26]   This report draws from research by Quirk, and McLaughlin 1996.

[27]   The idea of a policy being 'facially neutral but purposefully inclusionary' is raised in McCrudden 1986, 223. Although McCrudden is specifically referring to exclusion in general, the concept is also useful for an understanding of TSN.

This comprehensive approach – unifying equality rights in a single piece of legislation; and incorporating and linking anti-discrimination, affirmative action, mainstreaming and other equality tools – affirms the universal relevance of equality and enables greater acceptance of measures. Fitzpatrick et al. believe that remedial measures 'are more likely to be palatable if they emerge out of comprehensive equal opportunities policies than if they are invoked in isolation from such an approach' (Fitzpatrick et al. 1997b, 164).[28]

Some groups, the Equality Commission for Northern Ireland for instance, argue that the SEA should build on the good practice of affirmative action in fair employment. Lessons from fair employment point to important elements of an affirmative action programme that should be extended to other equality groups: setting goals and timetables, monitoring, reviewing policies, practices and procedures and reporting to an oversight body. The Equality Commission suggests that this approach should be married with a consultation approach that brings those affected by inequality into the debate, as developed under Section 75. This, argues the Commission, 'recognises that each ground of inequality brings with it its own practical issues' and would enable 'some degree of variation on grounds of diversity' (ECNI 2004, §2.2). The Commission is pressing the Office of the First and Deputy First Minister to shift its thinking on affirmative action from a 'narrow exception to non-discrimination principles' towards a 'major vehicle for promoting equality of opportunity' (ECNI 2004, §8.5.1).

Concluding Remarks

There are of course serious difficulties in measuring the degree to which socio-economic inequalities in and beyond the labour market are a result of discrimination. There is strong evidence that differentials between Catholics and Protestants *are* a result of discrimination however as argued for example by V.K. Borooah (Borooah 1999; Borooah 2000). Fortunately, these differentials have reduced over time.

Employment differentials are, perhaps not surprisingly, the measures that have equalised most over time. Northern Ireland's labour market experienced significant structural change from the 1970s to the 1990s. Absolute growth in jobs was not significant, amounting to an annual average rate of 0.5 per cent, with male employment actually falling, by about 0.3 per cent per annum (Dignan 2003, §3.30). In the 1990s, however, employment began to rise. During this period, as opposed to the 1971–91 period, 'the Catholic share of employment increased at a faster pace than the Catholic labour force share'. The Catholic employment share rose from 38 per cent in 1990 to 41 per cent in 1999, leading to a fall in the employment gap between Catholics and Protestants, from 3 per cent to less than 1 per cent through the 1990s (Dignan 2003, §3.66–3.68).

---

[28]   Quoted in ECNI 2002.

In 1990, McCrudden *et al*. note, 73 per cent of firms that had been partners to FEC agreements drew less than 25 per cent from one section or other of Northern Ireland's community in their workforces. By 2000, this had fallen to 63 per cent of firms (McCrudden et al. 2004, 134). In other words, there had been a 10 per cent drop in the number of firms that disproportionately hired from one or other section of the community. McCrudden et. al. point out that 'agreement firms' were more segregated than firms across the economy in general. They tended to have more unbalanced workforces. These firms also experienced the greatest drop in segregation, however. The percentage of Catholics in the monitored workforce increased across the 1990s from 33 per cent to 37.8 per cent, a higher increase in participation than experienced in the economy in general (McCrudden et al. 2004, 139). It does seem that directed affirmative action programmes were having a considerable impact.

This is not the end of the story, however. Despite their greater opportunities in the labour market, Catholics remain far more likely to be in poverty and/or to be unemployed. 9 per cent of Catholic men and 6 per cent of Catholic women, as opposed to 5 per cent of Protestant men and 3 per cent of Protestant women, are unemployed (*Labour Force Survey* 2004). Catholics are far more likely than Protestants to live in deprived areas (Dignan and McLaughlin 2002, 18). 35 per cent of Catholics live in the bottom 30 per cent of the income distribution, as opposed to 21 per cent of Protestants. 50 per cent of Catholic children live in poverty, as compared to 32 per cent of their Protestant counterparts (Dignan and McLaughlin 2002, 206).[29]

It is clear that structural inequalities play a role in the distribution of poverty and unemployment. It is also clear that there are areas of structural inequality that labour force affirmative action programmes cannot reach. Equality mainstreaming is required if social change is to be brought about. The addressing of inequalities across a wide front, from directed formal affirmative action to equality-mainstreaming programmes like TSN, is far more likely to resolve the deeper, fundamental difficulties that disadvantaged groups experience in playing a full and equal role in Northern Ireland's society.

Of course, the equality-mainstreaming programmes are still in a formative stage. The strength of their impact in the future depends on the interpretations that politicians, judges and policy-makers place on them. In this light, the greatest threat to these programmes is the set of conservative responses that are coalescing in opposition to mainstreaming. These responses are often methodological, where actors seek to weaken equality-mainstreaming legislation, removing its relationship with directed affirmative action and setting it solely within the context of anti-discrimination initiatives. Sometimes, however, political actors object to the very idea that equality should be the subject of policy. Either they deny that structural inequalities exist, or they fear that policies focussing on these inequalities will undermine the positions of their clients and constituents.

---

[29]   15 per cent of those marked as 'other' and 27 per cent of those marked as 'not known' also live in this group.

Nevertheless, the equality issue has transformed the political debate on the structures of Northern Ireland's society. It is generally acknowledged that the status quo in pre-affirmative action Northern Ireland was not acceptable and that steps had to be taken to construct a more inclusive environment for all disadvantaged, including minority, groups. Policy makers have recognised that disadvantage cannot be thought of solely in the context of Catholic-Protestant divisions. Divisions and disadvantage within and between these sections of the community must be addressed, as well as those suffered by other groups. Equality is best served through the employment of a range of strategies and tools. As we have suggested, affirmative action and the other strategies and tools should be conceived of as sitting on a continuum.

The general political consensus in Northern Ireland until the late 1990s was that little action was required regarding the position of minority groups. The binary Catholic-Protestant distinction remained the central plank of the equality agenda, driven in part by the small proportion of members of minority groups in the population, and by the ongoing urgency of Northern Ireland's traditional divisions.

In a 1998 survey carried out by the Northern Ireland Statistics and Research Agency, relatively high (compared to similar surveys carried out across the UK) numbers of people expressed prejudicial attitudes regarding minorities. Approximately 35 per cent expressed discomfort with the idea of working with members of minorities (with 66 per cent expressing discomfort with the idea of working with Irish Travellers), 25 per cent regarding members of minorities living in their neighbourhoods (57 per cent regarding Irish Travellers) and 54 per cent regarding members of minorities marrying into their families (77 per cent regarding Irish Travellers) (Connolly and Keenan 2000).[30] Moreover, the fact of racism in Northern Ireland was and is highlighted by orchestrated and violent incidents aimed at members of minority communities, in Belfast and beyond.

Although the Catholic-Protestant distinction has driven debates on affirmative action in the region, legal frameworks have largely been extended towards members of minority groups. Section 75 duties, as described in Section 5 of this chapter, relate to race to the same extent that they relate to religion etc. The Race Relations (Northern Ireland) Order 1997 made provisions for members of minorities to be given preferential treatment 'in regard to their education, training or welfare, or any ancillary benefits' (Race Relations Order 1997). Northern Ireland's late emergence as a multicultural society requires that the position of minority groups in the community be attended to. There is growing pressure to ensure that any forthcoming Single Equality Act extends to minority groups and other disadvantaged groups the

---

[30] Comparison with the rest of the UK is difficult because questions asked vary, but it does seem that attitudes are significantly less tolerant in Northern Ireland. By way of comparison, a 2000 MORI poll, commissioned for the Readers' Digest Magazine, identified 8 per cent of people in Great Britain as either agreeing or agreeing strongly with the sentence 'It would upset me if my neighbour was of Asian or Afro-caribbean origin' and 12 per cent with the sentence 'It would upset me if a close relative married a person of Asian or Afro-caribbean origin'. (*Reader's Digest* 2000).

benefits of effective affirmative action pioneered for the Catholic community under fair employment legislation.

Disadvantage and discrimination merit attention in and of themselves. The status of Northern Ireland as a divided society, however, also means that there is an instrumental imperative in addressing inequality: the conflict cannot be resolved without making Northern Ireland a more equal society.

The role of affirmative action and equality-mainstreaming in conflict resolution also raises the question of the degree to which the political process itself is or should be influenced by affirmative action approaches. It is certain that in Northern Ireland, the governments of the UK and Ireland, as guarantors of the Agreement, established commitments to equality, including in the political process itself. Decision-making power in the Northern Ireland Assembly was to be distributed so that one group could not dominate another.[31] Both main sections of the community were afforded equal status in the constitutional structures of the Agreement.

Affirmative action is more than a set of programmes. It is also a moral and philosophical agenda, recognising that egalitarian imperatives underpin a stable and just society. Northern Ireland has become the major testing ground for such a wide range of initiatives because it is so profoundly and violently divided. This should not detract from the democratic import of the policies that have been put in place. As we said, an unequal society is a divided society. It stands to reason, then, that reconciliation requires an addressing of inequalities. This is true not just of societies like Northern Ireland. It is true everywhere. Tackling inequalities in the round is not solely about conflict resolution. It is about justice.

Glossary

AFL–CIO:	American Federation of Labor and Congress of Industrial Organizations
DED:	Department of Economic Development
EQIA:	Equality Impact Assessment
FEA:	Fair Employment Agency
FEC:	Fair Employment Commission
MP:	Member of Parliament
NI:	Northern Ireland
NICRA:	Northern Ireland Civil Rights Association
NICS:	Northern Ireland Civil Service
OFMDFM:	Office of the First Minister and Deputy First Minister

---

[31] This was achieved through a new voting mechanism, the allocation of ministerial posts on a proportional basis across four political parties, and through the requirement for cross-community consent for key decisions.

PAFT:	Policy Appraisal and Fair Treatment
PSNI:	Police Service of Northern Ireland
RUC:	Royal Ulster Constabulary
SACHR:	Standing Advisory Commission on Human Rights
SEA:	Single Equality Act
TSN:	Targeting Social Need

Chapter 6

Australian Multicultural Equity and Fair Go

Martine Piquet

If Australia today officially takes pride in its ethnic plurality and is committed to a multicultural policy that recognises the social, cultural and economic benefits of diversity, this was not always so. Until the immediate post-war period Australia's record was discriminatory when it was not openly racist. Only the irreversible changes in immigration patterns from the 1950s onward made Australia aware that it should alter its approach, and led it to adopt first more inclusive, then multiculturalist policies. Since 1945, over six million people have migrated to Australia as new settlers, and the population has risen from about 7 million at the end of World War II to just under 20 million in 2003. Today, nearly a quarter of Australia's population was born overseas, and a total of 43 per cent were either born overseas or have at least one parent born overseas. Since 1999, New Zealand has replaced the United Kingdom as the largest source birthplace of migrants. The number of settlers arriving in Australia between July 2001 and June 2002 totalled 88,900. They came from over 150 different countries. Most were born in New Zealand (17.6 per cent), the United Kingdom (9.8 per cent), China (7.5 per cent), South Africa (6.4 per cent), India (5.7 per cent) and Indonesia (4.7 per cent). Until 1971, Australian Indigenous people (Aborigines and Torres Straight Islanders) were not included in national census counts. 410,000 (i.e. 2.2 per cent of the total population) identified as such in the 2001 census.[1]

Nevertheless, in spite of the inevitable problems of inclusion and equity related to ethnic plurality, the terms 'positive action', 'protective discrimination' and 'positive discrimination' have been absent from the multicultural debate. Australia has a broad legislative framework prohibiting racial discrimination, but the term 'affirmative action' refers to measures targeting women, and Australian law refers to it exclusively in terms of women's employment rights. The only piece of federal legislation using the term 'affirmative action' was the *Commonwealth Affirmative Action (Equal Employment for Women) Act 1986*, interestingly renamed *Equal Opportunity for Women in the Workplace Act* when amended in 1999.

---

[1] Source for all figures: *Australian Bureau of Statistics*, <http://www.abs.gov.au>.

Federally, questions relating to ethnic minorities[2] presently fall within the province of the *Department of Immigration and Multiculturalism and Indigenous Affairs* (DIMIA for short). Concurrently, the application of anti-discrimination laws is monitored by the *Australian Human Rights and Equal Opportunity Commission* (HREOC), a national independent statutory government body, established in 1986 under the provisions of the *Australian Human Rights and Equal Opportunity Commission Act*. Similar dispositions for the monitoring of enforcement of local anti-discrimination legislation exist at state level.[3] Generally speaking, the promotion of equity and respect among the ethnic groups making up the Australian society was, and remains, the foundation of the multiculturalist policies introduced in Australia in the early 1970s. Nevertheless, while there has been a continuous bipartisan political consensus on multiculturalist principles, there also seems to have been a gradual erosion of the assistance to ethnic minorities, and quite deliberately so under the present conservative Coalition government of John Howard.

Before going into these questions, it is useful to cast a quick glance at how Australia evolved from early discriminatory and exclusionary practices towards non-Anglo-Saxon minorities to multiculturalism.

---

[2]   The term 'ethnic minority' applies to all non-Anglo-Saxon immigrant and Indigenous groups, and is not just a euphemism for what might be called 'visible' minorities in other countries. In fact, some critics even insist that the 'Anglo-Celtic' majority (people of British and Irish descent) be themselves regarded as 'ethnic'. In everyday usage, however, 'ethnic' tends to refer primarily to non-Indigenous groups, while such an expression as 'race relations' will usually be spontaneously understood as referring to relations with Aborigines.

[3]   Australia is a federation of six states (New South Wales, Queensland, South Australia, Tasmania, Victoria, Western Australia) and a number of territories (among which the Australian Capital Territory and the Northern Territory). The colonies federated in 1901 under the name of 'Commonwealth of Australia'. The Head of State of the Commonwealth is the British Monarch, represented by the Governor-General. It has two legislative houses (Senate [76], House of Representatives [150]). Sometimes dubbed '*Washminster*' (from Washington and Westminster), the political system is a combination of American federalism and British parliamentarianism. As in Britain, the head of government is the Prime Minister, who is also the leader of the party that won the legislative elections. Ministers are chosen among the members of Parliament. In the early days of Federation, the scope of federal power was limited to foreign affairs, defence, immigration, currency, foreign and inter-state trade and transport. Other fields, such as health, education, justice etc. were exclusively state business. Gradually, however, and particularly since World War II, the federal government has extended its sphere of power at the expense of the states. Each state has its own constitution and parliament. On the federal level, the states are represented in the Senate by an equal number of Senators, regardless of their population. For the election to the House of Representatives, the number of constituencies in any given state is in relation to its population. The High Court [of Australia] is the final court of appeal from State and Federal Courts, and it determines matters arising under the Constitution or involving its interpretation.

Racial Discrimination and Exclusion in Australia

In Australia, racial discrimination may safely be dated back to the beginning of British settlement (1788), with the peak of discriminatory legislation being passed roughly from the last decade of the nineteenth century to World War II. The earliest victims were the aboriginal occupants of the continent,[4] but non-European immigrants, as well as some 'undesirable' European groups were not spared.

The Marginalisation of Indigenous People

Like similar societies, Australia was built on the massive arrival of settlers who shared the same intolerance towards the Indigenous nations living on the territories they were conquering. Like their Zulu, Maori or Native American counterparts, Australian Aborigines were dispossessed of their ancestral lands, their culture was despised and thought to be backward. They soon found themselves relegated to the margins of the colonising society, the consequence today being their strikingly low standard of living, their life expectancy well below national averages, their high rates of unemployment, crime, infant mortality and school drop-outs. Their contribution to national history was long obliterated, when not fiercely negated, to the benefit of pioneering mythologies highlighting the figure of the intrepid settler overcoming both a hostile environment, and ill-disposed 'savages'.

In Australia as elsewhere, the settlers' feeling that they were rightfully entitled to colonise overseas territories arose from various elements. First came the assurance that those lands had been lawfully acquired by the mother country. But the most consequential factor was probably the completely opposing conceptions settlers and Indigenous nations had of their relationship to the land. To Europeans, the connection was necessarily linked to work: the land belonged to he (more rarely she...) who toiled on it. Not to exploit the land was a sin. As hunter-gatherers, leading a nomadic or semi-nomadic way of life, Aborigines did not share agriculturists' or pastoralists' sense of having to *subdue* their environment, and had no notion that the land might be *earned* by toiling on it. The invading agriculturist and pastoralist settler society itself could not conceive of a different relationship to the land than the one it had imported from the mother country. The Australian continent was thus deemed *terra nullius* (literally 'nobody's land'), Indigenous people were dispossessed of their lands and natural rights, and marginalised.

Superimposed on this was the European people's linear conception of progress, from a primitive to an advanced civilisation, itself corroborated by the dogmas of social Darwinism and the Puritan ethic. The British settlers who came to Australia were convinced that Indigenous communities and 'races' were inexorably doomed to

---

⁴   The native inhabitants of Australia are made up of two groups: Aborigines proper, from the continent, and Torres Strait Islanders who are Melanesians in origin. They are sometimes referred to collectively under the acronym 'ATSI' *(Aborigines and Torres Strait Islanders)*, while 'Indigenous people' is in more common use.

extinction. By the end of the nineteenth century Australian Aborigines were almost universally depicted as a relic of human evolution with no prospect of survival in the modern world. Relations with them were thus perceived as being transitory: it would be enough to take the right measures either to assimilate them or, as the saying went, '*smooth their dying pillow*'. The policies set up to achieve these ends were more or less radical depending on location and time. A whole array of discriminatory legislation gave authorities widespread powers, for example, to reduce Indigenous people's freedom of movement and oblige them to live in specific areas, including government reserves they could not leave without due permission; prohibit certain customs and traditional practices; control marriages; forcibly remove children from families without right of appeal; control terms of employment and wages. An important economic motive for continuing discrimination was the desire of some employers, particularly in the cattle industry, to retain a source of cheap labour.

The Exclusion of Non-Europeans

Controlling and excluding non-European immigrants was another of Australia's obsessions well into the twentieth century. The earliest European arrivals were not migrants but convicts and their warders. Those free people who had accompanied the convicts and stayed on, or those who migrated in the 1820s and 1830s to take advantage of free land and labour, saw themselves as 'colonists' extending the British Empire in the Pacific. When transportation ceased, free immigrants provided the labour the colonies badly needed. By 1850 there were 187,000 free migrants in Australia. Most of them were British and had their passages paid for. The gold rush of 1851–60 brought a further 622,000 cosmopolitan migrants to the colonies, and for the next 40 years immigration intakes varied according to economic fluctuations. Between 1861 and 1900 a further 765,000 migrants arrived. Colonial censuses first recorded a majority as native-born in 1871.

With Federation in 1901, immigration policy control passed to the federal government. By then the rationale for immigration had changed. British Australian nationhood had become clearly identified with the preservation of the 'racial purity' of a White Australia, and development was linked to the somewhat paranoid fear of an invasion of the continent by supposedly overflowing 'teeming millions' of Chinese and Japanese. Meanwhile, fear of cheap 'coloured labour' led unions to demand restriction on the Chinese[5] and Pacific Island[6] labour which had become a strong feature of gold mining, sugar cane farming, and certain urban trades.

In the decades immediately after World War I, governments tried to organise British immigration on a large scale both to strengthen Australia in the face of a supposedly rising Japanese threat, and make up for the war losses. Between 1919 and 1929, 221,000 British (mostly English and Scots) migrated to Australia, many attracted by land settlement schemes many of which, unfortunately, subsequently failed. Ironically, it was the unassisted and unwanted South-European migrants (mostly Italians, Greeks and Maltese) who were most successful, as small farmers, market gardeners, winegrowers, woodcutters, or contractors.

After World War II and the Pacific War, Australia's immigration priorities evolved significantly. The Japanese had come dangerously close,[7] and the feeling that Australia had escaped invasion by the skin of its teeth convinced Australia's first Minister for Immigration, Labor's Arthur Calwell, that the country must indeed 'populate or perish'. In August 1945, he announced a large-scale immigration programme meant to increase the meagre population of just over 7 million, and strengthen national security and economic development. The goal became an annual population increase of two per cent: half from natural increase, the rest from migration, with a ratio of 'ten Britons to one foreigner'.

Contrary to expectations, however, it proved impossible to attract enough British migrants. Australia agreed to take Displaced Persons from Europe's refugee camps and, gradually but reluctantly, the concept of 'acceptable European races' developed and widened to include Eastern and Southern Europeans, who were only grudgingly accepted. Non-Europeans were not admitted at all. Asians in particular remained almost totally excluded for years. It was only from the mid-1950s, as the economy boomed, that tight controls began to ease, but entry remained limited to those non-whites who were 'specially qualified to integrate'.

---

[5]   The Chinese had come to Australia early on and formed a tiny community. From 1851, many thousand Chinese were attracted to the gold fields of Victoria and New South Wales. Their presence caused racial tension and occasional severe riots (Buckland River in 1857 or Lambing Flat in 1860–1861). This resulted in the first local restrictions on Chinese immigration. In 1888 a colonial conference introduced drastic, although not uniform, limitations on further Chinese immigration. With the Immigration Restriction Act of 1901 and Naturalisation Act of 1903 imposing a de facto bar on all non-Europeans, the number of Chinese in Australia dropped from 38,000 in 1880 to less than half that number 40 years later.

[6]   Often recruited by fraud or force ('blackbirding'), Pacific Islanders were used as indentured labourers in the last decades of the nineteenth century. From 1863 to 1904, 62,000 were imported to work on the sugar and cotton plantations of Queensland. This aroused hostility from the trade union movement and was condemned by religious and humanitarian reformers. The new Commonwealth parliament legislated in 1901 to outlaw the practice and repatriate the labourers.

[7]   The northern towns of Darwin and Katherine were bombed, and midget submarines sailed into Sydney Harbour in 1942.

The White Australia Ideal

Underlying the treatment of Indigenous people and non-British migrants until the middle of the twentieth century was the White Australia ideal.

'White Australia' as a national ideal and policy only developed in the last decade of the nineteenth century, when politicians and journalists began to articulate a vision of a future 'white' Australia, preferably made up of an overwhelming majority of Britons. While the White Australia Policy is commonly said to have its roots in the reaction to the influx of Chinese to the gold fields in the 1850s and the concern over the importation of indentured Pacific Island and Asian workers by the Queensland sugar industry and the West-Australian pearling and fishing industries, its origins can be traced back to the early nineteenth century, when the British government's policy was to keep Australia as 'a preserve for the English race'. In time Australians came to think of themselves not just as 'Britons from the Southern seas' but as 'better Britons than the British themselves'. Pride in being of British stock and sharing with Britain an unequalled democratic heritage prevailed, but there was also a strong sense of having achieved a number of 'Anglo-Saxon' democratic ideals – in particular in the field of social justice – more successfully than the 'old' class-ridden British society. At the time of Federation in 1901, Australia was commonly boasted of as '98 per cent British'. By then 'British' Australians had developed a clear sense of themselves as different from and superior to non-Europeans, a conviction nurtured by racial theories, particularly Social Darwinism, at a time of apparent global dominance of the British Empire.

One the first pieces of legislation passed by the new Commonwealth parliament in 1901 was the *Immigration Restriction Act*, meant 'to place certain restrictions on immigration and to provide for the removal from the Commonwealth of prohibited immigrants'. Among these were the insane, the bearers of contagious diseases, prostitutes, and criminals. Most of all, it included the dictation of 'a passage of 50 words in length in a European language directed by the [immigration] officer' – which amounted to the effective banning of most non-Europeans. Similar expedients had been used in American southern states to bar Blacks from the franchise and in Natal against unwanted immigrants. After World War I the definition of '*white races*' of superior and inferior European racial stock was refined and narrowed, leading to quotas on southern European and Jewish immigration. The White Australia Policy was also directed at non-European residents. It sought to control the movement of Aboriginal people within the country, and led to the reinforcement of policies likely to hasten their 'inevitable' extinction, in particular though the forcible removal of children from their communities and their institutionalisation or adoption.

The ethnic prejudice and intolerance expressed through the White Australia Policy were to persist well into the twentieth century. They were particularly strong in the inter-war period, with the poor economic conditions of the twenties and thirties, and with the rise of nationalism in many parts of the world. If there were some minor indications of change (the idea that Aboriginal people would become extinct was gradually abandoned; the notion of assimilation, as opposed to that of forthright exclusion, slowly gained ground), the outbreak of hostilities with Japan during World War II reinforced the exclusionary philosophy of the White Australia policy, and Prime Minister John Curtin did not hesitate to declare that Australia would 'remain forever the home of the descendants of those people who came here in peace in order to establish in the South Seas an outpost of the British race'.

Australian Multiculturalism

From White Australia to Multiculturalism

The retreat from White Australia began after 1945 as several factors, including the revelation of the horrors of Nazi death camps, dealt a decisive blow to policies openly based on ideas of racial superiority and rejection. The policy that sought to isolate Aboriginal people was abandoned. Prime Minister Holt's decision in 1949 to allow a number of non-European refugees to stay in the country, and to let in the Japanese brides of war veterans or of soldiers then stationed in Japan, was the first step towards a non-discriminatory immigration policy.

All major parties agreed that a high level of continuing immigration was essential to the health of the economy, but the impact of the policies and the needs of migrants, especially those who did not speak English, was recognised only gradually. In the 1950s, once it became clear that mass non-British immigration was inevitable, the government introduced a policy of assimilation, based on the idea that immigrants could be culturally and socially absorbed, and become indistinguishable from the Anglo-Australian population. Measures to encourage successful settlement included some special services for new arrivals. But the centrepiece of assimilationism was the treatment of migrants as 'New Australians', who were to live and work with, and like Anglo-Australians as quickly as possible (which also meant they were supposed to learn English and forget their own language as soon as they set foot on Australian soil), and eventually become citizens. There was no special educational provision for migrant children, who were to be brought up as Australians. Cultural pluralism and the formation of 'ethnic ghettos' were to be avoided at all costs. By the 1960s, however, it became clear that assimilationism was not working. Migrants were *not* being changed into 'Australians' overnight. Their poor command of English often restricted them to low-status jobs with little prospect, made their relationships with public services difficult, not to mention their contacts with the rest of the population. Many felt they could not cope, and a growing number of them were leaving the country. By the 1970s, political parties began to discover the political potential of the 'ethnic vote'. The result was the abandonment of assimilationism and the shift to multiculturalism.

Concern for the problems faced by migrant minorities only really started to be expressed in the late 1960s and early 1970s, in particular by sociologist Jerzy

Zubrzycki[8] who argued for a 'modest commitment to cultural diversity through the maintenance of immigrant languages and the development of studies in European cultures'. By then, Australia had become ethnically diverse through a broadening entrance policy. Immigration had ceased to be mainly British, and immigrants had not only become more 'visible', but also increasingly vocal. Assimilationism was eventually officially abandoned in 1973 when the pluralist term '*multiculturalism*', borrowed from Canada, was adopted by A.J. Grassby, Minister for Immigration in the Whitlam Labor government (1972–1975). In his own words, this meant that Australians were embarking '*upon a new stage of [their] history, the search for [their] national identity*'.[9]

Multiculturalist Policy Pronouncements

In Canada, the existence of a plurality of ethnic communities had led sociologists and anthropologists to develop the notion of 'ethnic mosaic', a metaphor for a harmonious synthesis achieved by the juxtaposition of distinct ethnocultural groups, from which a feeling of national identity might emerge: the paradox of the creation of unity from diversity.

The adoption of multiculturalism in Australia, however, was based on a less idealised and more pragmatic stance. When Labor's Gough Whitlam – whose party had removed any reference to the White Australia Policy in 1965 – spoke of Australia as 'a multicultural nation', he merely seemed to be describing the demographic reality of his country, and acknowledging the peaceful coexistence of its diverse ethnic groups. Al Grassby had a slightly wider vision. Championing the democratic right of migrants to preserve their distinctive cultural background, he likened the nation to a 'family' whose members, while united, might be diverse. He stressed the implications of cultural pluralism as including child migrant education, ethnic group organization, and migrant participation in the political process. The most significant structural change introduced at this time was the *Telephone Interpreter Service*, in 1973. Expenditure on education and welfare increased greatly under the Whitlam government. While most programmes were not directed specifically at migrants, they were among the main beneficiaries of measures designed to assist the disadvantaged, such as *Medibank*, the universal health insurance scheme. A number of changes occurred within mainstream services, such as the appointment of hospital interpreters, the growth of Community Health Centres, and changes in school curricula. The government also funded important research on migrant issues.

---

[8]   *Progress report: Inquiry into the departure of settlers from Australia*/Immigration Advisory Council, Committee on Social Patterns, Commonwealth Immigration Advisory Council, 1972 Professor Jerzy Zubrzycki, CBE, former Professor of sociology, an influential figure in Australian immigration. Chairman of the Australian Ethnic Affairs Council in 1977.

[9]   Preface to A.J. Grassby, *Australia's Decade of Decision, Immigration Reference Paper: 11 October 1973*, (Canberra, AGSP 1973), quoted in John Lack and Jacqueline Templeton, *Bold Experiment*, p. 219, (Oxford, Oxford University Press, 1995).

Two significant measures were taken during what proved to be Whitlam's last year of office: the creation of an experimental ethnic broadcasting service and the passage of the *Racial Discrimination Act* in 1975.

By the late 1970s, multiculturalism had become the basic principle of policies for managing ethnic diversity at both federal and state levels, and enjoyed bipartisan support. All Whitlam's successors (Malcolm Fraser, Liberal 1975–1983; Bob Hawke, Labor 1983–1991; Paul Keating, Labor 1991–1996; and even the current Liberal Prime Minister John Howard, for all his lack of enthusiasm) supported multiculturalism.

After Labor's defeat in 1975, Malcolm Fraser's Liberal government set itself the task of giving shape and structure to multiculturalism in Australia. Building on its predecessor's initiative, the new government created a permanent ethnic broadcasting service, the *Special Broadcasting Service* (SBS). Communities were encouraged to organise themselves to voice their needs. Direct channels of communication with government were opened with the formation and official recognition of *Ethnic Community Councils* (EECs), which formed the *Federation of Ethnic Communities' Councils of Australia* in 1979, a body with official government support and funding which gave ethnic communities a voice at national level. In 1978, the consequential *Galbally Report*[10] on migrant services and programmes recognised that migrants had special needs but unequal access to services and resources, and put major emphasis on the necessity of involving ethnic organisations in the provision of such programmes. It also stressed the importance of the promotion of multicultural education in schools and the community in general. The implementation of Galbally's recommendations proceeded very rapidly. Among the important measures arising from the report were an expanded *Adult Education Programme*, grants-in-aid distributed among a large network of ethnic associations, and the establishment of *Migrant Resource Centres*.

In the early 1980s, public discussion of immigration and settlement policies was to be dominated by two issues: (1) the levels and ethnic composition of the immigration intake, and (2) the implications for Australian national identity and unity. In the late 1970s and early 1980s, Australia had started accepting increasing numbers of Southeast Asian refugees. There was a resurgence of xenophobia and a number of incidents increased hostility against immigration and multiculturalism.

In 1984, a 'great immigration debate' was initiated by historian and writer Geoffrey Blainey, who launched a campaign to reduce immigration, in particular from Asia. In *All for Australia*,[11] he argued that the intake of non-Europeans was testing community tolerance, and the debate suddenly became public, populist and

---

[10] After the name of the chairman of the group of four appointed to report on the post-arrival programmes and services provided to immigrants by Commonwealth and NGOs supported by Commonwealth funding. Official title: *Review of Post-arrival Programs and Services to Migrants.*

[11] Geoffrey Blainey *All for Australia* (Sydney, Methuen Haynes, 1984). Prominent historian, Professor of History at Melbourne University, author of many books, the best known being *The Tyranny of Distance* (1966). He was chairman of various governmental bodies, including the Australia-China Council.

polarised. The opponents of multiculturalism feared that in the context of ethnic and religious conflicts overseas, multiculturalism might entrench cultural differences and create a fertile breeding ground for social strife in Australia. For a time some Liberals (under the leadership of Andrew Peacock) flirted with the idea of taking up Blainey's crusade, but in the end caution prevailed, and the controversy died down.

Hawke's Labor government responded to criticism of the scale and pace of immigration, and a succession of changes were introduced. Bob Hawke accepted the need for a major examination of immigration policy, and appointed the *Committee to Advise on Australia's Immigration Policies* (CAAIP) after the 1987 election. The ensuing *FitzGerald Report* of 1988[12] reaffirmed the principle of a racially non-discriminatory immigration policy, called for the rejection of an immigration debate conducted on racial grounds, and recommended a coherent policy of immigration as it saw mistrust and failing consensus threatening community support for immigration. The report further argued that the official definition of multiculturalism no longer corresponded with the popular concept of it because its original ideals ('justice, equality and esteem') had become obscured by a multiplicity of meanings that now made the term a liability, and it even suggested that the term *multiculturalism* be abandoned.

In 1989, the *Advisory Council on Multicultural Affairs* (ACMA), under Sir James Gobbo, produced a carefully worked *National Agenda for a* Multicultural Australia. It guaranteed cultural rights and social justice to all Australians 'whether [of] Aboriginal, Anglo-Celtic or non-English-speaking background' and wherever they were born, subject to 'an overriding commitment to Australia'. This dispassionate approach was not maintained by the Keating Labor government who flamboyantly declared multicultural Australia to be resource-rich in its ethnic and linguistic diversity, an invaluable asset vital in a sophisticated regional and global economy. But Keating's depreciation of Anglo-Australia and of the links with Britain unsurprisingly annoyed many among the British-descended majority. There was also mounting criticism of the patterns of patronage in multicultural programmes.

The 1996 federal election, which brought back a Liberal-National coalition to power after 13 years of Labor rule, marked a low point for multiculturalism. Although John Howard led the Coalition to victory praising Australian diversity, endorsing multiculturalism, and backing pluralist social policies, the first measures introduced by this government (such as the abolition of the *Office of Multicultural Affairs* and the *Bureau of Immigration, Multicultural and Population Research*) appeared to initiate a swift move away from multicultural policies. This, together with the Prime Minister's persistent dislike for the notion of multiculturalism ('*I'm a one-nation man*'), and his obvious yearning for a return to the monoculturalism of the good old 1950s, encouraged resurgent right-wing racism, as shown both by the rise of Pauline Hanson's populist *One Nation* party and her racially inflammatory

---

¹²   After the name of CAAIP's chairman, Dr. Stephen FitzGerald, The official title was *Immigration: A Commitment to Australia.*

statements against government assistance to Aborigines and the 'swamping' of Australia by Asians.

Yet opinion polls continued to show strong support for multiculturalism. By 1999 the *National Multicultural Advisory Council* (NMAC) in a report entitled *Australian Multiculturalism for a New Century: Towards Inclusiveness*, strongly recommended the strengthening of multiculturalism. It thus signalled a change of emphasis by showing the relevance of diversity to *all* Australians, and emphasising 'its unique Australian character'.

In response to the report, the Government's policy statement, entitled *The New Agenda for Multicultural Australia,* generally acknowledged the NMAC's recommendations. It redefined Australian multiculturalism, created the *Council for Multicultural Australia* (CMA, established in 2000 for an initial period of three years, 'to raise awareness and understanding of Australian multiculturalism'), and announced a plan to put into practice four principles: (1) civic duty, concerned with support for the basic structures and principles of Australian society; (2) mutual respect; (3) social equity, i.e. equality of treatment and opportunity; and (4) productive diversity, to maximise the significant cultural, social and economic dividends arising from the diversity of the Australian population. The 2003 update, entitled *Multicultural Australia: United in Diversity* reaffirmed the Government's commitment to the 1999 *Agenda*, and articulated the strategic directions for multicultural policy for the period 2003–2006, giving emphasis to 'promoting community harmony and the benefits of (Australia's) cultural diversity for all Australians'. It reaffirmed the same principles, under slightly different headings that stressed the importance of the individual's role in the national community, through a revealing alternating use of 'all Australians' and 'each person'. 'Civic duty' still came first under the heading 'Responsibilities for all'; 'mutual respect' became 'respect for each person'; 'social equity' came under 'fairness for each person' in a paragraph calling for a 'social, political and economic life … free from discrimination, including on the ground of race, culture, religion, language, location, gender or place of birth'; 'productive diversity' came under 'benefits for all'.

Equity?

The declared aim of multiculturalism as a national policy has been to facilitate inclusion and full participation of ethnic minorities in the life of the Australian community. Australian multiculturalism has evolved from a merely benevolent stance, consisting essentially in encouraging migrants to retain and celebrate their cultural identity ('spaghetti and polka' multiculturalism), to a stage where its central objective was to achieve 'equitable access' by fighting discrimination, facilitating relations with local, state and federal institutions, promoting transcultural communication etc., to the present position where it is presented primarily as an *individual civic duty* essential to the preservation of the fundamental democratic structures and principles of Australian society.[13] Ethnic minorities' welfare and rights now clearly come second

---

[13]   <http://www.immi.gov.au/multicultural/australia/principles.htm>.

to the fulfilment of their social duties and obligations, as if the question no longer is how Australia can facilitate inclusion but what benefit it can draw from ethnicity.

Ideally, the discourse on multiculturalism producing greater social cohesion in Australian society through the promotion of migrant and Indigenous people's equality of opportunity may be seen as the expression of Australia's egalitarian tradition, with the stress put on the notions of what Australian call 'a fair go'[14] and 'mateship'.[15] As Gary Hardgrave, Citizenship and Multicultural Affairs Minister put it:

> In many ways, it is the Australian ethos of a fair go that allows us to live with not just cultural and language differences, but our different political views, religious devotions and affiliations. And our commitment to a fair go is consistent with our desire to retain the idea of mateship and egalitarian community spirit.[16]

This may give a hint as to why the terms '*affirmative action*', '*positive discrimination*' and the like have been mostly absent form the multicultural debate. By definition, multiculturalist policies have been meant to provide services and programmes geared to set ethnic minorities on their way and facilitate equitable access to economic and social opportunities. In fact, the term 'equity' is the one most often used in relation to multiculturalism, along with 'equal opportunity'. Political parties are well aware that migrant and Indigenous minorities have specific needs that require specific responses. The latter must, however, remain 'fair dinkum',[17] as the popular saying would have it. 'Positive discrimination' and its conspicuous contradiction in terms obviously wouldn't be. On the other hand, Australians are also renowned for their mistrust of 'tall poppies',[18] and receiving 'special treatment' may easily place the recipient in that category. Although it might look more acceptable, the term 'affirmative action' has its own negative connotations, because of its perceived adverse record in the United States. The *Equal Opportunity Commission of South Australia* has made this interesting comment about the federal *Equal Opportunity in the Workplace Act 1999*:[19]

---

[14]   Australian and New Zealand colloquialism: '1. A fair or reasonable course of action: *do you think that's a fair go?* 2. A chance to get on with something without interference or distraction: *the chairperson pleaded for silence and a fair go for the speaker.* 3. Interjection: an appeal for fairness or reason: *fair go mate!*', *Macquarie Concise Dictionary*, The Macquarie Library Pty, Macquarie University, NSW, Third Revised and Updated Edition, 1998 [1982].

[15]   'A code of conduct among men stressing equality and fellowship', Macqurie Concise Dictionary, *ibid.*

[16]   'Central to our welcoming policies – the fair go', *The Australian*, 9 May 2002.

[17]   Australian and New Zealand colloquialism: 'Dinkum: 1. also dinky-di: true, genuine: *dinkum Aussie* 2. Seriously interested in a proposed deal, scheme, etc. 3. Truly'. – 'Fair dinkum: 1. True, genuine, dinkum: *are you fair dinkum?* 2. Interjection, also fair dink, an assertion of genuineness: *it's true, mate, fair dinkum*'; Macqurie Concise Dictionary, *ibid.*

[18]   Conspicuously successful people.

[19]   The principal objects of the Act are 'to promote the principle that employment for women should be dealt with on the basis of merit; and to promote, amongst employers, the elimination of discrimination against, and the provision of equal opportunity for, women in

Affirmative Action: in Australia, means the taking of positive steps to remove barriers that have stopped women from doing some jobs, or from having the Chance to advance to higher levels within organizations. (In the United States, Affirmative Action applies to Afro Americans and ethnic minorities as well as to women. Another difference from Australia is that in the United States, Affirmative Action legislation imposes quotas; that is, organizations have to hire a certain proportion of women, Afro Americans and ethnic minorities) (...). This Act does NOT mean that a certain number of women must be employed. And the Act does Not mean that women must be given jobs over more skilled or better qualified men. This Act DOES mean that if there are barriers which are unfairly blocking the roles women can play, those barriers must be removed.[20]

In other words, awareness of all partners' rights and duties under the existing federal and local legislation and regulations, informed persuasion, consultation, and if that fails lodging complaints with the monitoring bodies or the courts of justice, should be the norm rather than trying to force quotas and reverse discrimination down people's throats.[21] Indeed, when individual institutions decide to implement ethnically inclusive employment policies, they clearly adopt this line of conduct. The Australian National University's *Aboriginal and Torres Strait Islander Employment Strategy Report* of 2002, for instance, proposed an Indigenous employment target equivalent to the percentage of Indigenous people in the total population (2.2 per cent), but to be achieved over a ten-year period, with 'performance indicators and accountability mechanisms (...) to monitor progress and to effectively manage the strategy'.[22] In the same way, the report pointed out that "Equity' does not mean that all staff should be treated the same' and that 'special conditions are sometimes required to deliver equality of opportunity'. While it recommended the creation of 'identified and earmarked positions' this was done with an abundance of precautions:

relation to employment matters; and to foster workplace consultation between employers and employees on issues concerning equal opportunity for women in relation to employment'.

[20]   *Equal Opportunity Commission of South Australia*, 'Australia: The National Situation – Federal Laws', <http://www.eoc.sa.gov.au/eo02.html#fedlaws>.

[21]   Cf. The Equal Opportunity for Women in the Workplace Agency of Western Australia defines its strategy to remove barriers as follows: 'Strategic interventions (...) include networking, career tracking, mentoring and succession planning that pay particular attention to the situation of women. Objective and unbiased recruitment and promotion procedures are vital in attracting and retaining a skilled female workforce (...). Strategies to speed up the advancement of women will need to focus on the following areas: enacting quality laws and rendering complaint procedures more effective; providing family care assistance; revaluing 'feminine' occupations; moving women into more scientific areas; insisting on objective criteria in recruitment; insisting on objective criteria in recruitment and promotion; questioning organisational structures in terms of their efficiency and treatment of both men and women; and raising awareness and changing social attitudes', <http://www.eeo.gov.au/AboyurtEqual Opportunity>.

[22]   The Australian National University. *Aboriginal and Torres Strait Islander Employment Strategy,* Report of the Aboriginal and Torres Strait Islander Employment Working Party, 19 September 2002, pp. 16–17<*http://www.anu.edu.au*>.

references to the federal legislation on racial discrimination and equal employment opportunity, and very strict, unquestionable criteria, of self-identification, knowledge, experience, and understanding of Indigenous cultures.[23]

Beyond considerations of vocabulary, however, the persisting concern for social cohesion must be taken into account. Since World War II there has been an on-going debate about the appropriate form of government assistance to migrants and ethnic minorities. Views have oscillated between two poles: either special services should be 'mainstreamed', with migrants and ethnic minorities treated the same as all other Australians; or, because of their distinctive language and cultural needs, there should be a provision of ethnic specific services. While facilitating the inclusion of ethnic minorities has been the underlying philosophy of Australian multiculturalism, the way it has been implemented has undergone subtle, but inexorable changes towards less social provision from the government, and a return to 'mainstreaming'.

Since the introduction of multicultural policies, a recurring criticism has been that access to social provision should depend upon assimilation into Australian mores and social practices. By extending entitlement to people who are not citizens, and by encouraging them to retain their cultures of origin, critics have argued, the government was abandoning its role as the defender of core values. Elements of this view were formulated by Professor Jerzy Zubrzycki in his 1977 report, *Australia as a Multicultural Society*. Multiculturalism in federal government policy, he thought, should be based firstly on a policy of social cohesion, amplified by concerns for equality and cultural identity. To him, equality meant '*equal access to social resources*'. In other words, social cohesion could only be maintained if social institutions were effectively open to the immigrant communities on the same terms as the long-established populations. At the time of the *Galbally Report* of 1978, however, and for a few years thereafter, the emphasis was on ethnic specific services. From the mid-1980s, government settlement policies began to move away from providing such services, to removing discrimination and dismantling the barriers confronting migrants trying to gain access to mainstream services: the *Access and Equity* policies initiated in 1985 required all government departments to report annually to the prime minister on their efforts to facilitate access to their services by all Australians. But there was no mention of affirmative action. Following the recommendations of the *FitzGerald Report* of 1988, the government further reduced its involvement in the provision of settlement services to migrants – now to be selected for their skills, business experience and relatively high education level, and therefore presumed to need less assistance than immigrants who had arrived under past programmes.

A further shift occurred when the *National Agenda for a Multicultural Australia* of 1989 introduced the notions of 'social justice' and 'productive diversity' as twin bases for multiculturalism. 'Social justice' was defined as 'the right of all Australians to equality of treatment and opportunity, and the removal of barriers of race, ethnicity, culture, religion, language, gender or place of birth' – nothing particularly new. The associated concept of '*productive diversity*' seemed to have been invented to make its

---

[23]   *Vid. ibid.*, pp. 18, Appendix 8, pp. 41–43.

counterpart more palatable. The idea was that cultural difference should be welcomed as an addition to the economic and intellectual capital of the country. In other words, if immigrants were seen as making an immediate cultural contribution of economic value (through their language, knowledge of how to approach a particular foreign market, etc.) then there would be little objection to their accessing the full range of social provision. Nevertheless, it was suggested that access and equity processes should be more firmly institutionalised. As a consequence, in the early 1990s, the DIMIA increasingly focused its settlement services on refugees and new arrivals.

With the coming to power of the Liberal John Howard in 1996, government-funded services were to be restricted mostly to migrants accepted for humanitarian reasons, and due to the 1996 budget deficit, almost immediate swingeing cuts were to be made to government spending, particularly welfare programmes. Thus migrants were identified as a potential source of expenditure reduction. Under the provisions of the *Social Security Legislation Amendment* (*Newly Arrived Resident's Waiting Periods and Other Measures, Act 1997*), immigrants became ineligible to apply for social welfare benefits for the first two years after their arrival. Many previously free and unrestricted government-provided services for migrants, such as those relating to language or employment, were transferred to private agencies, required fees, or were restricted to certain categories of applicants. On the other hand, the government agencies that had managed ethnic social issues were closed down. The effects of these changes were soon apparent and significant hardship was reported in immigrant communities.

With its 1999 report *Australian Multiculturalism for a New Century: Towards Inclusiveness*, the *National Multicultural Advisory Council* attempted to reinvest the multicultural debate with a more inclusive sense of the social sphere. Its chair, Neville Roach, a keen advocate of 'productive diversity', commended the virtues of 'Australian multiculturalism', a philosophy of inclusion relevant to all Australians, whose key-principle was '*Social Justice and Equity*', which meant that:

> all programs should be adjusted to address disadvantage or loss of entitlement arising out of ethnicity or cultural differences, just as other forms of disadvantage suffered by individuals or groups relative to other Australians are addressed.[24]

This, according to the report, required the re-establishment of a body to provide information and policy advice. The government's response, the *New Agenda for a Multicultural Australia*, released in December 1999, preferred the narrowly defined concept of 'Need and Social Equity' to the Council's '*Social Justice and Equity*':

> Need and Social Equity – subject to the eligibility criteria and within budgetary constraints for each program, where an individual or a group has need (including suffering disadvantage or loss of entitlement) arising out of ethnicity or other cultural difference it ought to be addressed, just as all other special needs are addressed within our social infrastructure.[25]

---

[24] *Australian Multiculturalism for a New Century: Towards Inclusiveness*, (National Multicultural Advisory Council, AGPS, 1999), The chair of the NMAC, Neville Roach, was CEO of Fujitsu Australia.

[25] *New Agenda for Multicultural Australia*, AGPS, 1999.

This confirmed the disappearance of '*social justice*' from the multicultural agenda, as part of the government's wider welfare reforms launched in September 1999 – and, in the process, also confirmed that ethnicity was not a factor for specific consideration.[26] However, the 2003 update defining the policy directions for 2003–2006 somewhat revised this position, with the announcement of the adoption of an '*access and equity strategy*', but while the *1999 Agenda* still mentioned '*groups*' in this chapter, the 2003 pronouncement only mentioned 'individuals', and the State's, not the individuals' interest appeared to take first place:

> There is a strong case for better developing even greater levels of government investments in vulnerable individuals. Otherwise, the cost of remedying the problems that stem from social dislocation and lost opportunities for personal advancement will be greater in the years ahead. This is particularly relevant for refugees with a history of torture and trauma and who may have had a chaotic educational background or those who do not have their qualifications recognised in Australia.
>
> In this regard, settlement programs to assist migrants and humanitarian entrants are positive investments that contribute to each person's ability to participate fully in our multicultural society, realise their personal aspirations and benefit Australia (...).[27]

The reference to refugees sounds bitterly ironic and hypocritical since by then, as will be seen below, their numbers had greatly diminished due to the drastic policies implemented in this field in the previous years. Besides, the document did not say just how much money the government was prepared to '*invest*', nor precisely on what and how. What seemed central in the wake of the attacks of 11 September 2001 in the US and 12 October 2002 in Bali was to make sure (1) that 'community harmony and social cohesion' be safeguarded and (2) that 'productive diversity' continued to help Australia forge links with the rest of the world that can deliver increased trade and investment through the expansion of markets and the development of diverse goods and services (...), capitalising on Australia's wealth of cultural and linguistic skills and on the social and business networks of Australia's migrants.[28]

The 'multicultural Australia united in diversity' of the 2003 statement plainly appeared as a dull community of diverse individuals merely connected together by their civic obligations, but whose only true worth for the authorities was their potential economic return.

As will also be developed in more detail below, Indigenous people have equally had to suffer from the effect of John Howard's dogmatic stance on the issue of reconciliation (the word does not appear in the 2003 pronouncement), as he has consistently refused

---

[26]   *Vid.* Andrew Jakubowicz, in James Jupp (ed.), *The Australian People*, (Cambridge, Cambridge University Press, 2001), pp. 854–56.

[27]   *Multicultural Australia: United in Diversity*, AGPS, 2003.

[28]   *Ibid.*

to express a formal apology in the name of the nation for the wrongs inflicted through colonisation. His favourite argument for refusing to do so is that the *current* generation of Australians cannot be blamed for the wrongdoing of *past* generations. Blind to the symbolical importance of a national apology, he has however repeatedly emphasised his preference for what he calls 'practical reconciliation', that is to say concrete measures to improve the appalling conditions Aboriginal communities face in matters such as health, housing, employment, education, etc. But since 1996, the drastic cuts in welfare expenditure and the stress put on obligations rather than rights have led to little improvement, and often regression.

Failings in the Multicultural 'Fair Go'

Migrants and Refugees

While difficulties experienced by migrants are of a very different nature to those of Indigenous people, and far less acute, there remain significant obstacles to their full participation in community and national life. This is particularly true of recent migrants of non-English-speaking backgrounds and of refugees.

A remaining difficulty is the lack of recognition for their skills and qualifications. Official figures for 1999 showed that the proportion of migrants with an overseas qualification recognised in Australia was only 49.4 per cent. Persisting discrimination by employers and private professional associations is also a major barrier. Skilled people arriving in the country are thus often unable to get work, which results in their higher unemployment or underemployment rates. Migrants from non-English speaking countries are all the more disadvantaged as they are less likely to engage in forms of training than the Australian-born or English-speaking migrants. The official literature warns them in advance:

> The Australian labour market is very competitive. Your success in gaining a job depends on prevailing economic conditions, which part of the country you live in or intend to live in, the type of work you are looking for, your skills and recognition thereof, and the unique circumstances of particular industries. Approval to migrate does not guarantee a job. It may take you some time to find work in Australia.[29]

In 2001–2002 there were 9.9 million people in the Australian labour force, of whom 24.6 per cent were born overseas. The labour force participation rate for the overseas-born was 57.9 per cent compared with 67.4 per cent for the native-born. Migrants from mainly English-speaking countries participated in the labour force at a higher rate (64.1 per cent) than those from predominantly non-English speaking backgrounds (54.3 per cent). The unemployment rate for migrants from mainly English-speaking countries (5.5 per cent) was lower than that for people born in Australia (6.5 per cent). The unemployment rate for migrants from mainly English speaking countries was

---

[29]   DIMIA, *Migrant Settlement in Australia: Help for People Settling in Australia, Working in Australia, Employment,* http://www.immi.gov.au/.

also much lower (5.5 per cent) than the unemployment rate among migrants from predominantly non-English speaking backgrounds (8.1 per cent). In 1999, 16.3 per cent of recent adult immigrants relied on government payment for their main source of income.[30] The lack of secure jobs and income in turn brings a number of personal and wider community costs including increased pressure on charities, and poor health due to lack of access to health care services. Recent migrants, particularly people from non-English-speaking backgrounds, can also be disadvantaged due to the inability of families to meet rising education costs, and lack of parental help with homework because of poor English language skills. Close to 20 per cent of new adult migrants spoke English 'Not Well' or 'Not At All' in 2000. They often also face specific burdens such as caring for aged relatives not eligible for pensions, repaying debts for passage money, sending money back home to support relatives, as well as the heavy costs of setting up a new household in a new country. This makes them particularly vulnerable to poverty.

There has also been much recent controversy over the treatment of asylum-seekers (particularly *boat people*) arriving in the country outside the official channels. An obsession that they might be economic scroungers 'misusing' refugee privilege, along with the determination to eradicate 'organised people-smuggling rackets' led the Government to grant them a special *'Temporary Protection Visa'* instead of the full protection visa available to other refugees. This prevents them bringing their families to Australia, and denies access to social security benefits and important settlement services for a period of three years. In addition, the present government has enforced a policy of systematic detention in centres where these asylum-seekers (men, women and children alike) are parked in appalling conditions, for indefinite periods of time (sometimes several years) while their applications for refugee status are being processed. This has been done in direct contravention of a number of international agreements and laws ratified by Australia, not to mention Australia's own family legislation as regards the welfare of children. By definition, refugees are not illegal immigrants, since it is in the nature of the status to arrive without permission, but boat people have been treated as potential criminals. In 1999–2000 and 2000–2001, there was a massive arrival of 4,175 and 4,137 boat people, respectively. By comparison, in 2001, it was estimated that just over 60,000 people were residing in Australia illegally, of whom the two largest groups were the British (10.5 per cent) and Americans (8.6 per cent). Those Anglo-Saxon *'overstayers'* obviously got a better deal and certainly far less media hype than asylum seekers from non-English-speaking countries. Australia's stringent policies have apparently achieved their aim as there were no new arrivals of boat people recorded in 2001–

---

[30]   *Year Book Australia 2003. Characteristics of the Labour Force; Australian Social Tends 2001: Population – Population Growth: Coming to Australia,* <http://www.abs.gov.au/Austats>.

2002 and 2002–2003, and there was a regular decline in the number of illegals held in detention (3,4000 in 2001, 1,282 in 2002 and 1,176 in January 2003).[31]

Indigenous People

While these issues urgently need to be addressed, the most blatant failure of multicultural policies is the enduring gulf of disadvantage between Indigenous and non-Indigenous Australians. This remains true in spite of the existence, since 1990, of the *Aboriginal and Torres Strait Islander Commission* (ATSIC) a Commonwealth statutory authority, set up under the *Aboriginal and Torres Strait Islander Commission Act 1989* to include Indigenous people in the processes of government affecting their lives. The creation of ATSIC came as the latest episode in a history of activism on the part of Indigenous organizations to gain greater autonomy for Aborigines and Torres Strait Islanders. Pressure from such organizations had led to legislation, including the *Aboriginal Councils and Associations Act of 1976*. Reform produced publicly funded Aboriginal service organizations such as medical, legal, and housing services; statutory land councils and government-sponsored national representative bodies. Under the Whitlam government, the *National Aboriginal Consultative Committee* (NACC) was formed to give Indigenous people a collective voice at the national policy level. Both the Consultative Committee, and its successor, the *National Aboriginal Council* (NAC), were weakened by the successive governments' suspicion of power in the hands of Indigenous people. The *National Aboriginal Council* was replaced in turn by ATSIC, which marked an important break with the past since it was not merely an advisory organization but a body with representative functions, albeit constrained by government supervision. It combined the functions of the *National Aboriginal Council* with the *Aboriginal Development Commission*, an organization established in 1980 to make grants and loans for land purchase, housing development, and Indigenous enterprises. Through ATSIC, a system of elected Aboriginal regional councils now provided Indigenous communities with access to decision-making and also funding. ATSIC's main functions thus included the formulation, implementation and monitoring of programmes for the social, cultural and economic advancement of Indigenous people; the protection of sacred sites and the publication of significant cultural material and information; and the collection and publication of statistical information relating to Indigenous people. Most of ATSIC's funding went to Indigenous community organizations for them to provide services to local people in areas such as community development and employment, housing and related infrastructure, legal aid, native title representation, and maintaining Indigenous culture and identity.[32]

In spite of specific programmes and of the process of reconciliation launched just over a decade ago, Australian Indigenous people remain the most substantially

---

[31]   DIMIA, *Australia's Refugee and Immigration Program*, <http://www.immi.gov.au/facts>.

[32]   <http://www.atsic.gov.au>.

disadvantaged section of Australian society. Obviously, but ambiguously, *Reconciliation* is more than just a process for dealing with Aboriginal disadvantage. To many non-Indigenous Australians, it is one of the most significant issues facing the nation: this has been consistently expressed in opinion polls and in the participation of hundreds of thousands of people in the walks and demonstrations across the country. *Reconciliation* is meant to bring about a better understanding of Aboriginal history, culture and society, mutual learning and collaboration, and thereby goes to the heart of questions of national identity. Yet, if there is less overt prejudice and narrow-minded bigotry towards Indigenous people than in the past, non-Indigenous Australians are still reluctant to accept both the conspicuous levels of disadvantage faced by Indigenous people in every area of basic human need, and the immensity of the effort needed to redress these problems.

Health is probably the most emblematic example of the extent of Indigenous deprivation. The current life expectancy of an Indigenous Australian is 51 years, a staggering 26 years less than the national average, and in some areas, it is lower than it was in the early 1900s. By comparison, life expectancies of Indigenous people in New Zealand (59), Canada (65) and the USA (63) are on average a good 11 years higher than those of Indigenous Australians, and this gap keeps on widening according to the *Australian Institute of Health and Welfare* (AIHW).[33] Major causes of death in the Indigenous community are cardiovascular diseases, injury, respiratory disease and endocrine disease (such as diabetes). Substance abuse, including alcohol, hard drug abuse and petrol sniffing, is also a major problem. Substance addiction is often paired with high levels of violence that may affect up to 90 per cent of families in certain communities. Many factors contributing to health disadvantage are specific to Indigenous people, such as poverty, poor infrastructure, the legacy of dispossession and the forcible removal of Indigenous children from their families whose effects include ongoing trauma, lack of self-esteem, lack of parenting skills, and generational disconnection. In 1997, the Minister for Aboriginal Affairs introduced an AUS$ 56 million package of initiatives in response to the *Bringing Them Home* report of the *Inquiry into the Stolen Generations.* The package included programmes to establish family link-up services, boost culture and language programmes, fund new counselling positions and family support programmes, and develop a national oral history project. Unfortunately, many recommendations from the inquiry have not been implemented. As part of the emphasis on '*practical reconciliation*', the Federal Government has developed bilateral *Aboriginal and Torres Strait Islander Health Framework Agreements* with each State and Territory. However, current policy approaches continue to suffer from inadequate funding, red tape and lack of attention to the specific health and cultural needs of Indigenous patients. There is a gross shortage of doctors working in Indigenous health, with an estimated 60 per cent increase required. The number of nurses also needs to increase by 25 per cent according to a recent study by the *Australian Medical Association*. Public expenditure on health services to Indigenous people is increasing, but the Federal Government

---

[33]   <http://www.aihw.gov.au>.

still spends 25 per cent less per capita on Indigenous people than it does on the rest of the population. Overall government health funding is 22 per cent higher than for non-Indigenous people, but the *Australian Medical Association* estimates a needs index of 200 per cent to adequately compensate for health disparities.[34]

Poor housing is also a crucial issue. Major housing problems include overcrowding, the lack of basic infrastructure, maintenance and municipal services. According to a 1999 study by the *Australian Bureau of Statistics*,[35] 23 per cent of dwellings in Indigenous communities required major repairs and a further 10 per cent needed replacing. Furthermore, over 13 per cent of dwellings were of a temporary nature (caravans, tin shacks, cabins, etc.). It found discrimination in access to housing, and a great disparity between Indigenous and non-Indigenous Australians in levels of home ownership. Only 31 per cent of Indigenous households owned or were purchasing their home, compared with 70 per cent for the rest of the population. Indigenous people are particularly vulnerable to homelessness, and received just under 13.5 per cent of all support provided by the *Supported Accommodation Assistance Program* (SAAP), despite constituting only 2 per cent of the population.[36]

Indigenous people are also substantially disadvantaged within the Australian education system. At the time of the 1996 census, nearly 50 per cent of Indigenous people of working age had no formal education at all, and only 2 per cent held a bachelor degree or above, compared with 10 per cent of the non-Indigenous population. According to the *Commonwealth National Indigenous Literacy and Numeracy Strategy* (NIELNS),[37] if participation in early childhood and primary schooling has improved dramatically, Indigenous children are still less likely to get a preschool education, and are well behind in literacy and numeracy skills development before they leave primary school: seven out of ten Indigenous students are below literacy and numeracy standards compared with three out of ten non-Indigenous students. Indigenous children have less access to secondary school in the communities in which they live; they are absent from school two to three times more often than other students; leave school much younger and are less than half as likely to go through to Year 12. Although Year 12 retention rates shifted from single digits thirty years ago to about 32 per cent in 1998, there was a 15 per cent decline in the number of Indigenous students starting university in 2000. If Indigenous participation in university courses increased from under 100 people 30 years ago to some 7,800 in 1998, Indigenous students are far more likely to be doing bridging and basic entry programmes in universities and vocational education and training institutions. They obtain fewer and lower-level education qualifications, and are far less likely to get a job, even when they have the same qualifications as others. Nevertheless, the participation rates of Indigenous 15 to 24-year-olds in vocational education and training have actually reached levels about the same as for other Australians.

---

[34]   <http://www.mja.com.au/public/issues>.
[35]   < http://www.abs.gov.au/Aussats>.
[36]   <http://www.facs.gov.au/saap>.
[37]   <http://www.dest.gov.au/schools/Indigenous/nielns.htm>.

Another important aspect of Indigenous disadvantage is the disproportionately high rates of imprisonment and deaths in custody experienced by Indigenous people. In 1997, the imprisonment rate for Indigenous people was over 14 times that of other adult Australians. The Indigenous prison population has more than doubled since 1988, with an annual growth rate of around 7 per cent, 1.7 times that of the non-Indigenous prison population. Young people are particularly affected – in 1996, 41 per cent of all children held in corrective institutions were Indigenous. Indigenous people removed from their families in childhood were twice as likely as other Indigenous people to have been arrested more than once in the previous five years. Of the 996 deaths in custody that occurred in Australia between 1990 and 2001 18 per cent were Indigenous Australians, a gross disproportion for only 2 per cent of the population. This was no real improvement on the findings of the 1991 report by the *Royal Commission into Deaths in Custody*, which covered the period 1 January 1980 to 31 May 1989. The lack of action taken by all levels of government in response to the *Royal Commission into Aboriginal Deaths in Custody* has allowed gross inequities in the criminal justice system to persist. The rates at which Aboriginal people come into contact with the criminal justice system have not improved, and law and justice remain a crucial area of concern. Furthermore, mandatory sentencing regimes introduced in the Northern Territory and Western Australia – supposedly to curb crime rates but which, in practice target mostly Aborigines – constitute blatant discrimination against Indigenous people and breach the provisions of the *International Covenant on Civil and Political Rights* (ICCPR).[38] For no useful purpose, as a study by the *Australian Institute of Criminology* has found that mandatory sentencing does not substantially reduce the rate of crime and is not the most cost-effective means of doing so.[39]

All these handicaps are obviously linked to the state of destitution a great many Indigenous communities find themselves in. Economic independence and sustainability are crucial to ensuring Indigenous people and communities can live in freedom and dignity, with the opportunity to pursue social, cultural and spiritual goals. The absence of a sound economic base in many Aboriginal communities, particularly for those living in traditional and often remote isolated areas, restricts job opportunities and the capacity for economic independence. Such inequities are increased by poor skill and literacy levels, overwhelming health and housing issues and poverty. Such social and economic forces effectively close the labour market to many Indigenous people. Unemployment rates are two to three times higher among Indigenous communities than among the rest of the population, reaching up to 75 per cent in certain areas. When there are jobs available, they are often community-based, or part of the *Community Development Employment Projects* (CDEP) – not an affirmative action programme, but a 'work for the dole' scheme in which one third of the Indigenous workforce was engaged on a part time basis in 2000. This prompted Geoff Clark, to blame Australia's labour markets and private sector employers for

---

[38]   <http://www.efc.ca/pages/law/un/intl-covenant-civil-political-rights.html>.
[39]   <http://www.aic.gov.au>.

not taking up the challenges of Indigenous employment (they provided only one third of the jobs for Indigenous people), and said if nothing changed he would call for affirmative action laws 'obliging large employers to ensure 2 per cent of their workforce was Indigenous', pointing out that 'to make it a legal obligation [to employ them] may be the only way to ensure Indigenous people will get a fair go'.[40] There have, however, been valuable initiatives and successes. The *Business Development Program* (BDE) offered by ATSIC[41] is an important initiative for promoting economic independence and sustainability by offering alternatives to mainstream financial assistance and a variety of other business development facilities. This is an indispensable condition to the promotion of self-determination, namely, the right to make decisions and control their implementation, shape policies that affect their lives, rather than simply to manage government programmes. The UN *Working Group on Indigenous Peoples* in the draft *Declaration on Indigenous Rights* includes the statement that Indigenous people have the right to self-determination, in accordance with international law. By virtue of this right, they freely determine their relationship with the states in which they live, in a spirit of co-existence with other citizens, and freely pursue their own economic, social, cultural and spiritual development in conditions of freedom and dignity.

But Australia lags behind other countries such as Canada, the United States and New Zealand where debates about autonomy focus on how it can be achieved, and not merely about whether or not autonomy is an option. The current structure of Indigenous affairs in Australia is still determined by non-Indigenous governance arrangements through the so-called 'directed community services model' which vests little or no control in the hands of Indigenous people themselves and continues to treat them as victims, in a very paternalistic way. This is obviously a major flaw in current policy approaches, and while this attitude prevails, many of the underlying causes and processes leading to disadvantage and marginalisation will remain.

This is particularly visible in the issue of land rights and native title. Native title was recognised by the High Court in 1992, in its historic Mabo judgement, as the survival of a system of Indigenous land tenure. It was the recognition of title that pre-existed European settlement, and the acknowledgement that it has survived annexation of lands by the Crown. Native title has done much to acknowledge Indigenous people as the original owners and custodians of lands in different parts of the country. It is not, however, available to all Indigenous people, but only to those who can prove a continuous link with a particular area – which communities driven out of their ancestral lands or children forcibly removed from families cannot. Land rights continue to be an issue of fundamental importance to Indigenous peoples. Amendments made to Commonwealth native title legislation in 1999 were an erosion of the provisions of the *Native Title Act* of 1993. These actions have undermined efforts and policies designed to achieve Indigenous self-determination, economic independence and cultural sustainability. To the UN *Committee on the*

---

40 ATSIC. Media release, 28 June 2000.
41 <http://www.atsic.gov.au/programs/Corporate_Strategies>.

Elimination of Racial Discrimination (CERD), 'the effects of Australia's racially discrimination land practices have endured as an acute impairment of the rights of Australia's Indigenous communities'.[42]

Australia may even be moving further backwards. At the time of completing this chapter, the Howard government had announced its decision to wind up ATSIC, and to have it replaced by an appointed advisory committee of 'distinguished Indigenous Australians', thus depriving the Indigenous community of its most emblematic representative body. In so doing, it had been quick to catch the ball on the bounce after Opposition leader Mark Latham had himself let it be known in March 2004, that should his party win the forthcoming general election, a Labor government would abolish a body 'no longer addressing endemic problems in Indigenous communities', that had 'lost the confidence of much of its own constituency and the wider community', and that had been damaged by the leadership of Geoff Clark.[43]

It must be said that ATSIC always was a controversial organization, the core of criticism bearing on its lack of representativeness (with a low electoral turn out rarely exceeding 40 per cent, and a large number of Indigenous people not even registered on the polling lists), and its structural inability to address the problems of Aboriginal disadvantage (with its subordination to the government hindering its action and causing continuous tension between the representative regional councils at a local level and the administrative arm that reported directly to the Minister in charge of Indigenous affairs). On the other hand, its last chairman, Geoff Clark, was himself a controversial figure. His involvement in a number of scandals,[44] played up by the Murdoch press, did tarnish the credibility of Aboriginal governance in the eyes of conservative critics and others. In any case, all this came as a good excuse for John Howard to declare that 'separate representation, elected representation, for Indigenous people [had] been a failure'. The Minister for Indigenous Affairs, Amanda Vanstone, indicated that the Government would 'make the tough decisions to ensure the interests of Indigenous Australians [were] protected rather than tied to a discredited and dysfunctional Board of Commissioners'. Among those was a plan to devolve Indigenous services and programmes to mainstream departments, the establishment of an appointed – rather than elected – National Indigenous Council and that of a Ministerial Task Force. Such reforms were developed, she explained, 'in response to Indigenous people across Australia expressing concern that they are not getting their money from the current model, centred on ATSIC'.[45]

---

[42]   <http://www.unhchr.ch/html/menu2/6/cerd.htm>.

[43]   ABC Online, *The World Today*, 30 March 2004. 'Labour announces intentions to abolish ATSIC'. <http://www.abc.net.au>.

[44]   Alleged financial torts involving overseas trips and grants where up to AUS$6 million was lost, claims of forgery and other financial mismanagement; accusations of sexual assaults; convictions for obstructing police and riotous behaviour in 2003 which owed him to be suspended from the chairmanship of ATSIC for a year.

[45]   Ministry for Indigenous Affairs, *Labor backflip on ATSIC*, vIPS 028/04, 1 June 2004, <http://www.atsia.gov.au>.

The outcome of the October 2004 election was very uncertain at the time of writing. ATSIC was still in operation but on its last legs as a Senate select committee was running an inquiry on how best to replace it. The bipartisan appreciation of its failure and the decision to get rid of it was a source of great concern to Indigenous people even if, unlike the conservative Coalition in power, Labor's intention was to create a new directly-elected national Indigenous body, which would have, in the words of Mark Latham 'responsibility for providing independent policy research and advocacy, delivering policy advice to government and private sector, and monitoring policy outcomes with a very, very strong sense of accountability and public interest'.[46] Many thought the scrapping of ATSIC was 'setting them back' and 'winding back their cause'. They felt they were being disempowered and gagged yet again as they were left with no effective voice to help shape national policy. Most of all, they were particularly bitter to see the issue being kicked around like a political football to win votes.

Conclusion

Australia has come a long way since the brazen days of British White Australia, unashamed race-based exclusionary policies and remarkable zeal in trying to 'soften the Aboriginal race's dying pillow'. Despite persistent trends in prejudice, and occasional eruptions of narrow-minded bigotry, tolerance, and respect for difference and equal rights are vigorously asserted as basic principles of Australian democracy. Multiculturalism is proudly proclaimed as a civic model. It is not seriously questioned in public discourse despite occasional retreats in multiculturalist positions, as seems to currently be the case.

Currently, however, Australian social relations are experiencing considerable strain. The gap has been widening between an urban, educated community benefiting from globalisation, and a more suburban and rural, poorly educated, inadequately skilled segment whose social needs are rising precisely as social provision is shrinking. Ethnic communities, migrant and Indigenous, fall across this divide. Migrants and Indigenous people in the top urban segments may be proof that multiculturalism does work and that no 'special treatment' is necessary for the bold and hardy. This is certainly the message the present government would like to get across since it justifies its political and economic stance. Thus the present stress put on the individual that conspicuously appears as a deliberate negation of the group or community. For those in neighbourhoods where unemployment is high, where the capacity to support those in need is falling because of the cuts in welfare spending, multiculturalism is useless humbug (not up to expectations from the point of view of ethnic minorities, a waste of money from that of other people). Much ground seems to have been lost under John Howard's leadership. Nevertheless, history seems to show that progress can only be achieved through tactful leadership and skilful governance. Paul Keating's

---

[46]   ABC Online, *The World Today*, 30 March 2004, *ibid.*

forceful promotion of diversity and John Howard's reluctant, nostalgic approach have been found detestable by many, as the pendulum swung too far, too fast, from one extreme to the other. But perhaps finesse is too much to ask for when what is at stake is not merely equity and the legendary 'fair go', but the definition of national identity and the social contract.

Glossary

ACMA:	Advisory Council on Multicultural Affairs
AIHW:	Australian Institute of Health and Welfare
ATSIC:	Aboriginal and Torres Strait Islander Commission
BDE:	Business Development Program
CAAIP:	Committee to Advise on Australia's Immigration Policies
CERD:	Committee on the Elimination of Racial Discrimination
CDEP:	Community Development Employment Projects
CMA:	Council for Multicultural Australia
DIMIA:	Department of Immigration and Multiculturalism and Indigenous Affairs
EECs:	Ethnic Community Councils
HREOC:	[Australian] Human Rights and Equal Opportunity Commission
ICCPR:	International Covenant on Civil and Political Rights
NAC:	National Aboriginal Council
NIELNS:	[Commonwealth] National Indigenous Literacy and Numeracy Strategy
NACC:	National Aboriginal Consultative Committee
NMAC:	National Multicultural Advisory Council
SBS:	Special Broadcasting Service

Chapter 7

Affirmative Action in South Africa: The Limits of History

Beverly Thaver

Introduction

Given the previously discriminatory setting in South Africa, the call for affirmative action from the early 1990s onwards has been intended to give substantive meaning to the principle of equality as contained in the new South African Constitution (1996). In light of this, affirmative action should be seen as an instrument for the achievement of equality, in order to create the conditions for the transformation of wider structural inequities. In other words, it is a means to an end and not an end in itself.[1] It provides the necessary leverage to correct past discriminatory practices and ultimately provide the appropriate conditions for addressing social, political and economic inequalities in the long term.

Any meaningful understanding of affirmative action policies and practices in pursuit of a democratic and equitable South African future would require insight into the complexity of the historical conditions. While some of the conditions had directly buttressed the injustices, others had in subtle ways created semblances of privilege for certain social categories. Thus, confronting the complexity of apartheid's hierarchy of opportunity is a key challenge for the democratic government's affirmative action strategy. In light of this, the article begins with an outline of the historical contingencies under apartheid and the establishment of the legislative instruments under democracy. This sets the backdrop for understanding some of the practices in the economic, public service and higher education sectors in the first decade of democracy. It concludes with a commentary on the emerging themes and accompanying tensions that arise out of the implementation dynamic.

Historical Backdrop

In the first half of the twentieth century, the English and the Afrikaners vied for control over the political economy of South African society. These struggles occurred on the one hand, between the colonizers (English and Afrikaners) and on the other, the colonizers and the colonized. With regard to the former, the banner of

---

[1]   Maphai (1992) makes this point in his studies on affirmative action.

volkskapitalisme provided a galvanizing force for Afrikaner ideological groupings to marshall a systematic affirmative action programme in order to increase their share of agricultural over that of mining (English) capital (O'Meara, 1983). With regard to the latter, the struggles were about determining the levels of political and economic power to be accorded to the colonized population. Following the Native Land Act of 1913 that had effectively limited the size of land to thirteen percent for Africans, there was also the vexed question of political power, which was maintained through the principles of assimilation and separation of Coloured[2] and African persons respectively.[3] Under the Union governments 'Coloured persons were perceived as resembling the European in almost every respect except colour, (and) differs fundamentally from the Native' (Liebenberg, 1981:429). As a consequence of this perceived view, the Coloured category was included on the common voters' roll (Liebenberg, 1981: 430). Effectively therefore, the struggles between the colonizers and the colonized were marked by forms of preferential policies that had favoured sections of the colonized population. On the eve of the Nationalist Party's assumption to power, the practice of affirmative action had started to embed itself in the South African social formation, manifest economically in terms of supporting Afrikaner capital and politically, through the granting of political rights to the Coloured category. It is important to note that this occurred both at the exclusion and further marginalisation of the Black category.

When the National Party came to power in 1948, it consolidated preferential socio-economic and cultural policies for the Afrikaner communities (O'Meara, 1983). Coupled with this, was its policy framework of 'separation of the races', which was underpinned by the principles of scientific racism. The latter argues that there is a biological basis to the intellectual attributes of individuals (aggregated as population groups) which in turn establishes the thesis of racial hierarchies of superiority and inferiority (Anthias & Yuval-Davis, 1992). Despite this set of ideas being scientifically debunked, the National Party nonetheless used these to inform their political and social visioning. It systematically set about formalising some of the social forms of stratification that were already present[4] in South African society during the first half of the twentieth century. To this end, it divided South African society initially into three racial groups through the enactment of legislation (Liebenberg, 1981:484).

---

[2]   The terms Coloured, White, Black and Indian are used in the social classificatory sense, as they were under apartheid. The author does not agree with these apartheid labels, but nevertheless uses them for the sake of clarity and out of necessity to refer to statistics thus defined. The use of upper case denotes official classification as per the Population Registration Act of 1950.

[3]   For example, Coloured persons were included on the common voters' roll while Africans were excluded.

[4]   For example, the Native Regulation Act of 1911 had already standardised Black employment by providing for certain procedures and penalties if Black workers were to be employed.

The Population Registration Act (No. 30 of 1950) classified every person in South Africa within one of three categories, namely, Blacks, Coloureds and Whites.[5] These broad categories also contained sub-divisions. For example, the category, Blacks contained sub-divisions based on language groupings that included Zulu, Xhosa and Sotho-Tswana; while the category Coloured included Cape Coloured, Cape Malay and Indian (Liebenberg, 1981). The Population Registration Act of 1950 in conjunction with a plethora of legislation (some of which included the abolition of political representation for the categories Coloured and Indian)[6] as well as the establishment of homelands[7] for the category Black, were used to regulate the public and private lives of people in South Africa. The establishment of the Nationalist Party government simultaneously ushered in a process that excluded and marginalized the Coloured and Indian categories from previous access to the political system.

For over three decades, South African society was socially engineered along the racial axis of (what subsequently became) four[8] population groupings. These racial cleavages with firm boundaries between them became the basis for structuring the social relations. This was supported by a plethora of legislation that sought to advance the interests and hegemony of the White category. Within the framework of segregated policies and practices, voting rights continued to be granted to those classified as White, whilst the remaining three categories were denied access to the common voters' roll. By the mid-seventies, when resistance began to heighten both internally and externally, the lack of voting rights became a key political issue for the categories to mobilize against the National Party government. At this point, the categories, Coloured, Black and Indian subsumed themselves under the banner of 'black',[9] and coalesced around the lack of voting rights in opposition to-what became defined as-the apartheid government.

By the mid-eighties within the context of increasing resistance by the popular political movements the government embarked on a political reform process that ended with the establishment of a three-chambered parliament for the categories White, Coloured and Indian. For the category Black, designated areas with local authority structures were set up in accordance with the government's Bantustan policy. However,

---

[5] Forthwith these terms will be used in the singular sense as referring to a social category.

[6] Some examples were the Asiatic Laws Amendment Act of 1948 and the Separate Representation of Voters Act No.46 of 1951.

[7] This was an expression of the Bantu Authorities Act of 1951 that had two aims: the abolition of the Native Representative Council and the expansion of self-government in the Black homelands.

[8] From the literature it appears that one of the sub-categories within the broad category 'Coloured', namely, Indian/Asian, assumed the status of a fully formed separate broad category 'Indian/Asian' in order to accommodate those individuals from Indian descent.

[9] I am using a small letter to denote the difference between the term 'black' as an inclusive category to signal the common experience of political marginalization (drawing on some of Stuart Hall's ideas) and subsequent resistance to apartheid (by Black, Coloured and Indian categories) and the apartheid category Black, as restricted to African-language speakers.

minimal participation by Coloured and Indian categories in the three-chambered political process combined with heightened insurrection activities, led to a political compromise between the National Party (representing apartheid) and what was to become the African National Congress-led government (representing democracy).

On the eve of this political settlement, South African society was highly stratified along racial lines. However, these polarised categories masked some of the underlying divisions inherent in them.

Under apartheid, the 'race' discourse was not homogenous[10] insofar as the resistance category 'black' encompassed different hierarchies in the race-based ladder. For example, (arising from the segregated labour policies and residential apartheid favouring the Coloured category in the Western Cape), the category Black was required to apply for permission to live in this province. This ultimately gave the Coloured category preferential status over that of Black in this region of South Africa. Similarly, the three- chambered parliament, although disputed and resisted by significant sections of the Coloured and Indian categories, was nonetheless perceived as a formal system by which these categories could accumulate privilege in relation to the apartheid category Black. Hence, notwithstanding the unity around the lack of common voting rights, the resistance category black was highly fragmented. By contrast, the apartheid category White appeared to be relatively more unified. But again, the categories masked differences especially in relation to class and gender.

What is interesting about this period is that systemically, the 'race' discourse was foregrounded over and above the class and gender discourse on both ends of the black and white racial spectrum. Since the 'race' discourse was institutionally and legally more pronounced the effect was to blur class divisions even though income and wealth disparities were very stark. To this end, South African society was marked by a small upper middle class grouping which was primarily white and a large middle class grouping which, although largely white was also beginning to include small sections of the black population. The latter was primarily from the Indian and Coloured categories, with yet smaller sections from the Black category. Further research is necessary to highlight the nature of wealth accumulation by the different categories under apartheid.

The 'race' and class-based discourse was closely related to a patriarchal discourse within each of the racial categories. Unequal relations, characteristic of patriarchal society, were evident in all sections of the 'ethnic streams'[11] including that of the white category. This was mediated by cultural beliefs and systems specific to different sections of the society. In other words, each 'ethnic stream' had its own cultural way of reproducing patriarchal relations. However, and this is where the difference resides, the social experiences of white and black women had been distinctly different under the apartheid framework.

---

[10]   This means that the category 'race' was not unified.

[11]   The term 'ethnic stream' (drawing on the ideas of Neville Alexander) denotes different language and cultural formations within the two broad categories of black and white.

All Coloured, Black and Indian women lived under the yoke of legislation that excluded them from the public political domain insofar as they were not allowed to exercise their political voting rights. For Black women, this political constraint was further compounded by the overt and at times, brutal forms in which segregated policies were implemented. For example, Black women (as well as Black men) were required by law to carry passes when they entered areas, designated for the Coloured and Indian categories. On the other hand, white women were allowed to vote and had relatively more freedom of movement in the public domain. In a nutshell, white- as compared to black women were not bound by the same discriminatory legislation under the apartheid government. Thus, women experienced multiple forms of advantage and disadvantage relative to the hierarchies of opportunity structurally embedded in each of the social categories.

Therefore, in apartheid society there was a complex intersection of race, class and gender. It is important to note that there was a subordinate 'place' for black men and women across the class spectrum in South African society, as present in both the public and the private domains. While there was a subordinate place for white women in relation to their white male counterparts, they were however, accorded higher status over that of black men and black women on the basis of their legislative and institutional advantage. For example, white women had been able to vote since the 1930s, whereas black women and men were afforded the vote six decades later.

These discriminatory and exploitative factors had accumulated over time to the extent that by the early 1990s, South African society was highly stratified along race, class and gender lines with deeply embedded structural inequalities inherited from past discriminatory laws (Department of Labour, 2001:3). These were the historical conditions that necessitated the formulation of a systematic affirmative action strategy (Sachs, 199–) for the politically marginalized categories. Against this backdrop, the new democratic government after 1994 with its mandate to redress the historical imbalances in the interest of creating a non-discriminatory and equitable society established the appropriate legislative and political instruments. This will now be addressed.

The Building of a South African Democracy

The New South African Constitution

In the transitional period, the new government formulated several legal instruments as a foundation from which a democratic society could be built. In this regard, the Constitution of the Republic of South Africa (Act 108 of 1996) became the principle platform to launch the different policy initiatives. One element that articulates directly with affirmative action refers to the equality provision (Section 9 of the Bill of Rights), which asserts that no one may be discriminated against on the basis of race. It is worthwhile to note that constitutionally, there is a tension between the non-discrimination clause and that of affirmative action. A second element refers to the establishment of mechanisms and structures required for the implementation of the democratic principles, one of which is that of affirmative action. Thus, the

Constitution provided the backdrop for the promulgation of further legislation applicable to the different social sectors.

Legislation and Regulation

Several new legislative instruments were introduced to redress the structural inequities in various sectors of South African society. Much of the ideas that have subsequently informed the final legislative pieces were generated through the production of White Papers. For example, in the higher education sector, the paper, *A Programme for the Transformation of Higher Education 1997*, drives the reform process. The public service sector is steered by two papers, namely, the *Transformation of the Public Service, 1998* and *Affirmative Action in the Public Service, 1998*. Unlike that of higher education, the public service has a designated affirmative action set of guidelines for the implementation of affirmative action in the bureaucracy. Nonetheless, the one piece of legislation that is directly related to affirmative action and applicable to all sectors, refers to the Employment Equity Act No. 55 of 1998.

The Employment Equity Act, 1998

The overall aim of the Employment Equity Act (EEA), 1998 is to achieve equitable representation in all occupational categories and levels in the workforce. It seeks to 'eliminate unfair discrimination through the implementation of affirmative action measures for people from designated groups such as black[12] people, women (black and white, *my emphasis*) and the disabled (black and white, *my emphasis*)'. The EEA (1998) has a strong equality principle insofar as it is intended to ensure that suitably qualified people from designated groups have equal employment opportunities and are equitably represented in all occupational categories and levels in the workforce (EEA, 1998, Section 2).

The EEA (1998) goes further to specify affirmative action measures that should be implemented in the workplace. These include the 'identification and elimination of barriers; the promotion of diversity; reasonable accommodation and, the retention, development and training of people from designated groups including skills development' (EEA, 1998, Section 15). The measures 'include preferential treatment and numerical goals, but exclude quotas' (EEA, 1998, Section 15). It is important to note that the measure 'preferential treatment' is not intended to advantage one, over another social category. Instead, it signals the need to include historically discriminated categories (with the attendant training strategies), into the overall employment pool. In this way, the relevant conditions are created for the implementation of equity in the workplace. A further point of note is that the measures provide leeway for employers to define goals for themselves rather than have quotas imposed centrally by the government.

Employers are also bound by several procedures some of which include consultation with employees and trade unions; an analysis of their employment

---

[12]   Interestingly, the term 'black' as used in the EEA (1998), is drawn from the political – resistance category 'black' (see Note 9).

policies, practices, procedures and the working environment in order to identify any employment barriers which adversely affect people from designated groups; and the preparation of Employment Equity Plans. These should include objectives, measures to be implemented, and numerical goals for equitable representation, timeframes, monitoring and evaluation. Finally, employers should ensure the overall organisation, management and reporting of plans (EEA, 1998, Section 20). It also establishes a Commission for Employment Equity,[13] which seeks to advise the Minister on codes of good practice, regulations and policy pertaining to the Employment Equity Act. It is important to note that the Commission also has powers to make awards to high achieving employers, dialogue with the broader public and conduct research on relevant aspects pertaining to the application of the Employment Equity Act.

From the above it is clear that the ultimate aim of the EEA (1998) is to give effect to the principles of South Africa's constitutional democracy. It sets the framework for creating the social conditions that would ensure fairness and equality within the workplace against a backdrop of deep-rooted structural inequalities that had marked South Africa under the apartheid era. It is important to note that the EEA (1998) complements other pieces of legislation that also seek to redress the past inequities. Some of these include specific Acts targeting labour, namely the Labour Relations Act of 1995 and the Basic Conditions of Employment Act 1997. There is also the generic Promotion of Equality and Prevention of Unfair Discrimination Act of 2000 that has as a focus the prevention of discrimination. The overall aim of this Act is to prevent and prohibit unfair discrimination and harassment, to promote equality and eliminate unfair discrimination. In terms of its main features, it prohibits unfair discrimination on the basis of 'race', gender and disability.

While there are sector specific policy texts that address affirmative action, such as the White Paper on Affirmative Action in the Public Service, the EEA (1998) has become the key lever for addressing affirmative action across the various sectors. Effectively, with the establishment of the EEA, that is from 1998 onwards, much of the discourse on affirmative action has been replaced with that of 'equity'. For example, in the higher education policy texts, the idea of 'equity' is foregrounded over that of 'affirmative action'. There are indications to suggest that the idea of 'equity' is assuming the form of a principle underpinning some of the transformation practices in South Africa. This complexity is also compounded by the practice of using equity interchangeably with that of affirmative action.

Compliance and Enforcement of Affirmative Action/Equity Policies: Employment Equity Reports

Having outlined the legislative context for the post 1994 period, the question to be posed at this stage is the extent to which employment equity has been implemented, or, put another way, the extent to which there has been compliance on the part of the

---

[13] This is a statutory body established in terms of Section 28 of the Employment Equity Act, 1998.

Race and Inequality

different sectors. To answer this question, the following section draws on aspects of a data set of workforce profiles compiled by the Department of Labour's Commission for Employment Equity for the period 1999–2001. Before proceeding to address the data, it is important to provide a demographic profile of South Africa in order to contextualise the data set and the emerging themes.

The total population of South Africa distributed across the population groups (as still defined by the Population Registration Act of 1950) is approximately 43.7 million in total (Statistics SA, 2000, cited in the Department of Labour Report 2002). In terms of the breakdown, Africans account for 33.9 million; Coloureds 3.8; Indians 1.0 and Whites 4.5 million. Of this total population, the economically active population constitutes approximately just over 16 million, with figures of 10.3 and 5.8 million for the employed and unemployed respectively (Statistics SA, cited in SA Survey 2000/2001). It is important to note that Africans account for over 90 per cent of those who are unemployed. This sets the backdrop for identifying the patterns from the data set.

As identified earlier, employers with more than fifty employees are legally required to submit Equity Plans to the Department of Labour. However, in terms of the regulations as promulgated by the Minister of Labour in December 1999, all employers with more than one hundred and fifty employees were required to report via the Commission for Employment Equity, to the Department of Labour on the status of their workforce profiles (Department of Labour 2002). In its first report, this Commission was able to glean data for just over eight thousand employers, with a total workforce of approximately 3.3 million for different occupational categories. The following section addresses itself to some of the statistics and patterns emerging from the data.

Table 1 provides an occupational level breakdown for the approximately 3.3 million employees as per the Employment Equity Reports (Department of Labour, 2002). It outlines the profiles in terms of the occupational categories of management (top, senior and professionally qualified); skilled and junior management (including supervisor profile); semi- skilled; unskilled and non-permanent.

Table 1   **A breakdown of occupational categories as it relates to gender and 'race' in South Africa**

Occupational Level		Men				Women				Total	
		Black		White		Black		White			
Management	Top	2,362	10%	17,766	77%	480	2%	2,399	10%	23,007	100%
	Senior	6,829	14%	31,275	65%	2,036	4%	8,064	17%	48,204	100%
	Mid (profess-ional)	48,008	19%	94,982	38%	62,484	25%	45,858	18%	251,332	100%
Skilled & technically qualified		274,031	36%	186,670	24%	159,013	21%	148,079	19%	767,793	100%
Semi-skilled		581,868	53%	64,495	6%	323,310	30%	122,696	11%	1,092,369	100%
Unskilled		627,828	70%	10,110	1%	247,393	28%	7,803	1%	893,134	100%
Other		128,995	43%	22,886	8%	122,216	41%	26,848	9%	300,945	100%
Total		1,669,921	50%	428,184	13%	916,932	27%	361,747	11%	3,376,784	100%

Source: Department of Labour, 2002

A comment on some of the patterns from the data

As shown in Table 1, 87 per cent of the positions in top management are held by white men and white women (77 per cent and 10 per cent respectively); while black men and black women together hold 12 per cent (10 per cent and 2 per cent respectively). In the senior management category, 82 per cent of the positions are shared between white men (65 per cent) and white women (17 per cent), while 18 per cent are shared between black men (14 per cent) and black women (4 per cent). In the professional category, there is a large decline (from the earlier occupational levels) in the representation of whites. For example, white men (38 per cent) and white women (18 per cent) together constitute 56 per cent. Similarly, there is an increase in the professional level in the representation of black men and black women. However, what is quite interesting from the above data is that black women (25 per cent) surpass both black men (19 per cent) as well as white women who come in at 18 per cent, in the professional category.

In the skilled category, black men (36 per cent) tend to dominate, followed by white men (24 per cent), with white and black women coming in at 21 per cent and 19 per cent respectively. What is interesting about this category is that there is an almost similar pattern of representation between black (21 per cent) and white women (19 per cent).

In terms of the semi and un-skilled categories, the previous pattern of white representation is inverted in these occupational categories, with black men taking the lead over that of white men. This pattern is replicated for black women. It is important to note that this reflects the historically racial and gendered division of labour.

Affirmative Action and the Economy

Given the legacy of economic marginalisation and disproportionate racial inequalities, the economic sector is, without doubt, the area where change has to be of paramount importance. Areas of the economy requiring concentrated and focused strategies include that of land redistribution, adequate housing, poverty alleviation, the creation of employment opportunities and the raising of wage levels commensurate with inflation. In other words, the quality of life has to be raised for all those sections of society, but more specifically for those below the poverty datum line. Since the mid-1990s, the state has developed strategies (such as the Reconstruction and Development Programme and the Growth, Employment and Redistribution Strategy) that seek to influence the transformation of the economy. One of the key questions is the level of articulation between processes in the economy and that of affirmative action policies and practices. In this regard, there are different levels at which the debate on affirmative action takes place.

One level at which the debate on affirmative action takes place is in terms of the South African government's approach to black economic empowerment of which one consequence has been the establishment of the Black Economic Empowerment

(BEE) Commission. Central to the BEE Commission are areas of economic redress and the need for putting 'socio-economic transformation' into context (Mbabane, 2003). Subsequent to the establishment of the Commission, the government released a strategy document on black economic empowerment, which aims to increase the number of black people who manage, own and control South Africa's economy. A further key dimension of the BEE is the reduction of the income-gap between the wealthy and poor sections of society (Mbabane, 2003). To this end, the strategy seeks to expand the base of beneficiaries of black empowerment beyond that of a small black elite, through the advancement of the interests of small and medium sized enterprises (Department of Trade and Industry, 2003). To enhance this sector, various strategies are posited such as 'financing and incentives focused on small and medium sized enterprises, on employee share ownership, the transformation of pension funds and the use of state-owned enterprises to vest assets in a larger pool' (Department of Trade and Industry, 2003).

From the above it is clear that the empowerment process as driven by the government, is viewed as one strategy to mobilize and accelerate the economic transformation agenda. The intention is that this will have a ripple effect on society in general.

At another level, there is a 'black advancement' perspective, which argues that the wealth in the macro economic domain has to reflect the demography of the society. In light of this, the argument is that addressing the racial imbalances of the economy is directly related to a sustainable political and social environment (Surve, 2003). This perspective suggests that the replacement of white captains of industry with black captains of industry, of itself ushers in a transformation of society. In this sense, transformation implies the deracialisation of capital accumulation.

A key principle underpinning the above approach is the empowerment of black individuals who own large capital bases. In the mid-1990s several black-led empowerment initiatives were established at different levels of the economy. Three such examples are New Africa Investments Limited, Real Africa Investments Limited and Sekunjalo[14] located within the business sectors. These initiatives were intended to establish control in the macro-economic domain, through the accumulation of large assets by black individuals. What is interesting about these big capital initiatives is that it cuts through the racial stereotype and intellectual bifurcation that advances the view that black business must be small (Surve, 2003) while white business has access to big capital. Interestingly, several black individuals, especially those who had been active in the liberation and trade union movement sectors during apartheid, are actively taking up the cudgels of these (big) capital accumulation initiatives. For example, it is noted that several of the Sekunjalo partners had been active in political structures nationally (Surve, 2003). This is generating much debate (see Bond, 2000) on the extent to which black economic empowerment initiatives are benefiting a very small section of the black population.

---

[14] The word, Sekunjalo means, 'now is the time'. This was the African National Congress's rallying song for the democratic elections in 1994.

From the above, the BEE initiatives have two strands. While the black economic empowerment and advancement initiatives in the private (business) sector focuses more on black advancement of individuals located at the apex of society, the black economic empowerment strategy, emerging from the government, has as a focus and priority, the consolidation of the middle section of society (Department of Trade and Industry, 2003). The extent to which all of this can be implemented is of course a huge challenge. As noted by Mbabane (2003), the scorecard approach-which weights the extent that businesses invest in black empowerment, some of which include the number of black persons in management and skills development, means that companies can choose where to make their investment. In the words of Mbabane (2003), 'there is an inherent risk of being reductionist and quantitative, with companies strategizing around the speediest ways to calculate points and in so doing only take on those targets that are less challenging'.

Affirmative Action and the Public Service

Historically, the public service, much like other sectors in South Africa, was structured as an instrument of the apartheid state. In this regard it was rooted in discriminatory practices, with a racially polarized occupational structure (Hugo, 1989; Reddy & Choudree, 1994). In order to redress the inequalities inherent in the sector, the government embarked on a series of measures. For example, the Public Service Staff Code (1994) included a special provision for affirmative action, which became the precursor to the subsequent *White Paper on Affirmative Action in the Public Service* (1998). These measures were intended to accelerate the disappearance of the deficiencies that had been identified in the system, of which a key one had been that of a racialised occupational structure. It is important to state that these measures draw their sustenance from the Constitution (1996), in particular from the principle that articulates directly with affirmative action in the public service, which reads as follows:

> That public administration must be broadly representative of the South African people, with employment and personnel practices based on ability, objectivity, fairness and the need to redress the imbalances of the past (White Paper, 1998).

The White Paper of 1998 provides a framework within which each department and provincial administration will develop its own affirmative action programmes and be held accountable for the results. In light of this, targets for the attainment of representivity in the public service had been established. For example, it was stated that by the year 2000, that departments should be 50 per cent black at management level and that at least 30 per cent of new recruits to the middle and management level should be women (White Paper, 1998).

The question that should be asked at this point is what is the extent of the changes? Indications are that the required target of 50 per cent black at the management level is being met. In a study conducted by the Public Service Commission (2000) on the extent of representivity in the public service, it was found that out of a total of 2319 employees, 1264 were black, representing just over 54 per cent. However, the finding for women's representivity in the management and senior management echelons was not very positive. Out of a total of 2319 employees, 424 were women, representing 18 per cent, which is below the required target of 30 per cent. What is interesting about this data is that it is not disaggregated in ways that could show more meaningfully the correlation of multiple factors such as race, gender and occupational levels. For example, it is unclear as to whether the figure of 54 per cent for black representation also includes black individuals at the senior management level. This could partially explain the qualitative finding of a subsequent report in which it was noted that white people still dominate top managerial levels while black people remain clustered at the lower levels (Public Service Commission, 2002:31).

Affirmative Action and Higher Education

Historically, the landscape of higher education in South Africa comprised of thirty-six institutions, spread across two institutional types, namely, universities (twenty-one) and technikons (fifteen). It was a fragmented system structured by the apartheid state for the four population groups (Black, Coloured, Indian and White). Much like the education sector in general, higher education was designed to reproduce apartheid-type social relations of white superiority and black inferiority. This was reflected in the architecture of the fragmented system which, geographically, situated institutions 'inside' their segregated locales. The historically white and black institutions were mainly located in urban, peri-urban and rural areas, respectively. These provided specific functions for the respective communities. Overall the thirty-six institutions, systemically, were in the service of the apartheid political and social project. This was also reflected in the enrolment patterns as well as staffing profiles in these institutions.

Historically black institutions had a preponderance of students that closely reflected the 'ethnic stream' of the institution. For example, the University of the Western Cape was legally obliged to accept only Coloured students; University of Durban-Westville, Indian students; Fort Hare, African-speaking[15] students; University of Cape Town, white students and so forth. While the staffing profiles were also structured along these 'ethnic streams', there was also a preponderance of white academic staff at historically black institutions, concentrated especially in senior-executive level positions. After the mid-1990s the government embarked on a series of policy initiatives in order to transform a system that bore the imprints of apartheid.

The transformation agenda was taken up in 1997, with the introduction of the White Paper called *A Programme for the Transformation of Higher Education.* Premised on the principles of redress and equity, it provided a framework for the

---

[15]   For example, Xhosa and Sotho-Tswana speaking persons.

transformation of the system in South Africa, culminating in the Higher Education Act of 1997 and subsequently the National Plan for Higher Education of 2001. In terms of equity, the imperatives are to address representivity at the level of both students and staff. To what extent have these been met?

The late 1990s were marked by an increase in the number of black student enrolments at higher education institutions. For example, in 1993, on an enrolment total of just under half a million (473 000) the racial distribution was 40 per cent Black, 13 per cent Coloured and Indian and, 47 per cent White. In 1999, out of just over half a million (564, 000), the proportion of Black students was 59 per cent, Coloured and Indian 12 per cent and, 29 per cent White (Council for Higher Education, 2000/1). The important point for the purpose of this paper is that the black enrolments were not bound to institutions from their previously segregated locales, but instead went beyond their immediate locales, into previously white institutions. It may be worthwhile noting that this may not be a direct result of affirmative action policies but more a marker of the opening-up of public spaces across the previously racialised boundaries after 1994. For example, after 1994 students were able to exercise individual choice as to their selection of universities. Nonetheless, black student enrolment is certainly a feature of the first decade of democracy, a pattern though, that is not replicated at the level of academic staff.

Changes in the staffing profiles have not been commensurate with that of the student body. *The White Paper on A Programme for the Transformation of Higher Education (1997)* states that there are indefensible imbalances in the ratios of black and female staff compared to whites and males (White Paper, 1997:8). The redress of academic staff (especially at the level of permanent employment status) is a recurring issue in subsequent policy texts and initiatives such as the Size and Shape Report 2000/1 and the National Plan for Higher Education 2001. This is against a backdrop of an academic staff profile for 1999 that had approximately 80 per cent white representation in the entire system (Council for Higher Education 2000/1). The under-representation of black academics is similarly replicated for that of women. Women are under-represented in the overall system and more specifically in the higher ranks as well as in areas that traditionally are not service-related positions. From this, it is clear that affirmative action in relation to the transformation of the staffing profiles at certain institutions has not been fully optimised. Indications are that affirmative action in relation to staffing is also being compromised by the merger processes currently underway. In seeking to reduce the number of higher education institutions from 36 to 22, through merging some of the institutions (for example, in the Western Cape, two historically black and white technikons) large amounts of financial and human resources are being absorbed by the restructuring process. A key question for further research is the extent to which the merger process is promoting the transformation of staff profiles in ways that are commensurate with the new democracy.

Themes Emerging from the Data

From the above discussion several themes related to the policy and practices of affirmative action/equity are emerging. The following section identifies and analyses some of these themes.

There continues to be an over representation of white males in the middle to senior level occupational categories

Given the designated categories implicit in the EEA (1998), the continuing pattern of over-representation of white individuals (men and women) in the top and senior management categories has to be questioned. In light of this, what factors harness this phenomenon?

One of the key factors that will continue to entrench this approach is the view that 'there is a limited pool of suitably qualified black persons' from which to recruit. This approach, which argues for the lack of appropriate skills, arises in the higher education sector but can similarly be applied to other sectors. This supply and demand approach basically makes a case for the fact that there are too few skilled black persons for senior-level positions in institutions. Furthermore, market forces are identified as impacting negatively insofar as companies tend to 'poach' senior level individuals by offering them more attractive packages.

Other complex factors that hamper the mobility of black persons into top and senior positions are that of inadequate succession planning (Department of Labour, 2002). This means that few black persons and women are accorded the opportunity to be trained and groomed inside companies. The complexity of succession could also be mediated by the familial factors. For example, in certain instances the succession line in private companies is reserved for family members. Given the legacy of wealth distribution in South Africa, it is very likely that chief executive officers are from white families. Effectively therefore, this process would militate against any non-family member entering the succession line.

Coupled with familial barriers, is the common practice for companies to headhunt suitable candidates internationally. Inadequate succession planning is also related to the fact that companies seek to make their investment in human resources at the senior level competitive with global processes. Effectively, their recruitment and selection processes take them beyond the national borders, to international countries, in their search for the right candidate (*Sunday Times*, March 2003).

The aforementioned practices beg two questions. On the one hand, what is the extent of public accountability expected of private companies operating in South Africa? Related to this, is the extent to which public legislation could substantively influence the strategic positioning of private companies. Although all companies operating in South Africa with more than fifty employees are bound by the legislation, the former continue to have a great deal of leeway around strategic appointments at the senior level.

Beneficiaries: Given the hierarchy of opportunities under apartheid, who should benefit from affirmative action?

Another aspect of implementing affirmative action pertains to the complex implementation tension arising from the 'designated group' that should benefit from the appointment process. This tension occurs around levels of entitlement.

As identified at the start of this article, the category black is not a homogeneous one insofar as it embraces multiple ethnic streams, each of which have been subject to different policies and legislative frameworks under apartheid. As identified earlier, the Coloured category was given preferential treatment in employment policies in the Western Cape.

Furthermore, the National Party's segregated policies and subsequent three-chambered reform process undoubtedly created a formal system, by which Coloured and Indian categories could potentially accrue relative privilege in relation to Black.[16] In other words, on average, the Coloured and Indian categories have had more economic and social leverage to access resources over and above those classified as Black under apartheid.[17]

Furthermore, some of the preferential policies afforded to Coloured and Indian under apartheid fuels the growing perception that for the purposes of affirmative action, the designated group black (as outlined in the EEA, 1998) in effect refers to Black/African.[18] As a consequence, there is a growing perception that preferential treatment should be accorded to Black/African over and above that of Coloured, a phenomenon that has generated an enormous amount of angst among the Coloured category. Similarly, there is also a growing view that those from the Indian stream within the designated group black have had relative privilege during the apartheid period and as such are not entitled to benefits (as Black/African) under affirmative action practices. Thus, there is a growing perception that these 'ethnic streams' should not be accorded the same entitlement under affirmative action practices, as Black/Africans. The affirmative action discourse has in effect splintered the earlier resistance category black. As a result, African geographical, linguistic and cultural phenomena have been invoked to denote those who are Black/African. This process signals the return to the original apartheid category Black, as demarcated from that of Coloured and Indian. As a result, a plethora of tensions have been ushered in around notions of entitlement with a pecking order of Black/African, Coloured and Indian categories.

---

[16] Further research could highlight the extent to which both Coloured and Indian categories have utilized this as a point of accumulation.

[17] Clearly, this contributed to further economic stratification within the Coloured category, however, for the purpose of this paper, the issue is really the ways in which the different population groups (in a generic sense) experienced the effects of the apartheid policies.

[18] From the mid 1990s onwards, as the discourse of affirmative action and employment equity started to embed itself in South African society, the term 'Black' increasingly started to denote that of African and started to be used interchangeably as Black/African.

The entitlement tension is also evident in terms of the designated group that refers to 'women'. Similarly, as is the case with the category black, the category women is not homogeneous insofar as it embraces other social categories such as class and in the South African context, that of 'race'. The old apartheid categories (of Coloured, Indian and Black) have fragmented the solidarity of those women originally subsumed under the political resistance category black.

Given the legacy of institutionalized racism, there exist hierarchies of beneficiaries as noted earlier, which in turn should afford different forms of entitlement. Consequently, the perception is that, in theory in terms of affirmative action policy, Black/African women have a higher form of entitlement to that of the other 'ethnic streams' (Coloured and Indian). However, in practice what tends to happen in certain employment sectors is that white women are favoured over and above that of black women and black men. As evident from Table 1, in the top-management category, the representation of white women is on par with that of black men; while in the senior-management category, white women take the lead; and then trail black men by a small percentage in the mid-professional category. This may suggest that white women have higher levels of skills for this occupational category. It is important to note that this situation has arisen from the legacy in which the apartheid state had afforded white women political opportunities, which gave them the leverage to access resources. In other words, white women were legally entitled to employment opportunities that were not applicable to black men and least of all, black women. Consequently, 'patriarchy did limit the opportunities for all women in South Africa, (but) apartheid and poverty worsened the situation for black women, elevating the status of white women in relation to black women' (Msimang, 2001). This historical advantage gives white women the edge over that of black men and women in certain categories of jobs.

These conditions have generated a set of challenges for the implementation of affirmative action in South Africa. In terms of recruitment and retention of staff as well as the distribution of resources (for example, in terms of small business empowerment initiatives) there is a political issue at stake as to who are the legitimate beneficiaries of affirmative action. For example, should white women take preference over black men, or, inversely should black women be accorded higher selection status to both white women and black men? To complicate matters even more, should a particular ethnic stream within the black category, have higher political status to that of the other 'streams'? Clearly, these tensions are manifest in concentrated forms on both inter-and intra-race and gendered levels.

Legal Challenges to Affirmative Action

In certain instances the tensions have resulted in legal challenges to the principles of affirmative action. From this perspective, there have been instances in which white women have instituted legal cases for being discriminated against on the basis of both race and gender under a company's affirmative action policy (Butterworth's, 2000). Briefly stated, two women from Eskom, who had applied on two occasions for the same advertised posts within their unit, were not appointed to the positions 'despite the fact that Eskom had acknowledged that they had the necessary work experience and skills' (Butterworths, 2000). On filing a grievance against the company, they were informed that the posts contained the statement 'this position will be filled in line with Eskom's stance on affirmative action policy' (Butterworths, 2000). Consequently, the union acting on behalf of the women entered into an arbitration process with Eskom. After detailed consideration of the evidence, which had included reports on Eskom's affirmative action framework and policies, the arbitrator ruled in favour of Eskom (Butterworths, 2000), on the basis that:

> Eskom had demonstrated that it has adopted an aggressive approach to rectifying the injustices of the past. It has adopted and applied employment equity practices and an affirmative action policy in a rational and consistent manner.

It is also important to note that there is a tension between the implementation of affirmative action/equity policies as it gets interpreted in the context of the new Constitution. There have been several cases where arguments have been made for certain employment practices that run against the grain of the Constitutional principle of non-discrimination (Maykuth, 1997). In this vein, the promotion of those from the designated groups is viewed as being against the non-discrimination clause in the South African Constitution and in effect constitutes unfair labour practices.

All of the above has occurred in the context of heated debates around legal challenges to affirmative action. On the one hand, there is a 'reverse discrimination' argument, which states that 'sex, religion and race are morally irrelevant characteristics' used to arbitrarily discriminate against individuals. In other words, the differences in persons have been based on immoral grounds. Consequently, it is argued that it is not morally permissible to take into account the same (irrelevant) characteristics in order to compensate for the initial act of discrimination (Gross, 1977, cited in Faundez, 1994: 4). It is important to note that advocates of this perspective are not opposed to compensation for the victims of discrimination but merely argue for a different form of compensation (Gross, 1977 cited in Faundez, 1995). On the other hand, there are those who defend affirmative action and the need for corrective action on the grounds 'that the differential treatment is not based on irrelevant characteristics, but on the fact that members of a group were treated unfairly because of their race' (Nickel, 1977, cited in Faundez, 1994).

Implementation Tensions and Challenges

In South Africa, affirmative action practices tend to be fraught with tension regarding the best candidate for the job. Much of the debate is clouded by a bifurcation approach, which implies that the appointment of black and white individuals brings, respectively, a low and high standard (Thaver, 2003). In fact, very bluntly stated, the issue of quality is invoked which results in the black candidate perceived to be an equity appointment, with the denotation of tokenism while the white candidate is viewed to be one of merit with the denotation of excellence. This has generated much debate and tension around the extent to which equity practices are compromising issues of standards and quality.

The employment sector is thus faced with several challenges, one of which is intellectual, regarding the conceptualisation of what constitutes an equity appointment. Debates within the recruitment processes have ushered in a plethora of binaries some of which include that of equity/merit; capacity building/professional development;[19] lack of quality/excellence. What happens is that the left and right sides of the binary refer respectively to black and white individuals suggesting that quality/high standards are located in the former and lack of quality/low standards, in the latter. In other words, there is a racial conflation between on the one hand, notions of quality and whiteness; and on the other, capacity building and blackness. This framework, arising from the scientific racism model as outlined at the start of this paper, has its own set of racial stereotypes that harness this type of thinking. Further research is needed to explore the meanings of excellence as being historically embedded within an apartheid racialised structure. A diverse and robust democracy requires that issues of excellence, standards and competencies be unhooked from a 'race'-paradigm. In this way, these qualities are judged on their own terms rather than on racial or even gender grounds.

Conclusion

This article began by mapping the historical context of apartheid as a backdrop for discussing the South African case for affirmative action/equity. The discussion was limited to compliance at the level of labour generally (as reflected in the Commission's Equity Reports) and three broad social sectors. It is clear from the above that the implementation of affirmative action is rather uneven across the three sectors and somewhat small in scale.

Indications are that there is some movement in the public service towards the establishment of a representative bureaucracy that reflects the demographics of the society, although as shown, women and especially black women continue to be under-represented.

In terms of the economy, affirmative action is taking the form of black advancement that seeks to promote the participation and contribution of black

---

[19]   In the South African context, capacity development premised on the deficit-assumption model, denotes the need (for black persons) to acquire basic skills and competencies for an occupational position. On the other hand, professional development (for white persons) works from the premise that the individual has the basic skill and competencies for the profession and needs to enhance and strengthen the skills in the context of the profession. Capacity development implies that the individual is not yet capable and as such does not inhabit the occupational/professional space. On the other hand, the term professional development implies that the individual occupies the space and merely has to learn and acquire the 'tools of the trade'.

people to the economy of South Africa. This is a two-pronged approach. The one is a private sector initiative that seeks to promote a small layer of black individuals with an existing big capital accumulation base. The second aspect of black economic empowerment, as initiated by the government, is intended to promote a larger layer of black individuals who are culturally more receptive to capital accumulation but who lack the financial basis to do so. The intention is that through the promotion and enhancement of a middle group of small businesses, there will be a multiplying social and economic effect on the economy as a whole. Further research is needed to show the scale of the impact in terms of the different sections of society.

In terms of higher education, there have been some positive outcomes at the level of the transformation of student enrolments; however, this pattern is not similarly replicated at the level of permanent and tenured academic staff. The compliance in terms of transforming academic staff profiles in terms of race and gender at the different hierarchical levels of the sector is not as great as that of the other sectors. For example, an analysis of the profile of equity reports submitted to the Department of Labour in 2000, reveals that only 10 per cent of higher education institutions had submitted reports. It is likely that there will be more pressure on these institutions, given the recent announcement by the Minister of Labour. At the time of writing this article, the Minister announced that there would be more vigilant monitoring of the implementation of employment equity in higher education institutions.

Finally, the question has to be: towards what end is affirmative action being implemented?

Given the legacy of institutionalised racism in South Africa, the intention of affirmative action/equity has to be, to compensate for past discrimination. In other words, it is a mechanism for compensating groups in society who have experienced systematic and institutionalized forms of discrimination. To this end, the broad political category black encompassing men and women (from the apartheid categories Coloured, Indian and Black) should be the main beneficiaries of affirmative action/equity in the short term. This is important given the racial symbolisms that have characterized South African society for almost half a century. A clear message should be sent to South African society that 'race' should not be a criterion on which to build a new society. However, it is also important for groups that have not experienced overt insitutionalised forms of discrimination, to benefit from affirmative action/equity. In the light of this, women who have historically been classified as white (in South Africa) as well as all those who are disabled (and have borne the classification of white under apartheid) should also benefit from affirmative action/equity policies. This is important in order to accelerate their integration into society and thus avoid present or future discrimination (Faundez, 1994: 34). In other words, affirmative action/equity practices should seek to strike a healthy balance between prioritizing which categories from the designated groups should benefit. It is important to state that the benefits should not rest at the level of individuals in society. In this process it is important to keep in mind the overall principles of institutional and societal redress, which ultimately should steer the practices of affirmative action/equity. The benefit has to be for the broader society in the interests of not reproducing apartheid-type stereotypes and social relations.

In conclusion, affirmative action can only be a short-term strategy for a wider macro transformation project that seeks to address the problem of reproduction of the inequities in the system (Nzimande, 1996). While South African society is characterised by both 'race' and patriarchy, it is important to note that these social variables intersect with deep-rooted structural ones such as class. What is emerging from this study is that affirmative action/equity-related practices in the three sectors, are creating further spaces (material and psychological) for a small section of South African society, namely, those with access to material resources such as employment, education and finance. In order for South Africa's democracy to flourish redress policies need to speak to the unemployed and under-resourced sections of society, which – as the statistics at the start of this article have shown – constitutes half of the economically active population. Only in this way, could the equity practices begin to give substantive meaning to the constitutional mandate.

Glossary

AA: Affirmative Action
EEA: Employment Equity Act
SA: South Africa

Acknowledgements

I would like to thank Elaine Kennedy-Dubourdieu, Christina Lunceford and Lionel Thaver for commenting on drafts of this article.

Conclusion

Elaine Kennedy-Dubourdieu

While there is no universal agreement about a definition for affirmative action there are nevertheless certain broad underlying principles which the countries detailed in this book have subscribed to. In order to highlight the political choices they have made, and by way of conclusion, I would like to cite one counter-example of a country that has persistently taken an assimilationist, non-multiculturalist stance – a country that refuses to take into account the reality of race.

At the time of completing this book in November 2005 France was witnessing scenes of violence and rioting in its *banlieues* – those high-rise housing estates on the outskirts of the major cities, isolated geographically from the prosperous centres of towns. These *banlieues* are home to large numbers of France's visible minorities and have high levels of unemployment – in the region of 40 per cent, compared with 10 per cent for the population as a whole.

France, like Britain, had a colonial empire and the successive waves of migration from its former colonies make France a multi-ethnic country. However in many respects it appears to be a country in denial of this fact.

Denial firstly of this colonial past. At the instigation of the right wing party, *Union pour la Majorité Presidentielle* (UMP) in February 2005 the French government passed a law stipulating that the teaching of history in schools should recognise the positive role of French colonisation, 'to break with this permanent culture of repentance'[1] as the Minister of the Interior and Chairman of the UMP Nicolas Sarkozy put it. There was outrage at this prescriptive attempt to gloss over the negative aspects of colonisation and at the beginning of 2006 the government was forced to backtrack and repeal this measure. But in many respects the episode reveals that France has still not come to terms with its colonial past or the necessity of including in its national identity this multi-ethnic history which should embrace the whole memory of its empire, as well as that of its overseas departments and territories. France apparently still prefers to see its past and its identity in terms of Astérix the Gaul, or even Charlemagne.

Denial secondly of the reality of race as a defining factor. This refusal to come to grips with its multi-racial identity is reflected in the very absence of terms to satisfactorily designate these 'visible minorities'.[2] Since the revolution French identity has been built on what is described as Republican 'universalism': the

---

[1]   'Sarkozy fait faux bond aux Antilles', *Ouest-France*, 8 December 2005, p. 2.

[2]   Usually described as being of 'immigrant origin', *issu de l'immigration*. This expression is reserved for those who are somatically different. Nicolas Sarkozy, Minster of the Interior, is of Hungarian origin, but being white he is never described as being of immigrant

Republic is one and indivisible and all its citizens are free and equal before the law.[3] Although as the French comic Coluche pointed out (plagiarising George Orwell) some are more equal than others.

The French state recognises its citizens only as individuals, not as members of groups however these may be defined (whether they be racial, ethnic, religious, etc.). The state does not ask any questions on these grounds, nor does it permit employers or anyone else to do so. It should however be remembered that this has not always been so. Ethnic and racial data was kept by the state at the time of colonisation and during the occupation of France in the Second World War, which then made it possible for the French authorities in certain areas to track down and hand over French Jews to the Nazis. For many people today this is a good enough reason not to reactivate such a strategy. Indeed there is constant questioning of the use that could be made of such statistics and again this fear may be well founded. In 2006 the Minister of the Interior said that he would like the police to collect ethnicity data on delinquents, thereby opening up the possiblilty of reinforcing negative stereotypes were these figures to be presented as a sensationalist short cut, ignoring other socio-economic factors which would not have been collected at the same time. The police themselves expressed opposition to this and for the moment at least such ethnic and racial statistics remain illegal.

However the watchdog National Committee for Civil Liberties and Data Protection has authorised a few exceptions on an individual basis at the behest of researchers and the National Institute for Demographic Studies (INED).[4] These rare studies have testified to persistent discrimination and disadvantage (qualified by the French as forms of 'exclusion') in accommodation and employment particularly, revealing that France's visible minorities have scarcely more opportunities than their parents and grandparents.

Convinced of the need for such statistics, researchers and academics have in fact come up with ingenious ways of bypassing this prohibition, such as studies that use first or second names. A simple device, that is not totally accurate of course, but which has contributed to a greater understanding of the patterns of discrimination and disadvantage that France's visible minorities are embroiled in.[5] Another recent suggestion has come from the business sector that is starting to appreciate the need for employing staff that reflect the ethnic composition of potential consumers. In a report sent to the Prime Minister, the Chairman of Axa, Claude Bébéar suggested

---

origin. Obviously there are two types of immigrants – those whose children remain visibly different, and those that melt into the mass.

[3]   Declaration of the Rights of Man and of the Citizen, 26 August 1789. Article 1.

[4]   INED, *Mobilité géographique insertion sociale*, 1995, Published in shortened form: Michèle Tribalat, *Faire France*, (Paris, Editions la Découverte,1995).

– Dominique Meurs et al, *Mobilité intergénérationnelle et persistance des inégalités*, INED Working Document no 130, 2005, pp. 36, <www.ined.fr>.

[5]   See for example the study of 144,000 middle school pupils in the Bordeaux Education Area which constructed a statistical measure of ethnic origin using first names: Georges Félouzis et al, *L'apartheid scolaire*, (Paris, Seuil, 2005).

companies take a yearly photograph as a means of measuring the evolution of their diversity.[6] Since the 1990s, simple empirical testing has also been used to show that both post-code and name discrimination are a regular occurrence in France, making it difficult for France's ethnic minorities who do not have Camembert-French-sounding names to obtain jobs which correspond to their qualifications. Nevertheless these *ad hoc* studies cannot replace the systematic counting provided by a Census and all too often detailed information on disadvantage/'exclusion' is lacking.

Since the Second World War, French governments, both left and right, have refused to take race or ethnicity directly into account, as this they believe will lead to 'communitarianism' – the fragmenting of the nation into racial and ethnic sub-groups, set at each others' throats, competing for resources. Indeed racial and ethnic policies are believed to be the actual cause of strife and division and are thus to be avoided.

As the explanation of disadvantage/'exclusion' is believed to be purely socio-economic and not racial, France's response has traditionally been territorial, targeting geographical location and social class for supplementary resources and special treatment. This began in the 1960s and continues today – and in France it now often carries the nametag of 'positive discrimination'.

In 1981 educational priority areas (ZEPs) were set up following the British model. These were defined according to two types of criteria: the academic achievement of the pupils and the socio-economic structure of the catchment area. Being designated as a ZEP brought extra resources and the reduction in class sizes, but also led to greater concentrations of disadvantaged families, as the better off tended to move out to avoid what was often felt to be the accompanying stigmatisation of living in such an area. As a general principle the French republican system has relied heavily on education as a social equaliser to open up opportunity. This is a principle which France's ethnic minorities themselves have subscribed to, which makes the disappointment all the more acute for these young people who have educational qualifications and then discover the perverse effects of racial discrimination: they are not considered by many of their compatriots as fully French. Irrespective of their qualifications, the unemployment rate of young French citizens of North African origin is two and a half times higher than that of their white peers.

Nevertheless France persists in this strategy of territorial targeting. Urban development policies have also functioned in this way, singling out for specific help various geographical locations which have been defined variously as 'sensitive urban areas', 'areas designated for urban re-dynamisation' or those that are said to be 'tax free' (*zones franches*) to encourage businesses to set up there.

The urban violence in the autumn of 2005 focussed attention finally on the everyday reality of racial discrimination: holding French citizenship does not automatically open the doors of equality. In France police harassment of visibly different citizens is a well-known fact, as is discrimination in employment and housing. Despite France's constitutional idealism, simple observation reveals an

---

[6]   Claude Bébéar, *Des Entreprises aux couleurs de la France*, November 2004, <www.premier-ministre.gouv.fr>.

appalling lack of representation of France's visible minorities across the broad spectrum of social and political life. Here once again (and to re-state Albie Sach's formula) demography is not destiny.

In response to the violence the French Prime Minister declared that 2006 would be 'the year of equality of opportunity'. Yet it is hard to see how this will be brought about, as the policies he has announced so far do not constitute a fundamental change of tack.[7]

But these riots have led to the questioning of France's so-called model of 'integration'. There has been a frank airing of these questions by journalists, politicians and academics, as well as those at the receiving end of these discriminatory practices – the ethnic minorities themselves. Also particularly striking has been the opening up of the public debate over the use of 'positive discrimination' and the necessity – or not – to deal head on with the question of race. Although race and class seem inextricably mixed in the French *banlieues* they are nevertheless two distinct factors. Targeting social class and geographical location for greater economic fairness can only provide a partial solution – even though it is doubtless more comfortable in the short term for the state to declare itself colour-blind and refuse to recognise the diverse identities of its citizens.

This urban violence has also highlighted an emerging racial and ethnic identity and inter-ethnic solidarity amongst those who have the shared experience of everyday racism and discrimination in France. Not all French citizens recognise themselves in the French nation as it has been constructed thus far. Aimé Césaire for example has constantly rebelled against assimilation, and the adoption of a 'white masque'.[8] He has long advocated 'Liberty, Equality, Identity'[9] and a re-definition of the national motto that would take race and ethnicity into account. In order to create a truly non-racial society perhaps the French state should consider, like many of its researchers and academics, making a conscious use of racial distinctions and reconsidering the policy of affirmative action, not just in the stereotypical form of race quotas, but in the multiplicity of modes as detailed in the previous chapters.

We hope to have provided insights into the subtle differences and possibilities of the policy of affirmative action, thus enabling the debate to escape the confines of national mindsets and Manichean approaches.

We also hope that the book will provide an incentive for further discussion, research and imaginative policymaking.

---

[7] The state has announced greater severity as regards those found guilty of discrimination, as well as the use of testing to determine where discriminatory practices exist. It also intends to bring in the 'anonymous cv' – job centres will be called on to remove names and addresses from cvs before submitting them to employers. This will mean that candidates will at least have an equal chance of obtaining an interview, but it does not directly tackle employers' discriminatory attitudes.

[8] To use Frantz Fanon's expression.

[9] Aimé Césaire, 'Nègre je resterai', *Télérama*, no. 2931, 15 March 2006, p. 10.

Bibliography

(Britain) *Race Relations Amendment Act 2000.*
(Britain) *Race Relations Act 1965.*
(Britain) *Race Relations Act 1968.*
(Britain) *Race Relations Act 1976.*
(Britain) *Sex Discrimination Act 1975.*
(Canada) *Constitution Act 1982.*
(Canada) *Employment Equity Act*, S.C. 1986.
(Canada) *Job Quotas Repeal Act*, 1995.
(Canada) *Royal Proclamation 1763.*
(Canada) *Constitution Act 1867*, (UK).
(Canada) *Indian Act*, R.S. 1985.
(France) *Déclaration des droits de l'homme et du citoyen du 26 août 1789.*
<http://www.chrc-ccdp.ca/legislation _policies/aboriginal_employment-en.asp>.
<http://wwwisiswomen.org/pub/wia/wiawcar/affirmative.htm>.
<www.premier-ministre.gouv.fr>.
2001 Census, (London: The Statistics Office, 2001).

Abella, Rosalie Silberman (1984), *Report of the Commission on Equality in Employment*, (Ottawa: Ministry of Supply and Services).
Abramson, Joan (1979), *Old Boys, New Women, the Politics of Sex Discrimination*, (New York: Praeger).
Abu-Laban, Yasmeen and Gabriel, Christina (2002), *Selling Diversity: Immigration, Multiculturalism, Employment Equity, and Globalization*, (Peterborough: Broadview Press).
Agocs, C. and Michael, H.J., (2001), *Systematic Racism in Employment in Canada: Diagnosing Systemic Racism in Organizational Culture*, (Canadian Race Relations Foundation).
Agocs, Carol, (ed.) (2002), Workplace Equality: International Perspectives on Legislation, Policy, and Practice, (The Hague; New York: Kluwer International).
Ahmad, W.I.U and Atkin, K., (eds) (1996), '*Race' and Community Care*, (Buckingham: Open University Press).
Alibhai-Brown, Yasmin (2000), *Who Do We Think We Are?, Imagining the New Britain*, (London: Allen Lane-The Penguin Press).
America, Richard (1993), *Paying the Social Debt: What America owes to Black America*, (Westport, Connecticut).
Anthias, F. and Yuval-Davis N., (1992), *Racialized Boundaries: Race, Nation, Gender, Colour and Class and the Anti-Racist Struggle*, (London: Routledge).
Aylward, Carol A., (1999), *Canadian Critical Race Theory: Racism and the Law* (Halifax: Fernwood).

Backhouse, Constance (1999), *Color-Coded: A Legal History of Racism in Canada, 1900 – 1950*, (Toronto: University of Toronto Press).

Bakan, A.B. and Kobayashi A., (2000), *Employment Equity Policy in Canada: An Interprovincial Comparison*, (Ottawa: Status of Women Canada), < http://www. swc-cfc.gc.ca/pubs/pubspr/0662281608/200003_0662281608_e.pdf>.

Banton, Michael (1998), *Racial Theories*, 2nd edition, (Cambridge: Cambridge University Press).

Barbier, Marie-Claude, Bénédicte Deschamps and Michel Prum, (eds) (2005), *Tuer l'Autre: Violence raciste, ethnique, religieuse et homophobe dans l'aire anglophone*, (Paris: L'Harmattan).

Barbier, Marie-Claude, Deschamps Bénédicte & Prum Michel, (eds) (2005), *Tuer l'Autre : Violence raciste, ethnique, religieuse et homophobe dans l'aire anglophone*, (Paris: L'Harmattan).

Bardon, J. (1997), *A History of Ulster*, (Belfast: Blackstaff).

Barker, Martin (1981), *The New Racism*, (London: Junction Books).

Bastien, M. *et al.*, (1998), *Les programmes d'accès à l'égalité au Québec: bilan et perspectives*, (Québec: Commission des droits de la personne et des droits de la jeunesse du Québec).

Bébéar, Claude (2004), *Des Entreprises aux couleurs de la France*.

Belz, Herman (1994), *Equality Transformed: a Quarter Century of Affirmative Action*, (New Brunswick N.J.).

Bergman, Barbara (1996), *In Defense of Affirmative Action*, (New York: Basic Books).

Blackstone, Tessa, Parekh, Bhikhu and Sanders, Peter (1998), *Race Relations in Britain*, (London: Routledge).

Bloch, Farrell, *et al.*, (1977), *Equal Rights and Industrial Relations*, (Madison, Wisconsin: Industrial Relations Research Association).

Bond, P., (2000), *Elite Transition: From Apartheid to Neo-Liberalism in South Africa*, (London: Pluto Press).

Boorah, V.K., (1999), 'Is There a Penalty to Being a Catholic in Northern Ireland? An Econometric Analysis of the Relationship Between Religious Belief and Occupational Success', *European Journal of Political Economy*, 15:2, pp. 163–92.

Borooah, V.K., (2000), 'Targeting Social Need: Why are Deprivation Levels in Northern Ireland Higher or Catholics Than For Protestants?', *Journal of Social Policy*, 29:2, pp. 281–301.

Bowen, William and Derek Bok (1998), *The Shape of the River: Long-Term Consequences of Considering Race in College and University Admissions*, (Princeton N.J.: Princeton University Press).

Bradford District Race Review (2002), *Community Pride not Prejudice: Making Diversity work in Bradford*, (Bradford: Bradford District Council).

Brewer, J.D. and Higgins, G.I., (1998), *Anti–Catholicism in Northern Ireland 1600–1998: The Mote and the Beam*, (London: Macmillan Press).

Brouard, Sylvain and Tilberj, Vincent (2005), *Français comme les autres? Enquête sur les citoyens d'origine magrébine, africaine et turque*, (Paris: Presse de la Fondation nationale des sciences politiques).

Bullard, Robert, Grigsby, Eugene and Lee, Charles, (1996), *Residential Apartheid: the American Legacy*, (Los Angeles: UCLA Center for African American Studies Publications).

Burns, Stewart (1997), *Daybreak of Freedom*, (Chapel Hill: University of North Carolina Press).

Butterworths Law Reports, (2000), *Mineworkers Union obo Snyman and another/ Eskom (Distribution)* November, Vol 3., <http://192.102.9.101/Print/799f60f0. htm>.

Cabinet Office Strategy Unit Report, (2003), *Ethnic Minorities in the Labour Market*, (London: Cabinet Office).

Cairns Alan C *et al.*, (eds) (1999), *Citizenship, Diversity and Pluralism – Canadian and Comparative Perspectives*, (Montreal: McGill-Queen's University Press).

Canadian Bar Association Reports, <http://www.cba.org/CBA/cba_reports/ RacialEquality.pdf>.

Canadian Bar Association, *Racial Equality in the Canadian Legal Profession.*

Canadian Human Rights Commission Policy Statement on Aboriginal Employment Preferences, (25 March 2003), Canadian Human Rights Commission, *Annual Report 2002.*

Caribbean Ex-Service Women's Association, (1993), *Caribbean Women in World War II: 4 Black Women's History of War Time Service*, (London: Caribbean Ex-Service Women's Association and the London Borough of Hammersmith and Fulham).

Carvel, John (1985), 'Ministers clash on fair deal for blacks', *The Guardian*, (October 15).

Castles, Stephen and Miller, Mark J., (1993), *The Age of Migration — International Population Movements in the Modern World*, (London, Macmillan).

Castles, Stephen *et al.*, (1992), *Mistaken Identity — The Demise of Nationalism in Australia*, 3rd edn (Marrickville, NSW: Pluto Press).

Cedley, E., (2001), 'Getting Equality to Work: The South African Employment Equity Act', *Safundi*, Issue 4.

Center for Individual Rights, (1998), *Racial Preferences in Higher Education, The Rights of College Students, A Handbook*, (Washington, D.C.: Centre for Individual Rights).

Central Community Relations Unit, (1994), *Appraisal and Fair Treatment Annual Report*, (Belfast: SACHR).

Central Community Relations Unit, (1998), *New TSN: an Agenda for Targeting Social Need and Social Exclusion in Northern Ireland*, (Belfast: CCRU).

Central Procurement Directorate Northern Ireland, (2002), *A Review of Public Procurement; Findings and Recommendations*, (Belfast: Department of Finance and Personnel).

Centre for Individual Rights, *Racial Preferences in Higher Education. The Rights of College Students, A Handbook*, (Washington D.C.: Center for Individual Rights).

Césaire, Aimé (1972), *Discourse on Colonialism*, trans Joan Pinkham, (New York: Monthly Review Press).

Chicha, Marie-Thérèse (2000), *L'équité salariale: mise en oeuvre et enjeux*, 2nd edn (Cowansville: Yvon Blais).

Commission for Black Staff in Further Education, *Challenging Racism: Further Education Leading the Way*, (London: Commission for Black Staff in Further Education).

Commission on the Future of Multi-Ethnic Britain (2000), *The Future of Multi-Ethnic Britain: The Parekh Report*, (London: Profile Books).

Compton, P., (1981), *The Contemporary Population of Northern Ireland and Population Related Issues*, (Belfast: Institute of Irish Studies, Queen's University Belfast).

Connolly, P. and Keenan, M., (2000), *Racial Attitudes and Prejudice in Northern Ireland, Report 1*, (Belfast: Northern Ireland Statistics and Research Agency).

Cormack, R.J., and Osborne, R.D., (eds) (1991), *Discrimination and Public Policy in Northern Ireland*, (Oxford: Clarendon Press).

Council on Higher Education, (2001) *Annual Report 2000/2001*. (Pretoria).

CRE, (2001), 'Bringing it all back', *Connections*, (London: CRE, Summer).

CRE, (2003), 'Extend the duty, say public bodies', *Connections*, (London: CRE, Spring).

CRE, (2003), *Towards Racial Equality: Are public authorities meeting the duty to promote race equality?*, (London: CRE).

CRE (2004), *Racial Equality and the Smaller Business: A Practical Guide*, (London: CRE).

CRE/She Magazine, (2002), *Survey on Race*, (London: CRE).

Cronon, David (1972), *Black Moses, the Story of Marcus Garvey and the Universal Negro Improvement Association*, (Madison, Wisconsin: University of Wisconsin Press).

Daniel,W.W., (1968), *Racial Discrimination in England: Based on the PEP Report*, (Harmondsworth: Penguin Books).

Darity, William Jr. and Ashwini Deshpande (eds) (2003), *Boundaries of Clan and Color: Transnational comparisons of inter group disparit*, (London: Routledge).

Davidenkoff Emmanuel, (2005), 'Ecole : la sauvegarde d'un moule', *Libération*, (2 December), p. 5.

Department of Education, (1997), *Education White Paper: A Programme for the Transformation of Higher Education*, (Pretoria).

Department of Labour, (2002), *Commission for Employment Equity Report: 1999–2001*, (Pretoria).

Department of Trade and Industry, (2003), 'In search of the "missing middle"', in *Mail & Guardian*, (Pretoria, 4 April).

Desai, I.P., (1984), 'Should Caste be the basis for recognizing backwardness', *Economic and Political Weekly*, (14 July), pp. 1106–1116.

Deshpande, Ashwini, (2000), 'Recasting Economic Inequality', *Review of Social Economy*, Vol. 58, No. 3, (October), pp. 381–399.

Deshpande, Ashwini, (2001), 'Caste at Birth? Redefining disparity in India', *Review of Development Economics*, Vol. 5 No. 1, (February), pp. 130–144.

Deshpande, Ashwini, (2004), 'Identity and exclusion: Caste disparity under early liberalisation in India', (under submission).

Diamond Andrew and Magidoff Jonathan, (2005), 'A gauche, le racial impensé', *Libération*, (November 30) p. 35.

Dignan, T. and McLaughlin, E., (2002), *New TSN Research: Poverty in Northern Ireland*, (Belfast: OFMDFM).

Dignan, T., (2003), *Community Differentials and New TSN: Report Prepared for the OFMDFM Equality Directorate*, (Belfast: OFMDFM).

Dobrowolsky, A., and Hart, V., (eds) (2003), *Women Making Constitutions: New Politics and Comparative Perspectives*, (New York: Palgrave–Macmillan).

Driedger Leo (1996), *Multi-Ethnic Canada: Identities and Inequalities*, (Toronto: Oxford University Press).

Driedger, Leo and Halli, Shiva S., (2000), *Race and Racism: Canada's Challenge*, (Montreal & Kingston: McGill/Queen's University Press).

DuBois, W.E.B., (1935), *Black Reconstruction in America*, (Cleveland: Meridian, 1968).

Dubourdieu, Elaine (1998), 'The Theory and Practice of 'Positive Discrimination', in John Edwards and Jean-Paul Révauger, (eds).

Dubourdieu, Elaine (1998), 'The Wilson Years: A (Small?) Step Towards Racial Equality', in Bernard Gilbert (ed.), *Les Années Wilson, 1964–1970*, (Paris: Editions du Temps).

Dubourdieu, Elaine (2000), 'Droits des minorités : droits universels, droits particuliers, Le cas de la 'discrimination positive', in Martine Spensky, (ed.).

Dubourdieu, Elaine (2002), 'Enoch Powell, the "Rivers of Blood" Speech' in A. Kober-Smith and T. Whitton, *Civilisation Britannique*, (Paris, Editions du Temps), pp. 83–92.

Dubourdieu, Elaine, (2005), 'Violences 'raciales' en Grande-Bretagne : Perceptions du problème au vingtième siècle', in Marie-Claude Barbier, Bénédicte Deschamps and Michel Prum (eds).

Dudziak, Mary (2002), *Cold War Civil Rights*, (Princeton: Princeton University Press).

Dworkin, R., (1977), '*Reverse Discrimination*', *Taking Rights Seriously*, (London: Duckworth).

Eames, R., (1992), *Chains to be Broken*, (London: Weindenfeld and Nicholson).

Eboda, Michael (2001), 'It's a jungle out there ...', *The Observer*, (November 25).

Edwards, John (1987), *Positive Discrimination, Social Justice and Social Policy*, (London: Tavistock).

Edwards, John (1995), *Affirmative Action in a Sectarian Society*, (Aldershot: Avebury).

Edwards, John and Révauger Jean-Paul (eds) (1998), *Discourse on Inequality in France and Britain*, (Aldershot: Ashgate).

Elliot, M. (ed.) (2002), *The Long Road to Peace in Northern Ireland*, (Liverpool: Liverpool University Press).

Equality Commission for Northern Ireland, (1999), *Response to a New Beginning: Policing in Northern Ireland – The Report of the Independent Commission on Policing for Northern Ireland*, (Belfast: ECNI).

Equality Commission for Northern Ireland, (2000), *Guide to the Statutory Duties – A Guide to the Implementation of the Statutory Duties on Public Authorities Arising from Section 75 of the Northern Ireland Act 1998*, (Belfast: ECNI).

Equality Commission for Northern Ireland, (2001), *Section 75 of the Northern Ireland Act 1998 – Practical Guidance on Equality Impact Assessment*, (Belfast: ECNI).

Equality Commission for Northern Ireland, (2002), *Position Paper: Update on the Single Equality Act*, (Belfast: ECNI).

Equality Commission for Northern Ireland, (2003), *Report on the Implementation of the Section 75 Statutory Duties – 1 April 2002–31 March 2003*, (Belfast: ECNI).

Equality Commission for Northern Ireland, (2004), *Commission Response to OFMDFM Consultation Paper*, '*A Single Equality Bill for Northern Ireland*', (Belfast: ECNI).

Fair Employment, (Northern Ireland), Act 1989.

Fanon, Frantz (1967), *Black Skin White Masks*, (New York: Grove Press).

Fanon, Frantz (1967), *The Wretched of the Earth*, trans. Constance Farrington, (New York: Penguin Books).

Faundez, J., (1994), *Affirmative Action: International Perspectives*, (Geneva: International Labour Office).

Félouzis Georges *et al.*, (2005), *L'apartheid scolaire*, (Paris: Seuil).

Fitzgerald, G., (2004), 'Foreword', in Osborne, B. and Shuttleworth, I. (eds).

Fitzpatrick, B., Hegarty, A. and Maxwell, P. (1997a), 'A Comparative Review of Fair Employment and Equality of Opportunity Law', in Rose, S. and Magill, D. (eds).

Fitzpatrick, B., Hegarty, A. and Maxwell, P. (1997b), 'Fair Employment Law in Northern Ireland: Debates and Issues' in Magill, D. and Rose, S. (eds).

Forbath, William E. and Torres Gerald, (1997), 'The Talented Tenth in Texas', *The Nation*, (December 15) p. 21.

Ford, Richard, (2003) 'Ethnic Minorities become majority in two areas', *The Times*, (14 February), p. 4.

Foster, Lois and Stockley, David (1984), *Multiculturalism: The Changing Australian Paradigm*, (Avon: Multilingual Matters).

Foster, Lois and Stockley, David (1988), *Australian Multiculturalism: A Documentary History and Critique*, (Avon: Multilingual Matters).

Foster, R.F., (1989), *Modern Ireland 1600 – 1972*, (Harmondsworth: Penguin).

Fryer, Peter (1984), *Staying Power: The History of Black People in Britain*, (London: Pluto Press).

Gaffikin, F. and Morrissey, M., (1999), *City Visions*, (London: Pluto Press).

Galanter, Marc (1991), *Competing Equalities: Law and the Backward Classes in India*, (New Delhi: Oxford University Press).

Gilroy, Paul (1987), *There Aint No Black in the Union Jack*, (London: Hutchinson).

Gilroy, Paul (2004), *After Empire. Melancholia or Convivial Culture?* (London: Routledge).

Goldberg, David Theo (1994), *Multiculturalism — A Critical Reader*, (Cambridge, Mass.: Blackwell).

Goodman, David, O'Hearn D.J., Wallace-Crabbe Chris (1991), *Multicultural Australia, The Challenges of Change*, (Newham: Scribe Publications Pty).

Grant, Nancy (1990), *TVA and Black Americans: Planning for the Status Quo*, (Philidelphia: Temple University Press).

Grattan, Michelle (ed.) (2000), *Reconciliation*, (Melbourne: Bookman Press Pty Ltd).

Guhan, S., (2001), 'Comprehending Equalities' in S. Subramanian (ed.), *India's Development Experience*, (New Delhi: Oxford University Press).

Hall, Stuart (1999), *History Workshop Journal*, Vol 48, (London: Oxford University Press).

Hall, Stuart (2000), 'Conclusion: The Multi-Cultural Question', in Barnor Hesse (ed.), *Un/settled Multiculturalisms: Diasporas, Entanglements*, (London: Zed Press).

Harbison, J.J.M., (2002), 'Police Reform and the Equality Commission', *The Belfast Telegraph*, (2 January).

Harbison, J.J.M. and Hodges, W.J., (1991), 'Equal Opportunities in the Northern Ireland Civil Service', in Cormack, R.J. and Osborne, R.D. (eds).

Heffer, Simon (2002), *Like the Roman: the Life of Enoch Powell*, (London: Phoenix Grant).

Herbold, Hilary, 'Never a Level Playing Field', *Journal of Blacks in Higher Education*, 5 (Winter 1994/1995) pp. 104–108.

Hill, L., (2001), *Black Berry, Sweet Juice: On Being Black and White in Canada*, (Toronto: HarperFlamingo).

Hillyard, P. and Tomlinson, M., (2000), 'Patterns of Policing and Policing Patten', *The Journal of Law and Society*, 27:3, pp. 394–415.

Hinds, B., (2003), 'Mainstreaming Equality in Northern Ireland', in Dobrowolsky, A. & Hart, V. (eds).

Home Office, (2002), *Building Cohesive Communities. A Report of the Ministerial Group on Public Order and Community Cohesion*, (London: Home Office).

Home Office, (2002), *Community Cohesion.A Report of the Independent Review Team Chaired by Ted Cantle*, (London: Home Office).

Honeyford, Ray (1988), *Integration or Disintegration? Towards a Non-racist Society*, (London: The Claridge Press).

House of Commons Official Report, 1998, (London: TSO–Hansard).

Huggins, Nathan (1990), *The Harlem Renaissance*, (New York: Oxford University Press).

Human Rights Watch, (1999), *Broken People: Caste violence against India's 'untouchables'*, (New York: Human Rights Watch).

Hutson, N., (1996), *Policy Appraisal and Fair Treatment: A Contribution to the Debate on Mainstreaming Equality*, (Belfast: SACHR/TSO).

Independent Commission on Policing for Northern Ireland, (1999), *A New Beginning: Policing in Northern Ireland*, (Belfast: TSO).

INED (1995), *Mobilité géographique insertion sociale*, (Paris: INED).

Jack, John and Templeton, Jacqueline (1994), *Bold Experiment — A Documentary History of Australian Immigration since 1945*, (Oxford: Oxford University Press).

Jamrozik, Adam *et al.*, (1995), *Social Change and Cultural Transformation in Australia*, (Cambridge: Cambridge University Press).

Jordens, Ann-Mari (1995), *Redefining Australians. Immigration, Citizenship and National Identity*, (Maryborough: Hale & Iremonger).

Jupp, James (ed.) (1989), *The Challenge of Diversity — Policy Options for a Multicultural Australia*, (Canberra: AGPS).

Jupp, James (ed.) (2001), *The Australian People, An Encylopaedia of the Nation, Its People and Their Origins*, (Cambridge: Cambridge University Press).

Kahlenberg, Richard (1996), *The Remedy : Class, Race and Affirmative Action*, (New York: Basic Books).

Karim, Razia, 'Take care when being positive', *Connections*, (London: CRE., Winter 2004/05).

Kluger, Richard (1977), *Simple Justice*, (New York: Random House).

Kruman, Marc W. (1975), 'Quotas for Blacks: the Public Works Administration and the Black Construction Worker', *Labor History*, 16 no. 1 (Winter) pp. 50–51.

Kymlicka, Will (1995), *Multicultural Citizenship: A Liberal Theory of Minority Rights*, (London: Oxford University Press).

Kymlicka, Will (2001), *Politics in the Vernacular: Nationalism, Multiculturalism and Citizenship*, (London: Oxford University Press).

Labour Force Survey, (2003), *Labour Force Survey Quarterly Supplement*, (London: Summer).

Labour Force Survey 2002/3, (London: The Statistics Office, 2004).

Lawson, Steven (1996), *Running for Freedom: Civil Rights and Politics in America Since 1941*, (New York: McGraw Hill).

Li, Peter (ed.) (1999), *Race and Ethnic Relations in Canada*, (2d edn) (Don Mills, Ontario: Oxford University Press).

Liebenberg, B.J., 'Hertzog in Power, 1924–1939', in C.F.J. Muller (ed.), *Five Hundred Years, A History of South Africa*, (Pretoria: Academica).

Liebenberg, B.J., 'The National Party in Power', in C.F.J. Muller (ed.), *Five Hundred Years, A History of South Africa*, (Pretoria: Academica).

Logan, Rayford (1954), *The Betrayal of the Negro*, (New York: Collier, 1965).

Lubiano, Wahneema (ed.) (1997), *The House That Race Built*, (New York: Pantheon Books).

Macpherson, William (1999), *The Stephen Lawrence Inquiry: Report of an Inquiry by Sir William Macpherson of Cluny*, Cm 4262–1, (London: Home Office).

Magill, D.S. and Rose, S.A., (1997), *Comparative Review of Fair Employment and Equality of Opportunity Law*, (Belfast: SACHR).

Maguire, Daniel (1980), *A New American Justice*, (New York: Doubleday).

Malamud, Deborah C., (1996), 'Class Based Affirmative action: Lessons and Caveats', *Texas Law Review* 74, 1847–1900.

Malik, Kenan (1996), *The Meaning of Race: Race, History and Culture in Western Society*, (Basingstoke: Macmillan).

Mann, Patricia (2003) *Employment Equity in South African Universities*, (Unpublished manuscript).

Maphai, V., (1992), 'The Civil Service: Transition and Affirmative Action', in P. Hugo, *Redistribution and Affirmative Action: Working on South Africa's Political Economy*, (Pretoria: Southern Book Publishers).

'Margaret Thatcher Interview', *Women's Own*, (October 31, 1987).

Markus, Andrew (1994), *Australian Race Relations 1788–1993*, (St Leonards, NSW: Allan & Unwin).

Markus, Andrew (2001), *Race: John Howard and the Remaking of Australia*, (Crows Nest, NSW: Allen & Unwin).

Maykuth, A., (1997), 'South Africa Struggle on Affirmative Action', in *Philadelphia Inquirer*, <http://www.maykuth.com/africa/affirm428.htm>.

Mbabane, L., (2003), 'Equity goals need to be set against numerical benchmarks', *Sunday Times: Business Times*, (Pretoria: March 30).

McCrudden, C., (1986), 'Rethinking Positive Action', *The Industrial Law Journal*, 15:1, pp. 219–243.

McCrudden, C., (1996), *Mainstreaming Fairness? A Discussion Paper on Policy Appraisal and Fair Treatment*, (Belfast: CAJ).

McCrudden, C., (1997), *Commentary on Mainstreaming Fairness? – A Discussion paper on Policy Appraisal and Fair Treatment and on Policy Appraisal and Fair Treatment in Northern Ireland: a Contribution to the Debate on Mainstreaming Equality*, (Belfast: CAJ).

McCrudden, C., (1998), *Benchmarks for Change: Mainstreaming Fairness in the Governance of Northern Ireland*, (Belfast: CAJ).

McCrudden, C., (1999), 'Mainstreaming Equality in the Governance of Northern Ireland', *Fordham International Law Journal*, 22:4, 1697–1775.

McCrudden, C., (2004), *Mainstreaming Equality in Northern Ireland 1998–2004: A Review of Issues Concerning the Operation of the Equality Duty in Section 75 of the Northern Ireland Act 1998*, (Belfast: OFMDFM).

McCrudden, C., Ford, R. and Heath, A. (2004), 'The Impact of Affirmative Action Agreements', in Osborne, B. and Shuttleworth, I. (eds).

McKittrick, D., and McVea, D., (2000), *Making Sense of the Troubles*, (Belfast: Blackstaff Press).

McLaughlin, E. and Quirk, P., (eds) (1996), *Policy Aspects of Employment Equality in Northern Ireland Vol. 2*, (Belfast: SACHR).

McNamara, K., (2002), 'Give us another MacBride Campaign: An Irish–American Contribution to Peaceful change in Northern Ireland', in Elliot, M. (ed.).

Meier, August and Rudwick, Elliot (1973), *CORE*, (New York: Oxford University Press).

Melleuish, Gregory (1998), *The Packaging of Australia, Politics and Culture Wars*, (Sydney: University of New South Wales Press).

Mendes E.P., (ed.) (1995), *Racial Discrimination: Law and practice*, (Scarborough, Ont: Carswell).

Meurs Dominique *et al.*, (2005), *Mobilité intergénérationnelle et persistance des inégalités*, Working Document no 130, (Paris: INED) < www.ined.fr>.

Ministry for Public Service and Administration, (1997), *Green Paper: A Conceptual Framework for Affirmative Action and the Management of Diversity in the Public Service*, (Pretoria).

Mitchell Claire, (2006), *Religion, Identity and Politics in Northern Ireland*, (Aldershot: Ashgate).

Modood, Tariq and Berthoud, Richard (eds), (1997), *Ethnic Minorities in Britain, Diversity and Disadvantage*, (London: Policy Studies Institute).

Modood, Tariq and Werbner, Pnina (eds) (1997), *The Politics of Multiculturalism in the New Europe*, (London: Zed Books).

Mokgoro, T., (1996), 'Implementing Affirmative Action and Culture Change in the Public Service', in Nzimande, B. and Sikhosana, M. (eds), *Affirmative Action and Transformation*, pp. 255–262, (Durban, South Africa: Indicator Press).

Moreno, Paul (1997), *From Direct Action to Affirmative Action*, (Baton Rouge, Louisiana: Louisiana State University Press).

Mori, Poll *Readers' Digest*, (November, 2000).

Msimang, S., (2001), 'Affirmative Action in the new South Africa: The Politics of Representation, Law and Equity', *Women in Action*, No 2.

Nalbandian, J., (1989), 'The US Supreme Court's 'Consensus' on Affirmative Action', *Public Administration Review*, 49:1, pp. 38–45.

Nesiah, Devanasan (1997), *Discrimination with reason? The policy of reservations in the United States, India and Malaysi*, (New Delhi: Oxford University Press).

New York City Employees' Retirement System v. American Brands Inc., 634 F. Supp.1382, (SDNY), 1986.

Northern Ireland Act, 1998, Section 75 and Schedule 9, (Belfast: TSO).

Northern Ireland Affairs Committee, (1999), House of Commons Session 1998–99, Fourth Report *The Operation of the Fair Employment (Northern Ireland) Act 1989: Ten Years on*, Volume 1, (London: Report and Proceedings of the Committee, TSO).

Northern Ireland Economic Council, (1998), *Growth with Development: A Response to New TSN*, Occasional Paper, (Belfast: NIEC).

Northern Ireland Executive, (2001), Northern Ireland Programme for Government: Making a Difference, (Belfast: TSO).

Nzimande, B., (1996), 'Black Advancement, White Resistance and the Politics of Upward Mobility in South Africa's Industrial Corporations', in B. Nzimande, and M. Sikhosana (eds), *Affirmative Action and Transformation*, (Durban, South Africa: Indicator Press), pp. 187–202.

Ooiman Robinson, Jo Ann (ed.) (2001), *Affirmative Action. A Documentary History*, (Westport, Connecticut: Greenwood Press).

Office of Population Censuses and Surveys, (1990), *Why is this Information Needed?*, (London: HMSO, October).

Office of the First and Deputy First Minister (2001), *Promoting Equality of Opportunity: A Single Equality Bill for Northern Ireland. Initial Consultation Document*, (Belfast: OFMDFM).

Office of the First and Deputy First Minister, (2004), *A Single Equality Bill for Northern Ireland: A Discussion Paper on Options for a Bill to Harmonise, Update and Extend, where Appropriate, Anti–Discrimination and Equality legislation in Northern Ireland*, (Belfast: OFMDFM).

O'Leary, B., (2000), 'What a Travesty: Police Bill is Just a Parody of Patten', *The Sunday Business Post*, (11 June).

O'Meara, D., (1983), *Volkskapitalisme 1934–1948*, (Braamfontein: Ravan Press).

Ontario Human Rights Commission, *Report of the Commission on Systemic Racism in the Ontario Justice System*, report written by David Cole and Margaret Gittens (Ontario: Queen's Printer, 1995).

Orfield, Gary and Eaton, Susan (1997), *Dismantling Desegregation: The Quiet Reversal of Brown v. Board of Education*, (New York: New Press).

Osborne, B. and Shuttleworth, I., (2004), *Fair Employment in Northern Ireland: A Generation On*, (Belfast: Blackstaff Press).

Osborne, R, Gallaghar, A. and Cormack, R., (1996), 'The Implementation of the Policy Appraisal and Fair Treatment Guidelines in Northern Ireland', in McLaughlin, E. and Quirk, P., (eds).

Patterson, James (2000), *Brown v. Board of Education: A Civil Rights Milestone and its Troubled Legacy*, (New York: Oxford University Press).

Pfeffer, Paula (1990), *Philip Randolph, Pioneer of Civil Rights*, (Baton Rouge, Louisiana: Louisiana State University Press).

Pinto, Ambrose, 'Saffronisation of Affirmative Action', *Economic and Political Weekly*, (December 25, 1999).

Piquet, Martine (2004), *Australie plurielle. Gestion de la diversité ethnique en Australie de 1788 à nos jours*, (Paris: L'Harmattan).

Piquet, Martine, Redonnet, Jean-Claude, and Tolron, Francine (2002), *L'Idée de réconciliation dans les sociétés multiculturelles du Commonwealth*, (Paris: Armand Colin).

Pons, Xavier (1996), *Le Multiculturalisme en Australie – Au-delà de Babel*, (Paris: L'Harmattan).

Povinelli, Elizabeth A., (2002), *The Cunning of Recognition, Indigenous Alterities and the Making of Australian Multiculturalism*, (Durham & London: Duke University Press).

'Powell attacks "colour count"', *The Independent*, (November 22,1986).

Prum Michel (ed.) (2000), *Exclure au nom de la race*, (Paris: Syllepse).

Public Service Commission, (2000), *The State of Representativeness in the Public Service*, (Pretoria).

Public Service Commission, (2002), *A Report on the State of the Public Service*, (Pretoria).

Purdie, B., (1990), *Politics on the Streets: The Origins of the Civil Rights Movement in Northern Ireland*, (Belfast: Blackstaff Press).

Quebec Human Rights Commission, <http://www.cdpdj.qc.ca/en/home>.

Quirk, P. and McLaughlin, E., (1996), 'Targeting Social Need', in McLaughlin, E. and Quirk, P., (eds).

'Race in the Work Place, Is Affirmative Action Working?', *Business Week*, (July 8, 1991) pp. 53–56.

Radhakrishna, S., (2004), 'The Dhammapada', (Chapter XXVI, 'Brahmanavaggo') in *The Buddhism Omnibus*, (New Delhi: Oxford University Press).

Razack Sherene, (1998), 'Looking White People in the Eye: Gender, Race, and Culture in Courtrooms and Classrooms', (Toronto: University of Toronto Press).

Reddy, P. and Choudree, R., (1994), 'Public Service Transformation and Affirmative Action, Perspectives in South Africa', *Industrial Relations Journal of South Africa*, 14 (1): pp. 24–36.

Reverchon, Antoine (2005), 'Un trou énorme dans la statistique nationale', *Le Monde Economie*, (November).

Rex, John (ed.) (2004), *Governance in Multicultural Societies*, (Aldershot, Ashgate).

Robinson, Randall (2000), *The Debt: What America Owes to Blacks*, (New York: Dutton).

Rose, E.J.B., (1969), *Colour and Citizenship: A Report on British Race Relations*, (London: Oxford University Press/ Institute of Race Relations).

Rose, S. and Magill, D., (eds) (1997), *Fair Employment Law in Northern Ireland: Debates and Issues* (Belfast: SACHR).

Royal Commission on Aboriginal Peoples (1993), *Sharing the Harvest: The Road to Self-Reliance*, (*Report of the National Roundtable on Aboriginal Economic Development and Resources*), (Ottawa: Ministry of Supply and Services).

Royal Commission Report on Aboriginal Peoples (1996), *People to People, Nation to Nation*, (Ottawa: The Commission) <http://www.aincinac.gc.ca/ch/rcap/sg/sgmm_e.html.>.

Rubio, Philip F., (2001), *A History of Affirmative Action, 1619–2000*,(Jackson: University Press of Mississippi).

Russell, R. (2004), 'Employment profiles of Protestants and Catholics: A Decade of Monitoring', in Osborne and Shuttleworth, (eds).

Sachs, Albie [199–], 'Affirmative Action and the Constitution', (Johannesburg: ANC Department of Information and Publicity).

Saggar, Shamit (1992), *Race and Politics in Britain*, (London: Harvester Wheatsheaf).

'Sarkozy fait faux bond aux Antilles', *Ouest-France*, (8 December 2005) p. 2.

Satzewich, Vic (1992), *Deconstructing a Nation: Immigration, Multiculturalism and Racism*, (Halifax: Fernwood Publishing)

Scarman, (Lord) (1981), *The Scarman Report: The Brixton Disorders 10–12 April 1981*, (Harmondsworth: Penguin Books).

Scarman, Rt. Hon., The Lord (1981), *The Brixton Disorders 10–12 April, 1981*, Cmnd 8427, (London: HMSO).

Schnapper, Eric (1985), 'Affirmative Action and the Legislative History of the Fourteenth Amendment', *Virginia Law Review* 71, 753–790.

Schneider-Ross Report, (2002), *The Business of Diversity*, (London: Schneider-Ross).

Schneider-Ross Report, (2003), *Towards Racial Equality: An evaluation of the public duty to promote race equality and good race relations in England and Wales*, (London: CRE).

Seligman, Daniel (1973) 'How "Equal Opportunity" Turned into Employment Quotas', *Fortune*, (March) pp. 165–166.

Shah, Ghanshyam (1985), 'Caste, class and reservations', *Economic and Political Weekly*, Vol.XX, No.3, (January 19) pp. 132–136.

Sheppard, Colleen, 'The Promise and Practice of Human Rights Protection: Reflections on the Quebec Charter of Human Rights and Freedoms', in Paul-André Crépeau (ed.) (1996), *Mélanges*, (Cowansville, Quebec: Yvon Blais).

Sheppard, Colleen, *Litigating the Relationship between Equity and Equality*, (Toronto: Ontario Law Reform Commission Report, 1992).

Sitkoff, Harvard (1978), *A New Deal for Blacks: The Emergence of Civil Rights as a National Issue*, (New York: Oxford University Press).

Smith, Verne E., (1999), 'Showdown in Atlanta', *Emerge*, (November) p. 49.

Solomos, John (1995), *Race, Politics and Social Change*, (London: Routledge).

Sowell, Thomas (1990), *Preferential Policies: An International Perspective*, (New York: William Morrow).

Sowell, Thomas (2004) *Affirmative Action Around the World*, (New Haven & London: Yale University Press).

Spensky, Martine (ed.) (2002), Universalisme, particularisme et citoyenneté dans les Iles Britanniques, (Paris: l'Harmattan).

Srikanth, H., 'No Shortcuts to Dalit Liberation', *Economic and Political Weekly*, (March 25, 2000).

Standing Advisory Commission on Human Rights, (1987), *Religious and Political Discrimination and Equality of Opportunity: Report on Fair Employment*, (Belfast: HMSO).

Standing Advisory Commission on Human Rights, (1990), *Religious and Political Discrimination and Equality of Opportunity in Northern Ireland: Second Report*, (Belfast: HMSO).

Standing Advisory Commission on Human Rights, (1998), *1997 – 1998 Report*, (Belfast: TSO).

Standing Advisory Committee on Human Rights, (1997), *Employment Equality: Building for the Future*, (Belfast: TSO).

Statistics Canada, (1990), *Making the Tough Choices in Using Census Data to Count Visible Minorities in Canada*, (Ottawa: Employment Equity Data Program).

Statistics Canada, (1991), *Approaches to the Collection of Data on Visible Minorities in Canada: A Review and Commentary*, (Ottawa: Employment Equity Data Program).

Steinberg, Stephen (1997), 'The Liberal Retreat from Race During the Post-Civil Rights Era', in Wahneema Lubiano (ed.).

Stern, Mark (1992), *Calculating Visions: Kennedy, Johnson and Civil Rights*, (New Brunswick: Rutgers University Press).

'Stormont Report: Second Stage Defeat of Human Rights Bill – Conflict Over Discrimination in the North', *The Irish Times*, (February 8,1967).

Surve, I., (2003), 'Black Economic Empowerment takes up the Struggle', *Business Report*, (Cape Town: May 31).

Tarnopolsky, W.S. and Pentney William, (1995), *Discrimination and the Law*, (Toronto: Carswell).

Tarnopolsky, W.S., (ed.) (1975), *Some Civil Liberties Issues of the Seventies*, (Toronto: Osgoode Hall Law School, York University).

Task Force on the Participation of Visible Minorities in the Federal Public Service, (2000), *Embracing Change in the Federal Public Service*, (Ottawa: Treasury Board of Canada).

Thaver, B., (2003) 'Deracialising universities: reflexive conversations', *South African Journal of Higher Education*, Vol 17 (3) (Pretoria).

The Agreement: It's Your Decision, 1998, (Belfast: TSO).

The Fair Employment and Treatment (Northern Ireland) Order, 1998.

'The Landmark Bakke Ruling', *Newsweek*, p. 31, (July 10, 1978).

The Race Relations (Northern Ireland) Order, 1997, SI 1997/869 (NI 6).

Theophanous, Andrew C., (1995), *Understanding Multiculturalism and Australian Identity*, (Melbourne: Elikia Books).

Thomas, Roosevelt (1990), 'From Affirmative Action to Affirming Diversity', *Harvard Business Review*, (March–April) pp. 107–117.

Tribalat, Michèle (1995), *Faire France*, (Paris: Editions la Découverte).

Tumalla, K.K., (1999), 'Policy of Preference: Lessons from India, the United States and South Africa', *Public Administration Review*, 56:6, pp. 495–508.

Van Hattem, Margaret (1985), 'Government studies black quota plan', *Financial Times*, (October 14).

Wallace, Phyllis (ed.) (1976), *Equal Employment Opportunity and the AT & T Case*, (Cambridge, Massachusetts: MIT Press).

Walsh, Kate (2001), *The Changing Face of Australia – A Century of Immigration 1901–2000*, (Crows Nest, NSW: Allan & Unwin).

Walsh, Mark (1997), 'Supreme Court Case Plays Out in N.J. School Every Day', *Education Week*, p. 20, (October 8).

Weil, Patrick (2005), *La République et sa diversité, Immigration, intégrations, discriminations*, (Paris: Seuil/La République des idées).

Weiss, Robert J., (1977), *We Want Jobs: A History of Affirmative Action*, (New York: Garland).

Wieviorka, Michel (1995), *The Arena of Racism*, (London, Sage).

Willenz, June (1994), 'Invisible Veterans', *Educational Record* 74 (Fall), pp. 41–46.

Williams, Patricia (1995), *The Rooster's Egg*, (Cambridge: Harvard University Press).

Wilson, Reginald (1998), 'G.I. Bill Expands Access for African Americans', *Educational Record* 74 (Fall), p. 36.

Wilson, William Julius (1996), *When Work Disappears, the World of the New Urban Poor*, (New York: Alfred A. Knopf).

Wise, Tim (1998), 'Is Sisterhood Conditional?', *NWSA Journal*, (Fall), p. 22.

Working Party on Discrimination in the Private Sector of Employment: Report and Recommendations, (Belfast: HMSO (now TSO)1973).

Xaxa, Virginius (2002), 'Ethnography of Reservation in Delhi University', *Economic and Political Weekly*, (July 13).

Yarwood, A.T. and Knowling, M.J., (1992), *Race Relations in Australia, A History*, (Melbourne: Methuen Australia).

Yu, Corinne M. and Taylor, William L. (eds) (1999), *The Test of Our Progress: the Clinton Record on Civil Rights*, (Washington, D.C.: Citizens' Commission on Civil Rights).

Index

Abella, Rosalie Silberman, 46
Abella Report, 46–7, 51, 53, 54, 58
Aboriginals, 5
    of Australia, 9, 127, 129–30, 137, 145,
        148
    of Canada, 43–6, 48, 52, 57–61, 146
Adivasis, 65
    see also Scheduled Tribes
Afghanistan, 79
Africans, of Britain, 78, 79, 80, 83–5
African Americans, 7, 11–27, 30–32, 35–7,
        40–41, 132, 139
African National Congress (ANC), ix, 156
Afrikaners, 153–4
Alabama, 31
    Department of Public Safety, 30–31
Ambedkar, B.R., 66, 72
American Civil Rights Coalition (ACRC),
        36
American Federation of Labor (AFL), 14,
        16
American Telephone and Telegraph
        (AT&T), 26
Anglo-Australians, see Britons, of Australia
apartheid, x, 6, 9, 153–7, 163, 164, 167,
        168, 170, 171
Arkansas, 19n30
Aryans, 65
Asians,
    of Australia, 131, 132, 137
    of Britain, 80, 83–5, 91–2
assimilationism, 44–5, 57–61, 80–81, 130,
        132–4, 140, 154, 173, 176
asylum seekers, 79, 144
Ati-Sudras, 64–5, 75
    see also untouchables
Australia, 3, 7, 79
    Aboriginal Development Commission,
        145
    Aboriginal and Torres Strait Islander
        Commission (ATSIC), 145, 149,
        150–51

Aboriginal and Torres Strait Islander
        Commission Act (1989), 145
Aboriginals Councils and Associations
        Act (1976), 145
Advisory Council on Multicultural Af-
        fairs, 136
affirmative action in, 8–9, 127–52
colonial era in, 129–30, 132, 143
Committee to Advise on Immigration
        Policies, 136
Council for Multicultural Australia, 137
Department of Immigration and Multi-
        culturalism and Indigenous Affairs
        (DIMIA), 128, 141
Equal Opportunity in the Workplace Act
        (1999), 138–9
Federation (1901), 130, 132
Federation of Ethnic Communities
        Councils, 135
Human Rights and Equal Opportunities
        Commission, 128
Human Rights and Equal Opportunities
        Commission Act (1986), 128
National Aboriginal Consultative Com-
        mittee, 145
National Aboriginal Council, 145
National Agenda for a Multicultural
        Australia, 136, 140
    National Multicultural Advisory
        Council, 137, 141
Native Title Act (1993), 149
New Agenda for a Multicultural Aus-
        tralia, 137, 141–2
Racial Discrimination Act (1975), 135
Security Legislation Amendment Act
        (1997), 141
Special Broadcasting Service, 135
Telephone Interpreter Service, 134
White Australia Policy, 9, 130, 132–4,
        151
Australian National University, 139

Bakke, Allan, 28–9, 42
Bangladeshis, of Britain, 80, 83–5
Bébar, Claude, 174–5
Belfast, 107, 123
Belos, Linda, 97–8
Birmingham (UK), 92n45, 94
Black and Asian Police Officers Association, 92
Black Leadership Forum, 35, 36
blacks, 78, 80, 83–5, 91–2, 94, 95, 132
    of South Africa, 155–8, 161–8, 169–71
    see also African Americans, Africans, Blacks/Africans, West Indians
Blacks/Africans, of South Africa, 154–7, 160, 164, 165, 167–8, 171
Blackmun, Harry, 29, 42
Blainey, Geoffrey, 135–6
Blair, Tony, 81
Botha, P.W., 6
Brahmins, 64–5, 73, 75
Brennan, William, 29, 30
Britons, of Australia, 127, 129–34, 136, 144
Buddhism, 63–4
Buddhists, 63–4, 84
Burger, Warren, 34
Bush, George E.W., 33, 35
Bush, Jeb, 37

California, 7, 15
    Superior Court of, 28
    Supreme Court, 28
California Civil Rights Initiative, 36
Calwell, Arthur, 131
Canada, 4, 7, 79, 134, 149
    affirmative action in, 5, 7–8, 43–61
    Charter of Rights and Freedoms, 50
    colonial era of, 44
    Constitution, 57, 59
    Council on Social Development, 54
    Employment Equity Act (1986), 47, 52, 60
    Federal Contractor's Program, 48
    Human Rights Commission, 48, 60
    Royal Commission on Aboriginal Peoples, 57–8
    Royal Commission on Equality in Employment, 46
    Supreme Court, 50–52, 59

Canaday, Charles, 32
Cape Coloured, 155
Cape Malay, 155
Cardiff, 78
caste, 2, 4, 63–6, 71, 72–4
    jati, 64–6, 67, 74, 75
    varna, 64–5, 67, 74, 75, 76
Catholics, 4, 8, 104–8, 109, 111–15, 120, 121–4
Center for Individual Rights (CIR), 37, 38
Césaire, Aimé, 176
Chinese,
    of Australia, 130–31, 132
    of Britain, 83, 84
    of Canada, 45
Christianity and Christians, 63–4, 84
    see also Catholics, Protestants
Clark, Geoff, 148–9, 150
Cleveland, 30
Clinton, William, 35
Coalition to Defend Affirmative Action, 36
cohesion, 1, 100, 120, 140, 142
colonialism, x, 9, 57, 77, 129–30, 132
colour, 4, 11–12, 14, 19, 33, 50, 92, 94
Coloureds, of South Africa, 154–7, 160, 164–5, 167–8, 171
Commission for Black Staff in Higher Education, 98
compensatory discrimination, 2
Confederation of British Industry (CBI), 94, 100
Congress of Industrial Organizations (CIO), 16
Congress of Racial Equality (CORE), 17n21
Connerly, Ward, 36–7
contract compliance, 5, 16, 19, 22–3, 35–6, 48–9, 93–5, 98–9, 118
Crown-Zellerbach, 22, 27
Curtin, John, 133

Dalits, 2, 8, 9, 64, 65, 66, 68, 70–74, 75
data, *see* statistics
Desai, Ali, 92
Dickson, Brian, 51
Dirksen, Everett, 21
disability, 2, 11n, 43, 46, 47–8, 50, 58, 60, 112, 115, 117, 158, 159, 171
District of Columbia, 27
Dole, Robert, 32

Dravidians, 65

Eames, Lord Robert, 107–8
Eastern Europe, 79
Eastland, James, 19
education, 4, 5, 8, 9
　in Australia, 133, 134, 135, 143, 144,
　　147
　in Canada, 43, 47, 49, 52, 54–6, 57–61
　in France, 175
　in Great Britain, 84, 85, 89, 90–91, 96,
　　97
　in India, 66, 68, 69–71, 74–5
　in South Africa, 158, 159, 164–5, 166,
　　171, 172
　in United States of America, 11, 14, 17,
　　18, 20, 27–9, 32, 33, 36–40, 41, 105
Eisenhower, Dwight, 19n30
Eskom, 168–9
employment, 4, 5, 8, 9
　in Australia, 127, 129, 130, 133,
　　139–40, 141, 143–4, 145–6, 148–9
　in Canada, 43, 44–52, 54–6, 57–61
　in France, 173–6
　in Great Britain, 78, 84–5, 86, 93–5, 96,
　　97–100
　in India, 66, 69–71, 72, 74
　in Northern Ireland, 105, 107, 109–12,
　　115, 118, 120, 121–4
　in South Africa, 158–64, 166–72
　in United States of America, 11, 14,
　　15–17, 19, 20–28, 30–31, 36, 40
enforcement, 6, 22, 35–6, 45, 47, 69, 86, 90,
　　94, 128, 159–61
England, 83
English,
　of Canada, 44, 53
　of South Africa, 153–4
equality, 11, 42, 43–4, 61, 64, 67, 96, 97, 99,
　　103, 105–6, 115, 122–4, 136, 140,
　　153, 157–9, 175
　of opportunity, 1, 3, 22, 67, 81, 90, 92,
　　93, 96, 104, 106, 111–12, 115–21,
　　137–9, 140, 158, 176
　substantive, 50–51, 58, 61
ethnic groups, 2, 4, 5, 9, 11n, 50, 54, 83,
　　84, 87, 89, 90, 92, 94, 98, 100, 128,

　　134, 136, 137–8, 140, 151, 156, 164,
　　167–8, 173–6
ethnicity, 1, 64, 79–80, 81–2, 85, 113, 132,
　　135, 138, 140, 141–2, 173–6
European Union, 79, 87, 88n32, 119
　Directives, 99, 114
Europeans, of Australia, 131, 132
First Nations ('Indians'), 43n2, 57, 59
Fitzgerald Report, 136, 140
Fletcher, Arthur A., 23
Florida, 37
Ford, Gerald, 34
Fort Hare, 164
France, 4, 7, 173–6
　and colonialism, 173–4
Fraser, Malcolm, 135
French, of Canada, 44, 53

Galbally Report, 135, 140
Gandhi, M.K. 'Mahatma', 65, 75
gender, 8, 20, 21, 26, 34, 38, 40, 41, 49, 50,
　　51, 56, 69, 87, 112, 113, 116, 117,
　　137, 140, 156–7, 159, 160, 164,
　　168–9, 170, 171
goals, 5, 9, 48, 94, 100, 110–11, 121, 158–9
Gobbo, Sir James, 136
Grant, Bernie, 97–8
Grassby, Al, 134
Great Britain, 4, 6, 7
　affirmative action in, 5, 8, 77–101
　Central Office of Information, 87
　Commission for Racial Equality (CRE),
　　7, 79, 86–7, 90, 93, 95, 96, 97, 99,
　　100
　Commonwealth of, 7, 78–9, 81
　Department for Education and Skills
　　(DfES), 98
　Department of Employment, 93
　Empire, 77–8, 81, 130, 132
　Home Office, 87, 92, 94
　Local Government Act (1988), 94
　Race Relations Act (1965), 86
　Race Relations Act (1968), 86
　Race Relations Act (1976), 86, 87–8,
　　90–91, 92–3, 95–6, 99, 116
　Race Relations Amendment Act (2000),
　　8, 95–7, 99, 101
　Sex Discrimination Act (1975), 87
　see also Northern Ireland

Greater London Council (GLC), 93–4
Gujarat, 73
Gypsies, 88n35

Hanson, Pauline, 136–7
Hardgrave, Gary, 138
Harijans, 8, 65, 75
Hawke, Bob, 135, 136
Heath, Edward, 81
Hinduism, 63–4, 72
Hindus, 8, 63–4, 84–5
Holt, Harold, 133
Howard, John, 128, 135, 136, 141, 142, 150,
      151–2
Hull, 78

immigration and immigrants, 9
   in Australia, 127–8, 133–5, 137–8,
      140–44, 151
   in Canada, 53–4
   in France, 173
   in Great Britain, 78–9, 81, 85
India, 3, 4, 9
   affirmative action in, 2, 5, 8, 63–76
   British colonial era, 7, 66, 67
   Constitution, 8, 66, 67, 69, 72
   Supreme Court, 72
Indians,
   of Australia, 127
   of Britain, 78, 80, 83–5
   of South Africa, 155–7, 160, 164–5,
      167–8, 171
indigenous people, 5, 8–9
   of Australia, 127–8, 129–30, 132, 138,
      139–40, 142, 145–51
   of New Zealand, 146
   of USA, 146
      see also, Aboriginals, First Nations,
         Inuits, Torres Straits Islanders
Indonesians, of Australia, 127
Institute of Race Relations, 80
integration, 9, 19, 54, 58, 60, 79, 81, 131,
      176
Inuit, 43n2, 57
Iqbal Sacranie, 84
Iraq, 79
Irish-Americans, 110
Irish Travellers, 88n35, 103n3, 123
Islam, 63–4

Jainism, 63n
Japan, 133
Japanese,
   of Australia, 130–31, 133
   of Canada, 45
jati, *see* caste
Jenkins, Roy, 79–80
Jews, 84, 88n35, 132, 174
Johnson, Andrew, 12n4, 13
Johnson, Lyndon, 11, 20–22, 25, 42

Kaiser Aluminum, 30
Karnataka, 66
Keating, Paul, 135, 136, 151
Kennedy, Anthony M., 40
Kennedy, John F., 7, 19
Kennedy, Robert, 19, 25
Kerala, 66
Kerry, John, 39
King, Martin Luther Jr, 19n30, 24–5, 33
Kshatriyas, 64–5, 76
Ku Klux Klan, 18

language and language groups, 1, 7, 68, 134,
      136, 137, 138, 140, 141, 143–4, 146,
      155, 167
Latham, Mark, 150, 151
Lawrence, Stephen, 95
legislation, *see* policy and legislation
Lester, Anthony, 85
Lewis, John, 33
Liverpool, 78, 92n45
Livingstone, Ken, 93
London, 78, 83, 92n45, 94, 95
Louisiana, 30

MacBride Principles, 110
McConnell, Mitch, 32–3
McLachlin, Beverley, 51
McNamara, Kevin, 110
Macpherson, Sir William, 95–6
Major, John, 95
Manchester, 83, 92n45
Mandal Commission Report, 68, 73, 76
Mandela, Nelson, ix
Manitoba, 59
Mansfield, Mike, 21
March on Washington Movement, 16
Marshall, Thurgood, 29

Mbeki, Govan (Oom Gov), ix–xi
Mbeki, Thabo, ix
Métis, 43n2, 57, 59
migration, 1, 5, 78
   see also immigration
minority and minorities, 2, 8
   in Australia, 128, 133, 134, 137–8, 140,
      151
   in Canada, 43n1, 47–8, 52–5, 58
   in France, 173–6
   in Great Britain, 79, 83–5, 86, 87–9,
      90–92, 94, 98, 100
   in India, 63
   in Northern Ireland, 104, 114–15, 123
   in United States of America, 11n, 21,
      26–8, 31–2, 34–5, 36–8, 40, 105,
      139
   visible, 43n1, 47–8, 52–5, 58, 79,
      103–4, 134
Mitchell, Clarence, 25
Mitchell, Parren, 26
multiculturalism, 1, 3, 7, 9, 44, 54, 81, 84,
   100–101, 127–8, 133–43, 151–2
Murnaghan, Sheelagh, 107
Murphy, Paul, 119
Muslim Council of Britain, 84
Muslims, 63, 84–5

Natal, 132
National Action Committee on the Status of
   Women, 47n24
National Association for the Advance-
   ment of Colored People (NAACP),
   18n27, 25
National Committee on Immigrant and Vis-
   ible Minority Women, 56
Nepal, 72
New Jersey, 35
New York, 17
   Fair Employment Commission, 17
   State Law Against Discrimination
      (1945), 17
New Zealand, 79, 149
New Zealanders, of Australia, 127
Nixon, Richard, 22, 34
North Africans, of France, 175
Northern Ireland (NI), 4, 7, 83
   affirmative action in, 8, 103–25
   Assembly, 115n19, 120, 124

Belfast/Good Friday Agreement (1998),
   112, 113, 115–17, 124
Commission on Policing for NI (Patten),
   113–15
Commission for Racial Equality for NI,
   104
Department of Economic Development
   (DED), 110
Equality Commission for NI, 104, 112,
   114, 116–19, 121
Fair Employment Act (1976), 109
Fair Employment Act (1989), 88n,
   110–12
Fair Employment Agency (FEA), 109,
   110
Fair Employment Commission (FEC),
   110–12, 122
Fair Employment and Treatment (NI)
   Order (1998), 112, 114
Government of Ireland Act, 107
House of Commons NI Affairs Commit-
   tee, 112
NI Act (1998), 104, 114, 116–21, 123
NI Constitution Act (1973), 109
Parliament, 107
Police (NI) Act (2000), 114
Policy Appraisal and Fair Treatment
   (PAFT), 116
Race Relations (NI) Order (1997), 104,
   123
Single Equality Act, 120–21, 123–4
Standing Advisory Commission on
   Human Rights (SACHR), 109, 110,
   116, 118
Targeting Social Needs (TSN), 119–20,
   121
   and UK, 106–7, 108–9, 114, 124
   and USA, 110
Northern Ireland Civil Rights Association
   (NICRA), 108
Northern Territory, 148
O'Connor, Sandra Day, 32, 39, 41
Ontario, 49
Other Backward Classes, 8, 65, 66, 67–8,
   72, 74, 76

Pacific Islanders, of Australia, 131, 132
Pakistan, 63

Pakistanis, of Britain, 80, 83–5
Peacock, Andrew, 136
Pendleton, Clarence, 34
Philadelphia Plan, 22–3, 24
Philip Morris, 22, 23, 27
Phillips, Trevor, 79
police and policing, 6, 27, 55, 91–3, 95, 107,
    112–15, 175
Police Service of Northern Ireland, 103n3,
    113
policy and legislation, 3–6
    see also Australia, Canada, France,
        Great Britain, India, Northern
        Ireland, South Africa, United
        States of America
Policy Studies Institute, 86
positive action, 2, 77, 81, 87–90, 91–2,
    97–8, 101, 127
positive discrimination, 2, 77, 87, 89–90,
    94, 98, 100, 127, 138, 175, 176
positive positioning, 2
Powell, Enoch, 81, 82, 100
Powell, Lewis Franklin Jr, 39
preferential treatment, 2, 9, 21, 33, 158
Progressive Citizens of America, 15
protective discrimination, 2, 127
Protestants, 8, 106–8, 109, 111, 113–14,
    120, 121–3

Quebec, 49, 53
Queensland, 132
quotas, 2, 5, 7, 8, 9, 16, 20–21, 23, 28, 39,
    40, 47, 55, 66, 68–70, 72–4, 76, 82,
    92, 94, 104, 110, 111, 132, 139, 158,
    176
    see also reservations

race, x–xi, 1, 8–9, 11–14, 19, 21, 22, 26,
    28–9, 30–39, 40–42, 50, 53, 55, 56,
    65, 79, 80, 81, 85, 87, 92, 98, 112,
    116, 123, 129, 133, 136, 137, 140,
    151, 156, 157, 159, 160, 164, 168,
    169–70, 171–2, 173–6
race riots, 78, 91–2, 94, 97, 100
racial groups, 2, 4, 5, 8, 9, 50, 88–9, 104,
    117, 132, 154–7, 173–6
racialized communities, 46, 52–6
racism, x, 2, 3, 6
    in Australia, 127, 129, 133
        in Canada, 43–4, 45, 52–6, 60
        in France, 176
        in Great Britain, 81, 82, 92, 95–6
        in India, 75
        in Northern Ireland, 123
        in South Africa, 154–7, 168, 170, 171
        in United States of America, 16, 23, 25,
            42, 107
Rajasthan, 73
Randolph, A. Philip, 16, 19n30
Rastafarians, 88n35
Reagan, Ronald, 33, 34
refugees, 5, 79, 131, 133, 135, 142, 143–5
Rehnquist, William, 34, 39, 40
religion, 8, 50, 63, 68, 84, 88n35, 106, 107,
    109, 112, 114, 116, 117, 123, 137,
    138, 140, 169, 174
Republic of Ireland, 106
reservations, quota, 67–8, 70, 72–3, 76
reverse discrimination, 2, 7, 11, 47, 49–50,
    59, 139, 169
Reynolds, William Bradford, 34
Riggs, Frank, 33
Roach, Neville, 141
Roosevelt, Franklin, 15–17
Rowntree Macintosh, 93
Royal Ulster Constabulary, 113

Sarkozy, Nicolas, 173
Scalia, Antonin, 40
Scarman, Lord, 90n40, 92
Scheduled Castes, 8, 65–8, 69–74, 76
Scheduled Tribes, 8, 65–8, 69–74, 76
Schultz, George, 22
Scotland, 83, 97
segregation, x, 13–14, 17n21, 18, 40, 46,
    122, 157, 164
Sekunjalo, 162
sex, *see* gender
Sikhism and Sikhs, 63n, 84–5, 88n35
Simms, Glenda, 56
Singh, V.P., 68
Sinn Fein, 115n19
slaves and slavery, x, 5, 12, 13, 21, 45, 77
Smith, William French, 34
Social Darwinism, 1, 14, 129, 132
Sotho-Tswana, 155
South Africa, ix–xi, 3, 6, 7, 79, 110
    affirmative action in, 2, 3, 8, 9, 153–72

Affirmative Action in the Public Service (1998), 158, 163
Basic Conditions of Employment Act (1997), 159
Black Economic Empowerment Commission, 161–3
colonial era of, 153–4
Commission for Employment Equity, 159, 160
Constitution (1996), 9, 153, 157–8, 163, 169, 172
Department of Labour, 160
Employment Equity Act (1998), 9, 158–9, 166, 167
Higher Education Act (1997), 165
Labour Relations Act (1995), 159
National Plan for Higher Education (2001), 165
Native Land Act (1913), 154
Population Registration Act (1950), 155
Programme for the Transformation of Higher Education (1997), 158, 164–5
Promotion of Equality and Prevention of Unfair Discrimination Act (2000), 159
Transformation of the Public Service (1998), 158
South Africans, of Australia, 127
South Carolina, 18n27
Southeast Asians, of Australia, 135
Southeastern Legal Foundation, 37
statistics, 81–5, 174–5
collection of, 4, 65, 67–8, 81–2, 84, 89, 92, 93, 98, 174–5
Stormont, 107
Straubenzee, William van, 109
Straw, Jack, 92, 95
Sudras, 64, 67, 76
Sylvester, Edward, 22

targets, *see* goals
Tasmania, 9
Taxman, Sharon, 35, 36
Teamsters Union, 27
Tennessee, 30
Tennessee Valley Authority, 7, 16
terminology, x, 2–3, 5, 9, 47, 53, 79–81, 87–90

Texas, 37–8
Thatcher, Margaret, 77, 79, 81, 83, 93–5
Thomas, Clarence, 34, 40
Tobacco Workers International Union, 22
Torres Straits Islanders, 127, 129n, 145
Truman, Harry, 19n30
Twigg, Stephen, 98

Unionists, 107, 108, 109, 113–14
United Nations, Committee on the Elimination of Racial Discrimination, 149–50
United States of America (USA), 3, 9, 149
affirmative action in, 1–2, 3, 5–6, 7, 11–42, 88, 138–9
Bureau of Refugees, Freedmen and Abandoned Lands, 12, 13
civil rights, 7, 12–13, 19–22, 24, 30, 33–6, 38, 40, 108
Civil Rights Act (1875), 13
Civil Rights Act (1964), 20, 33n79, 34
Civil Rights Act (1991), 33, 40
Civil Rights Commission, 34, 36
Civil Rights Restoration Act (1998), 33
Committee on Civil Rights, 19n30
Congress, 6, 12, 13, 17, 19, 24, 26, 27, 31, 32–4, 36
Constitution and Amendments, 11, 12–13, 14, 28, 29, 39
Department of Justice, 34, 35
Department of Labor, 22–3, 35–6
Office of Contract Compliance, 36
Office of Federal Contract Compliance (OFCC), 22–3, 35
Department of Transportation, Disadvantaged Business Enterprise Program (DBE), 32–3
Equal Employment Opportunity Act (1972), 24, 25
Equal Employment Opportunity Commission (EEOC), 20, 23–6, 27, 34, 35
Fair Employment Practice Committee, 17
Federal Communications Commission (FCC), 31, 32
Federal Glass Ceiling Commission, 40
National Labour Relations Act (1935), 16

National Labour Relations Board, 16
New Deal, 14–16
Public Works Administration (PWA), 16
Public Works Employment Act (1977),
    26
Reconstruction, 13
Servicemen's Readjustment Act (1944)
    (G.I. Bill), 17
Supreme Court, 13, 15, 18, 23, 27, 28,
    30–32, 33–5, 38–9, 41
Voting Rights Act (1965), 20
United Steelworkers, 30
University of California, 28–9, 36
University of Cape Town, 164
University of Delhi, 70
University of Durban-Westville, 164
University of Maryland, 32
University of Michigan, 36, 38–40, 41
University of Texas, 32, 37
University of Washington, 28
University of the Western Cape, 164
untouchables, 64–5, 75, 76

Vaisyas, 64, 76
Vanstone, Amanda, 150
varna, *see* caste
veterans, 2, 17, 133
Virginia, 22, 31

Waddington, David, 94
Wales, 83
Weaver, Robert, 16
Weber, Brian, 30
West Australia, 132
West Indians, of Britain, 78, 80, 83–5, 86
West Midlands, 83, 92n45
Western Australia, 148
Western Cape, 156, 165, 167
White, Byron, 29
White Citizens Council, 18
whites, of South Africa, 156–7, 158, 161,
    162, 164–5, 166, 168, 169–70, 171
Whites, of South Africa, 155–6, 160, 164,
    165
Whitlam, Gough, 134, 135
Wirtz, Willard, 22
women, 2, 8, 11n, 12n3, 26, 27, 31, 33n79,
    36, 40, 43, 46, 47–8, 54, 58, 68–9,
    84, 87, 113–15, 117, 122, 127, 139,
    156–7, 158, 160–61, 163–4, 165,
    166, 168–9, 170, 171

Xhosa, 155

Yorkshire, 83

Zulu, 155